SILVER BAY PUBLIC LIBRARY
9 DAVIS DRIVE
SILVER BAY, MN 55614

16/(

D0668202

The Seven Secrets *of the* Prolific

The Definitive Guide to
Overcoming Procrastination,
Perfectionism, and Writer's Block

by Hillary Rettig

Illustrations *by* Barry Deutsch

The Seven Secrets of the Prolific

The Definitive Guide to Overcoming Procrastination, Perfectionism, and Writer's Block
by Hillary Rettig

Copyright © 2011 Hillary Rettig. All rights reserved.
hillaryrettig.com.

Illustrations by Barry Deutsch, amptoons.com.

9-4-15 OCLC

Cover design and layout by Lee Busch/LBDesign, lbdesign.com.

Design of interior by Chris Sturr/LeftUp Publishing, leftup.org.
Layout of interior by Juan M. Jaume.

Printing by Lightning Source, lightningsource.com.

To George Lewis

Table *of* Contents

Chapter 3: **Coping with Resource Constraints** 71

Chapter 4: Liberating Yourself from Time Constraints   97

Chapter 5: Optimizing Your Writing Process   *133*

Acknowledgments

I gratefully acknowledge the support of:

Christopher Castellani, Sonya Larson, Eve Bridburg, and the wonderful staff and students at Grub Street Writers in Boston, who helped me find my mission.

Carolyn Benedict-Drew, with gratitude and respect.

Richard Stallman, an inspirational activist and stalwart friend.

Dan Krotz, a valued friend and mentor extraordinaire.

David Karp, who made just one suggestion but it was prime.

My wonderful landlords, Dorothy and Jack Benoit. And the crew at John Smith's Auto Body, including John Smith and Lenny Petrone. And everyone in East Boston, MA, a community full of friendly people and interesting ships.

And Gunnar Engstrom.

Vocabulary and Text Notes

Procrastination is the problem of not being able to reliably do your writing as planned.

A writer's block is a severe, prolonged bout of procrastination.

Throughout this book, I use the noun forms of these words interchangeably. Whenever you see me refer to "writer's block," you should assume I'm also talking about procrastination, and vice versa, unless I specify otherwise.

When I need a verb form, I generally use "procrastinate," and my preferred adjective is "underproductive." With each word, I'm again referring to the entire spectrum of underperformance, from slight procrastination to being hugely blocked.

For reasons that will become clear, I avoid using labels like "procrastinator" and "perfectionist" in conversation or when teaching, but I do use them in this book for brevity and clarity.

I use the word "prolific" not to indicate some fixed arbitrary standard of productivity, but someone writing at their own full capacity. Everyone's situation and capacity are different, and your own capacity will probably differ at different times.

Ditto for terms like "successful" and "underproductive": their meanings relate not to some arbitrary measure but to what you achieve relative to your own goals.

I use phrases such as "your writing career" and "your writing profession" to indicate any path involving a long-term commitment to writing, whether or not that path earns money—although I hope it does!

Throughout the book, except for Chapter 4 for reasons I will explain, I use the gender pronouns interchangeably.

Disclaimer

The information in this book is presented without warranty of any kind. It has helped many people, and it is my sincere wish that it help you, but I can't accept responsibility for any negative result you feel you may have obtained from using it. If you are suffering from anxiety, depression, addiction, or any other psychological or physical condition, please seek professional help before following the advice herein. If you are making choices that affect your financial well being, please consult your accountant.

About the Author

Hillary Rettig is an author, coach, and workshop leader who specializes in helping people improve their productivity and build effective and empowering careers and businesses. She is also a vegan, kidney donor, former foster mother to four Sudanese refugees ("Lost Boys"), and lover of dogs and other animals.

The text for her previous book, *The Lifelong Activist*, a self-help guide for progressives, is available in its entirety at www.lifelongactivist.com.

For more information on Hillary and her work, including abundant free downloads, visit www.hillaryrettig.com. Hillary also invites you to:

Email her at hillaryrettig@yahoo.com
"Friend" her on Facebook: www.facebook.com/hillaryrettig
And follow her on Twitter: www.twitter.com/hillaryrettig

For more on Hillary's coaching or to invite her to give a class, workshop, or speech, see hillaryrettig.com.

Chapter 1

The Mechanics of Procrastination

I have known authors whose lives have been troublesome and painful because their tasks have never been done in time.
—Anthony Trollope, *An Autobiography*

Section 1.1 Procrastination is Disempowerment

People who procrastinate or are blocked almost always think it's because they're lazy or lack an essential character trait such as willpower, commitment, or discipline, but that's never the case. As the phrase "writer's block" implies, you aren't missing anything, but blocked from using what you already have: your skills, talents, energy, vision, commitment, etc.

A good synonym for "blocked" is "disempowered" (get it? disempowered), which also helpfully denotes that there are forces acting on you that are causing your underproductivity. In other words, you procrastinate not due to any intrinsic deficiency or deficit on your part, but to outside forces.

Because we can work to uncover and ameliorate (or eliminate!) the forces disempowering you—and rather easily, once we clear up some misconceptions—the idea of disempowerment should bring hope. Regardless of how many years or decades you've struggled with your procrastination problem, it is solvable.

In the productivity classes I run for writers, we do an exercise where I say, "It's Monday at 10:00 a.m., and you're supposed to be writing your novel (or, nonfiction book, thesis, grant proposal, business report, etc.), only you don't feel like it. What might be some of the reasons?" The answers typically fall into eleven (!) categories:

Project-Related Problems and Feelings. You feel lost in your writing project, sick of it, overwhelmed by it, or alienated from it. Or, it feels boring or meaningless or futile. "Why do I even bother writing poetry when no one reads it any more?"

Fear of Failure or Success. You are afraid the project will fail, or afraid of the consequences of success. E.g., "My novel will never get published, but even if it does, my family will hate the way I portrayed them." Or, "This stupid grant will never get funded, and even if it does, I will hate working on the project." (Yes, the seemingly mutually contradictory fears of failure and success often do manage to coexist nicely.)

Note that I'm not describing the intense terror of failure and success borne of perfectionism (Chapter 2), but a more rational fear of one or more likely outcomes of your efforts.

Resource Deficiencies. The computer's flaky, or the printer is. You lack information you need to proceed, or someone who was supposed to help hasn't shown up.

Environmental Deficiencies. Your writing space is too crowded and noisy—or too isolated and quiet. Or, your writing desk and chair are uncomfortable.

Workplace Problems. (Specific to on-the-job writing.) Your workplace is poorly managed, chaotic, or abusive. This problem is far more common than most people realize, because even many "average" workplaces are dysfunctional. It's hard, if not impossible, to be productive when surrounded by dysfunction and chaos.

Boss Problems. (Specific to on-the-job writing.) Boss is unorganized, inept, negligent, abusive, or otherwise dysfunctional. Also a more common barrier than most people realize.

Competing Priorities. (On the job or with your own writing.) Other projects or people are clamoring for your attention. Or, perhaps there's something else you'd rather be doing.

Emotional Distractions. You're distracted by feelings of sadness or fear related to your personal life. Or, maybe feelings of happiness.

Happy is better, of course, but can still distract.

Physical Distractions. You feel tired, sick, hungry, or hyper.

Geopolitical Problems. You're upset at, or otherwise distracted by, current events.

Emotional/Cognitive/Learning Issues. You've got ADD or ADHD or another learning difference, or you suffer from depression or anxiety. These and similar conditions should be addressed promptly and with professional help, not simply because they are painful to live with, but because they can be huge barriers to productivity and success.

Five Key Lessons

There are five important things you need to know about the above list:

(1) All of the above barriers are totally, perfectly, 100% valid. It is perfectly legitimate, and even empowered, to not want to write when you're tired, ill, sick of the project, distracted by personal or family or geopolitical problems, under-resourced, abused at work, etc. Procrastination is even an okay response to those circumstances—once in a while. But as you no doubt know since you are reading this book, it's a terrible habitual response.

(2) The barriers are properly referred to as causes or reasons for not wanting to write—not excuses, complaints or whines. "Excuses," etc., are moralistic labels that do little but foment guilt and shame, thereby further impeding our productivity (Section 2.7).

(3) It's a long list, which tells us that our productivity is constantly under siege from many different directions.

(4) It's important, when reviewing the list of barriers, to distinguish between those that are obstacles and those that are triggers. An obstacle is an activity or circumstance that competes with your writing for time and other resources, or that otherwise impedes your ability to write. Childcare, relationships, community work, illness (your own or someone else's), a full-time job, and a deficient teacher, boss, or workplace are all obstacles. I'm not saying you shouldn't be doing childcare and some of those other activities, by the way: only that they compete with your writing. Chapter 4, on time management, will give you the tools to balance competing priorities.

Triggers, in contrast, are feelings that interfere with your ability to write. Fear is the big one, not just because it tends to be intense and disabling but because writers take constant risks, with fear being a natural consequence (Section 6.4). Fear is so disabling, in fact, that it's not surprising that one of the core differences between prolific[1] and underproductive writers is that the former feel much less fear around their writing—and, quite often, no fear.

Shame, guilt, disappointment, and anxiety are also common triggers.

The line between "obstacle" and "trigger" is not clear cut: most obstacles invoke triggers, both directly from their own emotional content and secondarily from the guilt and shame that arise from underproductivity; and most triggers are caused at least partly by present or past obstacles. Also, people with triggers often create obstacles: for example, they get in time-consuming, destructive relationships or create too-full schedules that don't allow time to write. Still, as you will see, the obstacle and trigger categories are useful for characterizing the complex causes of underproductivity, and can also point the way to solutions.

(5) Look at what's not on the list: laziness, lack of discipline, lack of willpower, lack of commitment, etc. Once in a while—rarely, really—a student does mention one of these as a cause of not wanting to write, and when they do, I say, "Tell us why one would feel lazy around this project." Then they promptly come up with one or more of the reasons listed above. This tells us that **laziness, lack of willpower, etc., are symptoms, and not causes, of underproductivity**—and, moreover, yet another set of moralistic labels that undermine us. One of the most important productivity techniques you can use—so important that I will be repeating it throughout this book—is to never apply labels such as "lazy" to yourself or anyone else.

Section 1.2 Procrastination vs. Problem Solving

The moralistic labels are always wrong—and yet don't we constantly use them when we fall short of our goals or are underproductive? "What's wrong with you?" we ask ourselves in a kind of self-abusive litany:

---

[1] I use the word "prolific" to indicate someone writing at full capacity, according to their own measure. Everyone's situation and objectives are different, and everyone's writing capacity will thus differ. (And your own capacity will probably vary at different times!) Ditto for terms like "successful" and "underproductive": their meanings relate not to some arbitrary measure but to what you achieve relative to your own goals.

How can you be so lazy? Don't you care about this project? Don't you care about your own success? And after all those thousands you spent on a new computer and writing classes! A total waste. You really are a loser. Etc., etc.

And if you do somehow manage to bravely write in the midst of all that self-abuse, procrastination is nothing if not adaptable:

Is that the best you can do? Those sentences are terrible! Whoever told you you could write? What a waste of time. Might as well give up now.

I'll have a lot more to say about the litany in Chapter 2. For now, let me just say that many writers have that obnoxious voice running through their heads more or less constantly. Sometimes it's in the foreground of their thoughts, sometimes in the background, but if it's in the background, it's always ready to leap to the foreground the moment you decide to write, or the moment the writing doesn't go well.

There's one group of writers, however, who don't indulge in the litany: the prolific. They understand that underproductivity is never caused by character flaws, but by disempowering obstacles and triggers from the eleven categories. And so they don't waste time belittling themselves when they're underproductive, but move promptly (automatically, really) into problem-definition and problem-solving modes:

From: "It's 10:00 a.m. and I don't feel like working on my novel."

(Skipping: "What's wrong with you? How can you be so lazy? Etc.")

To problem definition: "Okay, so I don't feel like writing—what's going on? First of all, I'm sick to death of this chapter: I've been working on it forever and it's still going nowhere. Also, I got really discouraged last night when that guy at the party told me that space-vampire novels were 'out' and I wouldn't ever be able to get published. And, finally, I'm distracted because the phone keeps ringing and I can't stop myself from Internet surfing!"

Followed by problem-solving: "Okay, let's take those one at a time—easy stuff first. Starting right now, I'm going to shut off the phone every time I sit down to write. I'm also going to disconnect the Internet while I'm writing (Section 3.6). As for space vampires being 'out,' I've never heard anyone say that before so that was probably just that guy's unfounded opinion. I'll call my critique buddy (Section 3.11) and see what she thinks. I know she'll tell me to ignore the guy and just focus on having fun with my book. And in the future, I'll avoid talking to that guy about my work. He sounded so sure of himself and that caught me off guard, but he's not in publishing—he doesn't even read much!—so how does he know anything?

"As for being sick to death of the chapter, why don't I just set it aside and work on another one (Section 5.4)—maybe that fun one where the characters are all partying in Antarctica! Or, I could journal about the problems I'm having, or start it over from scratch."

Here's how that process looks graphically:
Because the prolific person is focused on problem-solving instead

Three ways to respond to a barrier.

of remorse and self-recrimination, she will typically either, (a) recover quickly from obstacles and triggers, or (b) not even perceive them in the first place! (She will automatically and almost reflexively unplug the phone and Internet, dismiss the obnoxious guy's comment, etc.) Some problems, of course, take longer than others to solve, even for adept problem-solvers. What we can safely say is that the prolific tend to solve their problems in less time—and usually, much less time—than procrastinators, many of whom tend to do more dithering (unproductive worrying, complaining, etc.) than actual solving. (The reason for that will become clear in Section 1.8).

Procrastinators, in contrast, follow path (c), where the initial obstacle or trigger launches another powerful trigger: panic about the possibility of failure. That's bad enough, as panic pretty much obliterates your ability to solve problems, but the "solution" the procrastinator then employs to try to get back on track makes things far worse: it's the self-abusive litany, which she uses in a desperate attempt to shame or terrify herself back into writing. Unfortunately, that litany not only leaves her even more defeated and disempowered, but also escalates her terror to the point that she needs to escape—and procrastination provides the easiest route for doing so.

All this can happen in a flash the moment you encounter a problem with your writing, and it can even happen the moment you contemplate writing. You have probably been procrastinating for decades, after all, and so both your fears and your escapist response to them are pretty well ingrained.

The use of shame and coercion as motivational tools, even on yourself, is not just immoral, but futile. They yield not growth and evolution, but,at best, short-term compliance. They also sabotage the creative process. Related problems with bullying are that: (1) we inevitably come to resent the bully, even if it happens to be us ourselves (Section 1.11), and (2) we become habituated to bullying, so that over time it loses its effectiveness. (The first time you get scolded for missing a deadline it's horrible; the tenth time, not so bad.)

It's not surprising you would turn to bullying to solve your procrastination problem, because our culture—and especially our media—relentlessly promotes that approach (Section 2.8). But the true solutions are all based on compassion and nonviolence.

Section 1.3 The Seven Secrets of the Prolific

In the previous section, I discussed how prolific writers solve problems much more quickly than underproductive ones—in some cases, not even perceiving a problem as a problem. This is particularly true of many of the ordinary problems that afflict writers. A prolific writer is not going to waste time if her computer is flaky, her workspace distracting, or she's feeling discouraged; she's going to solve the problem as soon as possible so she can get back to work.

The prolific, in other words, have the gift of perceiving mountains as molehills—only it's usually not a gift, but something they have learned over time. (Some lucky writers learn it early on from enlightened parents or teachers.) Moreover, the prolific know that **the best strategy is to minimize the possibility of obstacles and triggers to begin with**, and so they take steps to do that. Specifically, they:

1. Identify and Overcome Perfectionism (Chapter 2)
2. Abundantly Resource Themselves (Chapter 3)
3. Manage Their Time (Chapter 4)
4. Optimize Their Writing Process (Chapter 5)
5. Understand and "Own" Their Identity as a Writer (Chapter 6)
6. Minimize the Chances of Toxic Rejection, and Cope Strenuously With It When It Happens (Chapter 7); and
7. Create Liberated and Empowered Careers (Chapter 8)

These are the Seven Secrets of the Prolific, and each of this book's remaining chapters covers one of them. Before we get to them, however, let's delve more deeply into the nature and mechanisms of procrastination.

Section 1.4 **Procrastination's Quintuple Punch**

Why would anyone persist in a self-defeating strategy such as the harsh litany described in Section 1.2? Because of **perfectionism** (Chapter 2), which:

(1) Convinces us that writing is easy and, therefore, that if we're having trouble doing it, it must be because we're lazy or otherwise deficient.

(2) Leaves us terrified (not merely afraid) of the possibility of failure. To a perfectionist, as awful as underproductivity feels, it is still more palatable than the "ego death" that would result if she somehow managed to finish her work but it fell short of her goals. And since perfectionists set goals that are pretty much unattainable, "falling short" is pretty much guaranteed.

(3) Perceives only one "solution" to procrastination: bullying. You'd think that after years of trying that and seeing it not work, a writer would try something else, but: (a) bullying is the only strategy most of us are taught, and (b) perfectionist psychology is fundamentally rigid and inclined toward self-punishment (Section 2.7). (In contrast, note how the prolific writer in Section 1.2 didn't bother with blame and self-punishment, but flexibly created options for herself.)

In the end, **it's mainly perfectionism-fueled fear (or terror, really) that fuels procrastination**, because at the moment of writing, or even when the writer is merely contemplating writing, it creates an overwhelming need to "escape" to a safe place, and procrastination is the easiest and most obvious route to do so.

The fear usually has four components:

- Fear of failure (or success) around the current writing session
- Fear of failure (or success) for the project as a whole
- Fear of failure (or success) for one's overall writing (or academic) career
- Fear and anxiety around the act of writing itself

Given that even one fear is a powerful barrier to writing productivity, you can imagine how powerful four combined are.

A final, devastating component is procrastination's addictiveness.

An addiction is a self-reinforcing destructive habit that, the more you partake of it, the more you need to. Procrastination definitely qualifies, since every time you procrastinate you increase your fears around your writing and, consequently, your need to procrastinate.

Procrastination and "traditional" addictions do, in fact, share a common core of perfectionism. In *The Heart of Addiction*[2], Lance Dodes, M.D., writes, "Severe, unrealistic self-criticism is a very common precipitant of addictive behavior." Of one of his patients, he writes, "His use of a drug to deal with the self-condemnation of such a punitive conscience ... [is] a way to create an identity free of the 'tyranny' of this internal hanging judge." And at least four of the twelve attitudes and behaviors that Allen Berger discusses in his book *12 Stupid Things That Mess Up Recovery* are perfectionist symptoms: trying to become perfect, "feeling special and unique" (Section 2.2), selective honesty, and "believing that life should be easy." I discuss each of these, and many more symptoms, in Chapter 2.

Procrastination's "quintuple punch" is one reason it's such a difficult habit to overcome, but another is that it is sneaky and deceptive and doesn't fight fair (Section 1.8). It can be overcome, however, and relatively straightforwardly, once you move past dithering and on to actual problem-solving.

The first step is to get a handle on the precise nature of your obstacles and triggers, which we begin to do in the next chapter.

---

[2]For more information on the books I discuss check out http://hillaryrettig.com.

Section 1.5 Block vs. Spaghetti Snarl

One of the worst impediments to overcoming writer's block is the word "block." Many of us, hearing it, consciously or unconsciously envision a giant boulder or a monolith a la *2001: A Space Odyssey*—and how the heck are you going to get around that? At best, you might scale it like a mountain climber or chisel away at its edges.

"Uh oh."

Fortunately, your block isn't a monolith; it's a giant spaghetti snarl

A minor impediment...

with at least a dozen (or, more likely, two or three dozen) "strands," each representing a particular obstacle or trigger. Some strands are probably immense hawsers, while others are tiny shoelaces or dental floss.

The strands are all snarled together, and that's your block. The fact that your block is really a snarl is great news because a snarl can be untangled far more easily than a monolith scaled or chiseled. And that's exactly what you need to do—identify the strands so you can start coping with (and ultimately eliminating) them. Another wonderful difference between snarls and monoliths is that while chipping away at a monolith never gets any easier, with a snarl the more you untangle the easier and faster subsequent untangling gets. (And you can start with the easiest strands.)

Here's a typical spaghetti snarl from a blocked fiction writer:

> Not sure about the direction of my novel
> Not sure if I'm any good at writing
> Not sure if I can finish
> Not sure if people will like it or if it will sell
> Not sure it will get published
> Worry that since I'm not that familiar with the publishing industry I'll be taken advantage of
> Afraid that the questions I want to ask my writing group will be stupid, annoying, or pointless
> Afraid I won't be a success, or that if I am I won't be able to repeat it
> Afraid if I get published that people will judge my appearance
> Don't have a good environment for writing (stuck writing on the couch with laptop and lots of clutter)
> Get distracted by TV and Internet
> No time
> Family is a distraction
> Personal worries (including financial worries) get in the way of writing
> Worried that I may be judged for my choices in writing/ genres
> An ADD diagnosis that has left me insecure and ashamed, and also makes it harder for me to organize big projects

Afraid of losing privacy after being published

Last job (not writing-related) had both a negative environment and an abusive boss so there's some residual trauma.

The above strands map closely with the barriers to productivity discussed in this book—and especially with perfectionism.

Here's another snarl—this time a typical one from a graduate student unable to write her Ph.D. thesis:

Need to preserve "together" facade to colleagues; embarrassing to reveal I'm struggling

Confusion/conflict over the direction of thesis

Conflicts about writing about (and thus mentally reliving) some intense, shocking and possibly traumatizing field work experiences

Desire to cling to benefits of student life: health insurance, relative lack of responsibility/authority

Fear of not getting hired despite best efforts

Feelings of fraudulence and not belonging

Horror (justified based on the my experience) of work/success being stolen

Ambivalence about assuming authority

Rampant sexism/misogyny by thesis advisor and father

Discouraged that I can't write papers as easily as when I was an undergraduate

Keep comparing myself to others

Single-parent stresses; conflict between parenting and graduate student roles

No wonder these writers were blocked! Every time they tried to write, each strand became an internal voice that not only created fear but that argued persuasively that they should be doing something else. In the next chapter, I discuss the metaphor of a forest path that I frequently use to describe this problem.

Section 1.6 Who's on Your Path?
The Woodland Trail Metaphor of Writing

Picture your writing session as a stroll down a beautiful, sun-dappled woodland path. The path is wide and flat, the air warm and inviting, and on either side of you are banks of friendly plants alive with twittering birds. You're having a marvelous time!

All of a sudden someone pops up out of the underbrush and joins you on your path—it's your husband, full of opinions on your current piece of writing.

You walk on for a bit, your husband yammering in your ear—not just about the writing, now, but about how he wishes the house were cleaner and how you two never go out any more. It's an unpleasant distraction, but you're still mostly enjoying your walk.

Then someone else pops up—your parents, who are worried about how your writing will reflect on them.

And then your siblings parachute down onto the path asking whether you don't think you're wasting your time, and aren't you embarrassed to be driving around in that old car?

Then an old writing teacher pops up, reminding you of how "you really don't do dialogue very well."

And an editor who, twenty years ago, described a story of yours as "jejune." (You had to look the word up, and oy did it hurt when you did!)

And the author of a newspaper article you recently read that proclaimed that the market for epic family sagas, like the one you happen to be writing, is "dead."

Etc.

Soon, you're walking at the center of a clamorous crowd, none of whom you've invited. Naturally, you'll have a hard time writing in the midst of their harping, carping, and negativity.

The prolific handle things differently. They decide, with absolute authority (get it? author-ity), who comes on their path and how long they can stay. You're only allowed on if they want you on, and the minute you're no longer an asset to their process, you're gone. (I like to imagine that "gone" being either in the form of a vaudeville hook whisking the offender off stage right, or a giant boot sending him into orbit.)

And no free passes—*everyone* has to pass the "asset" test, including partners, parents, kids, and "important" teachers, editors, and the like. And those who fail a few times permanently lose their right to apply for entry.

They're banished, baby.

And so the prolific have a wonderful time strolling peacefully and productively through the hours, days, and years of their work.

Section 1.7 Write Out Your Snarl

It would be great if, right now or very soon, you would put this book down and make a list of all the strands in your snarl: meaning, all your fears, worries, resource deficiencies, and other barriers to productivity. Try to write something concerning each of the categories mentioned in Section 1.1: conflicts over the project, fears of failure and success, resource deficiencies, etc. Also be sure to cover the five elements of the quintuple punch: fear of failure (or success) around the current writing session, the project as a whole, your overall writing career, and the act of writing itself, as well as procrastination's addictiveness.

Try to distinguish between obstacles and triggers, and try to figure out what triggers your obstacles are creating, and vice versa. (The main use of the obstacle and trigger categories is to help you understand more fully the complex nature of your barriers.) Be sure to examine incidents going back to your childhood, as most cases of procrastination have early roots (Section 6.1). Cast as wide a net as possible, capturing both issues that seem monumental (the hawsers), and those that seem tiny or trivial (but may, in fact, not be).

Characterizing your snarl can be deep, intense work—one student described her list as a "grenade." You're looking at the types of hurtful incidents, losses, rejections, humiliations, mistakes, failures, and other stuff that many people strenuously avoid examining. And you might consequently experience rage, grief, remorse, shame, humiliation, or other difficult feelings. So please make sure you are doing this work with abundant support, including, if needed, professional support from a therapist.

And take heart, because what you are doing is very powerful and healing: you are moving beyond a moralistic and disempowering "blaming and shaming" mindset to one of calm objectivity, which is the precursor to effective problem-solving. The amazing thing is that often simply naming a fear will either alleviate it or immediately present a solution:

> "Not enough privacy? I guess I'll use the guest room for my writing room. It just sits there empty most of the time, anyway."

> "Not enough time? I'll call up some friends and see if we can swap babysitting, or if they can drop the kids off at school."

> "Distracted because my friend called and we fought? From now on, I'll tell her to only call after my writing time. She probably won't like that, so I will need to be strong in the face of her pressure. And maybe I ought to rethink this friendship, anyway—it's draining me."

And, finally:

> "I hate that I've been stuck on this stupid chapter for weeks. Well, let's just take a moment and see if I can figure out what's happening. OK, one thing is that my hero and heroine are supposed to be warming to each other in this chapter, and I just don't see it happening. WOW, I think I just hit it. They really do hate each other. I think I've confused the hero and villain, or maybe I need an entire new character for the romantic lead. Wait! What about George, that funny astronomer in Chapter 7? I really liked him, and the heroine really liked him. I would love to write more about him, and I could really see them together. OK, so where else could they meet? Maybe she's camping in the state park and he shows up one night making a racket with his big telescope, and then she freaks out in her tent, thinking he's a bear and so she throws her canteen at him and it hits him in the..." (Continues writing the scene.)

About that last example: YES, getting unblocked is frequently that easy—once you move past the moralizing and shame. As discussed in Section 5.4, **work often stalls when you either haven't thought it through enough, or are trying to force it in a direction it doesn't want to go.** Journaling will often solve these problems, and when you use it, even a piece of writing that seemed hopeless can come together almost magically.

So journaling will eliminate or shrink some strands of your snarl. Others will require more work, and probably the involvement of family, friends, writing colleagues, mentors, and professionals (e.g., a therapist or doctor). Some strands will require years to solve, and still others—such as a disability or chronic health problem—may not in fact be entirely solvable. But they are still worth working on.

Whatever you do, don't waste time feeling guilty or ashamed about your barriers. As mentioned in Section 1.1, they're all reasonable, and in nearly every case you didn't even cause them.

Section 1.8 Procrastination's Duplicitous Strategies

Charles Dickens famously called procrastination "the thief of time." (It was Micawber in *David Copperfield*.) In classes, I share this quote and then ask students what qualities they associate with thieves: common answers include sneakiness, stealth, exploitation, and a predatory nature.

Congruent with Dickens's view is that of Steven Pressfield in his book *The War of Art*:

> Resistance [his word for the force impelling procrastination—HR] will tell you anything to keep you from doing your work. It will perjure, fabricate; falsify; seduce, bully, cajole. Resistance is protean. It will assume any form, if that's what it takes to deceive you. It will reason with you like a lawyer or jam a nine-millimeter in your face like a stickup man. Resistance has no conscience. It will pledge anything to get a deal, then double-cross you as soon as your back is turned. If you take Resistance at its word, you

deserve everything you get. Resistance is always lying and always full of shit.

Allen Berger's characterization of addiction, in *12 Stupid Things That Mess Up Recovery*, also applies perfectly to procrastination:

> Addiction [or procrastination—HR] is like a tiger lying in wait for its prey. Unfortunately, *we are* the prey! ... [The tiger] is well camouflaged with denial, minimization, rationalization, and other psychological defenses ... Addiction is cunning and baffling. Many times its victims do not know they are being stalked until it is too late. ...
>
> What makes matters even worse is that our opponent—our addiction—knows everything about us. It is part of us; it has all the intelligence, capabilities, insights, and knowledge that we possess. It's like we are in a life-and-death struggle against a clone. Our disease anticipates our every move. It understands our strategies. It knows our strengths and weaknesses.

Put simply, **we don't have trouble overcoming procrastination because we're weak, but because it is duplicitous**. While we've spent years and decades vacillating fruitlessly between trying to reason with it and trying to coerce it, it's blithely ignored our efforts and gone about its business—all the while, brilliantly hiding its tracks via two main strategies: denial and deceit.

Denial is when emotional needs cause you to either selectively consider the data around a particular situation, or to limit the conclusions you're willing to draw. Someone who gives up on his writing because he tells himself it's incompatible with normal adult responsibilities is in denial, as is someone who gives up on other important priorities because he thinks writers should live only for their writing. Both of these strategies are dead ends, as you'll learn in Section 1.10: denial is never productive over the long term.

The purpose of this book and all my work is to help you live as consciously as possible: to make choices with as full as possible an awareness of their context and implications, and to help you live as much as possible in alignment with your values. Consciousness is not only admirable and desirable in its own right, it's essential for any kind of ambitious achievement. And it yields true happiness, contentment, and even joy.

The strategies that lead to productive writing are outlined in this book. You may not need all of them, but pretending you don't need one when you do is pure denial and self-sabotage. You might dislike having to do your time management, for instance, or having to end a drama-filled relationship that's taking up too much time and energy, but if you need to do those things, you should do them, and sooner rather than later. Prolific people take on these kinds of challenging tasks routinely because they know that, while there might be short-term pain, the long-term pain of underproductivity and underachievement is far worse.

Deceit is procrastination's most powerful strategy. Procrastination deceives us by mimicking productive work; and, as you will see, there is no shortage of ways for it to do so. The graduate student who researches his thesis to death but never gets around to writing it is a victim of the "deceit" form of procrastination, as are:

- The novelist who keeps revising her novel but never actually submits it;
- The blogger who keeps reading other blogs instead of writing his own;
- The writer who overinvests time and energy in her day job, so that she is too exhausted to write when she gets home;
- The writer whose time and energy go to an endless list of good deeds and community work, so that she never has time to write;
- The writer who spends all her time being a supermom and housekeeper instead of writing.

In all of these cases, the writer will easily justify the procrastination—much more easily than, say, if she were playing video games all day. There will probably be people cheering her on, and society as a whole supports many of the above choices. All of this outside reinforcement makes the deceit form of procrastination extremely hard to identify and solve.

The solution, in many cases, is not to stop doing those other activities (assuming that that's even an option): it's to do the work in this book, including overcoming perfectionism (Chapter 2) and time management (Chapter 4).

Section 1.9 Two Commonly Overlooked Barriers

(1) Physical Discomfort

Writers tend to live inside their own heads and deprecate their physical needs, but prolific writers know that procrastination often begins in the body, so they treat their body like a "writing partner." In particular, they learn to (a) create comfortable and safe (ergonomic) workspaces for themselves, (b) diligently maintain their health, and (c) deal with small aches and other physical distractions before they become larger.

An ergonomic workspace (Section 3.7) is essential, not just as a guard against carpal tunnel syndrome and other maladies, but so you can write comfortably for long periods. Ergonomic furniture doesn't have to be expensive: a new adjustable office chair costs less than $100, and of course you can also buy used. My former husband built a super-comfortable custom writing table for me that's exactly the right height; it cost $10 and took about an hour to build, and a decade later I'm still using it. [3]

Diligent attention to bodily health makes sense from a productivity standpoint and many others. Proper rest, exercise, and nutrition are also essential.

Even a healthy body is susceptible to small aches and discomforts from sitting too long, however, and those aches can subvert your best efforts to stay focused. The prolific therefore work to become conscious of, and responsive to, their bodies' signals. A tiny bit of fatigue or stiffness, and they're up doing a few quick stretches—and then, back to work. If they're too cold, they break out the heater and foot warmers—and keep writing. If they're too hot, they break out the fan or air conditioner. Many moderate their eating before a writing session to avoid drowsiness, and the coffee drinkers fine-tune their intake so they are energized but not hyper.

(2) Indecision

People often procrastinate when they're scared to make a decision, a problem that's often most severe and obvious when the decision is a big one, such as finding a new job or leaving a bad relationship. Indecision on even small decisions can also be debilitating, however—and it's a

---

[3] I used to tell people it was "a big wooden plank with four sticks for legs," but have since been informed that it is a sheet of medium-density fiber board and four 2x2" balusters supported by 1x3" pine crossbars.

particular problem for writers because writing is basically a continuous series of large and small decisions. If you procrastinate every time you need to decide which word to use, or which car a character drives, or whether he was born in Tuscaloosa or Tacoma, you're going to have a tortuous writing process. (In case you're wondering, it's perfectionism that makes these decisions scary, because the perfectionist believes she MUST GET IT RIGHT. A non-perfectionist, in contrast, would just stick in the first word/car/city that came to mind, content in the knowledge that, (a) the initial choice is often the right one, and (b) if it's not, she can always change it later. See Section 5.2.)

So, practice making quick—even immediate—decisions while writing, and in other areas of your life. Many decisions get delayed because they require just a bit of thought, or are a bit confusing, or because the right choice is mildly inconvenient or unpleasant. Just push through the reluctance, decide, and act. **Indecision is also often the root problem for people with overflowing email inboxes**—with the added complication that they are also probably trying to craft detailed, artful responses when a terse reply (or none!) is all that's required.

Some people are terrified of making the wrong decision, but the prolific (and other successful people) know that wrong decisions are inevitable. They therefore don't dwell on or punish themselves for their mistakes, but simply try to rectify them as quickly as possible and move on. They also know it's far better to make a lot of quick decisions, including some wrong ones, then to agonize over every decision to the point where your productivity grinds to a halt.

And they also know that important decisions are best made after input from as wide a range as possible of those involved or affected, as well as knowledgeable mentors and colleagues. "Random" input from those who aren't involved or knowledgeable is common in this world, but not particularly useful.

Section 1.10 Procrastination's Denial of Self: Selling Out and Stalling Out

The worst cases of writer's block manifest themselves as selling out and stalling out.

Selling out is when you sacrifice your writing dream to other activities, such as making money, raising a family, or doing community work. You can also, of course, sacrifice it to less worthwhile endeavors, such as compulsive housekeeping, television watching, Web surfing, or video gaming. I actually avoid using the term "selling out" in general conversation and classes because it's often used to moralistically label people who are simply doing their best to make difficult life choices. But we can apply it non-judgmentally to those who relinquish too much of their dream.

Stalling out is the opposite of selling out: it's when you sacrifice everything else to your writing. Basically, your interests narrow, and your life narrows, until you're doing little else other than your work—except that, since this strategy creates deprivation and denial, you're probably not doing much of that, either.

Selling out and stalling out are both perfectionist mistakes, reflecting grandiosity (Section 2.2), dichotomization (Section 2.7), and other perfectionist symptoms.

Section 1.11 The Heart of Procrastination

Despite the many ways procrastination may have impeded your life and success, it is important that you not see it as your enemy. For one thing, it's part of your own psyche, and it's not helpful to see a part of yourself as the enemy. For another, its motives are noble: as discussed in Section 1.4, it is only trying to protect you from failure and consequent ego demolition. True, it is doing so incompetently and destructively, but that's not its fault, either: procrastination is incompetent because it is a fear-based behavior, and fear tends to both regress us psychologically (more on that in a bit) and impair our judgment and effectiveness. Also, if no one taught you the elements of writing productively, and the solutions for underproductivity, how can you blame yourself for not knowing them?

You invoke procrastination when you perfectionistically try to coerce your vulnerable writing persona into writing. That persona is vulnerable not because it's weak or flawed, but because writing is a hugely self-exposing activity, and is often risky in other ways, too (Chapter 6). Your perfectionist self will tell you the opposite—that writing is easy, trivial, etc.—but, as you will shortly learn, you should never listen to the voice of perfectionism.

So: you ask your vulnerable writer self to "perform," but hold her to an unreasonable perfectionist standard of success (Chapter 2) AND deprive her of needed resources and support (Chapters 3–8). And then, when she doesn't instantly leap up and do your bidding, you try to coerce her via the self-abusive litany ("Why are you so lazy?" etc.), which only increases her fear.

In other words, you've already tried to write (or merely contemplated writing), encountered an obstacle or trigger, felt a quintuple-engendered terror that you're going to fail, attempted to get yourself back on track via coercion, and thus are even more terrified.

Or, expanding on the illustration from Section 1.2:

Prolific vs. Underproductive

That's when procrastination steps in. She's regressed, remember? So let's picture her as a fierce and determined fifteen-year-old with a strong sense of justice. She reacts to your unfair demands and bullying with outrage, and responds the way teens do: first by rebellion, and eventually (if you persist) helplessness.

Rebellion: "Why should I be stuck in here writing when everyone else is out having a good time? I'm out of here!"

Helplessness: "It's hopeless, so why should I even bother trying?"

Both reactions reinforce and justify your initial reflex to flee from the terrifying oppression.

Rebellion and helplessness are developmentally appropriate

and even liberated reactions—for a fifteen-year-old. An adult, however, should be able to respond more productively by problem-solving (Section 1.2) or changing her writing context in ways detailed in the rest of this book. Then again, there's no real adult in this scenario: only the vulnerable writer, perfectionist bully, and teenaged defender. The adult will show up when you start practicing compassionate objectivity (Section 2.10) and the other solutions to perfectionism.

As discussed in Section 1.2, the best bullying can achieve, in most cases, is short-term compliance. The more you try to bully, in fact, the more likely the teen is to dig in her heels. And it's important to realize that, although the procrastinator is regressed and therefore disempowered in terms of problem-solving, she nonetheless retains all your adult capacities for dissociation, denial, and deception.

And her cause is just. As explained way back in Section 1.1, your reasons for procrastinating are always valid, even if procrastination itself is a suboptimal response.

So don't reject your procrastinator, but embrace her as your courageous protector. Soon you won't need her anymore—and, like most teens who've been asked to take on too much responsibility, she will be happy to step back and let the adult take charge.

The first step is to overcome your perfectionism—which we'll do in Chapter 2.

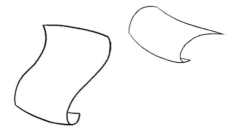

Overcoming Perfectionism

"You can believe that I would like this book, the child of my understanding, to be the most beautiful, the most brilliant, and the most discreet that anyone could imagine."
—Cervantes, *Don Quixote*

Perfectionism Characterized

Section 2.1 Perfectionists Hold Unrealistic Definitions of Success and Punish Themselves Harshly for the Inevitable Failures.

Many people think perfectionism is a destructive habit or way of thinking, but it's actually much worse than that: it's a kind of toxic filter through which you view yourself, your work, and the world. Perfectionists make six overarching mistakes:

1. They hold unrealistic definitions of success and punish themselves harshly for perceived failures.
2. They are grandiose.
3. They prioritize product over process.
4. They over-rely on external rewards and measures of success.

5. They deprecate the ordinary processes of creativity and career-building.
6. They overidentify with their work.

I discuss these in this section and also in Sections 2.2–2.6. In Section 2.7, I discuss a host of other serious perfectionist errors.

Then, in Sections 2.8 and 2.9, I discuss the causes of perfectionism.

And, finally, starting in Section 2.10, I start discussing the solutions.

Here are some examples of perfectionist writers:

• A novelist who believes he must sacrifice everything for his art, including family, friends, material comforts, and health. To not do so, he feels, makes him a "dilettante."

• A grad student who expects to write her thesis while still maintaining her full load of household, parenting, and teaching responsibilities. Anything less means she's being "lazy." Moreover, if her thesis doesn't rock her field, she'll know she "hasn't lived up to her potential."

• A community worker who plans to write a thirty-page grant proposal over the weekend, even though he's never written more than ten pages a day and is hosting out-of-town guests. If he fails, he'll feel "uncommitted."

• A short-story writer who has been blocked for years and decides to start writing again, setting a goal of three hours a day. If she fails, she knows she's destined to be a "loser."

All of these writers are making the fundamental perfectionist mistake of setting unrealistic goals and punishing themselves harshly, via self-shaming, when they fail to meet them. Please note that each has a rationalization for the crazy goal: the novelist tells himself that "sacrificing everything is what committed artists do"; the grad student thinks she's a "multitasker" and "has done so much research that the writing will be easy"; the community worker tells himself his guests are "low-maintenance"; and the short story writer tells herself "writing is easy." The rationalization occasionally contains a nugget of truth, but never enough to justify the perfectionist's inflated expectations.

It's important that you recognize just how far these writers are from the truth:

Nonperfectionist novelists know that chronic deprivation and isolation are not conducive to creativity—and, in fact, almost always work against it.

Nonperfectionist grad students know that the best way to write a thesis is to clear the deck of as many other commitments as possible before getting started. They also know that the goal should not be to set your field on fire—which almost no one does, anyway—but simply to finish as quickly as possible so that you can move on to the next stage of your career.

Nonperfectionist grant writers know it's crazy to try to increase your writing productivity 50% overnight, especially when you've got other commitments.

Nonperfectionist short story writers know that when recovering from a block, you should initially set extremely low productivity goals—say, five or ten *minutes* of writing time a day.

All of these perfectionist writers are probably also telling themselves that they're simply "setting a high standard." **But perfectionism isn't about setting high standards; it's about setting unrealistic or unachievable ones.** There's a *big* difference.

Most perfectionists struggle under a constant burden of failure and shame because they are constantly setting unrealistic goals and failing to meet them. "Time for a three-hour writing session. In which I have to write something fabulous. And each sentence needs to be superb. And all of this, pretty easily." Fail, fail, fail, fail.

"And the same thing tomorrow, and every day I try to write." Fail, fail, fail, fail.

And don't forget the harsh punishment side of the equation! It encompasses labels such as "dilettante," "lazy," and "uncommitted," which our writers will take very much to heart and feel deeply ashamed of, and more generally, our old friend the self-abusive litany ("What's wrong with you?," "Why are you so lazy?," etc.; see Section 1.2). An interesting thing about the litany is that, when I ask writers to recite it, they can almost always effortlessly do so, and this tells me it's a "living" presence within them. (Usually, their voice becomes harsh and strident, and sometimes, when I ask whose voice it is, it turns out to be that of a parent or teacher who harshly criticized them. Harsh words often live on for years or decades.)

The litany, as it turns out, is not merely the voice of

procrastination, but more specifically that of perfectionism, most writers' biggest barrier to productivity. Many writers refer it as their "inner critic." I call it the "inner bully." Anne Lamott, in *Bird by Bird*, cannily calls it "the voice of the oppressor," which fits in with the idea of procrastination as disempowerment, because oppressors by definition disempower you. *The voice of perfectionism is <u>always</u> wrong, and you should never listen to it.* In fact, the work of overcoming procrastination is largely the work of learning to ignore it.

Section 2.2 Perfectionists are Grandiose

Grandiosity, or the delusion that you're special and/or don't have to follow the normal rules governing productivity and success, underpins nearly every aspect of perfectionism. The writers in the previous chapter were all being grandiose, as are writers who believe they should be able to write polished first drafts (an oxymoron) or achieve commercial success without having to market or sell (Section 2.5). **Even reasonable goals can be grandiose if you're not willing to pursue them strategically, or make the needed investments of time, money, and other resources.**

Another group of grandiose writers believe that if they just publish the right book, all their problems will be solved. ("I'll be rich and famous *and* popular!") This is, basically, a gambler's strategy: writing as slot machine. Here's Steven Pressfield from *The War of Art*:

> Grandiose fantasies are ... the sign of an amateur. The professional has learned that success, like happiness, comes as a by-product of work. The professional concentrates on the work and allows rewards to come or not come, whatever they like.

Grandiosity is a problem for writers because our media and culture are permeated with grandiose myths and misconceptions about writing, which writers who are undermentored fall prey to. Red Smith's famous *bon mot* about how, to write, you need only "sit down at a typewriter and open a vein," and Gene Fowler's similarly sanguinary advice to "sit staring at a blank sheet of paper until the drops of blood form on your forehead," are nothing but macho grandiose posturing, as is

William Faulkner's overwrought encomium to monomaniacal selfishness, from his *Paris Review* interview:

> The writer's only responsibility is to his art. He will be completely ruthless if he is a good one. He has a dream. It anguishes him so much he must get rid of it. He has no peace until then. Everything goes by the board: honor, pride, decency, security, happiness, all, to get the book written. If a writer has to rob his mother, he will not hesitate; the "Ode on a Grecian Urn" is worth any number of old ladies.

Many of the most famous quotes about writing are grandiose. I'm not saying that all of these writers were posturing—perhaps that's how they truly perceived themselves and their creativity. **What I do know is that, for most writers, a strategy based on pain and deprivation is not a route to productivity.** In fact, it is more likely a route to a block.

I actually find quotes about how awful writing and the writing life are to be not just perfectionist, but self-indulgent. No one's forcing these writers to write, after all, and there are obviously far worse ways to spend one's time, not to mention earn one's living. All worthwhile endeavors require hard, and occasionally tedious, work; if anything, we writers have it relatively easy, given writing's few material requirements. (Contrast with, say, a potter's need for a wheel and kiln—not to mention, a place to house them—or a Shakespearean actor's need for an ensemble and stage.) Besides, writing, like all creative endeavors but unlike most noncreative ones, offers the possibility of transcendence—a fantastic reward for one's efforts and struggle.

Nonperfectionist and nongrandiose writers recognize all this. Flaubert famously said, "Writing is a dog's life, but the only life worth living," and Toni Morrison (I think it was) once said in an interview that, while she doesn't particularly enjoy writing, "without it, you only have life." Special kudos go to Jane Yolen, however, for her book *Take Joy*, which begins with a celebration of the inherent joyfulness of writing. She also responds to Smith's and Fowler's sanguinary comments with the good-natured ridicule they deserve: "By God, that's a messy way of working."

Even absent a self-sacrificial imperative, the idea that writing is a holy mission is fundamentally antiproductive, since it raises impossible expectations and puts huge pressure on the writer (see the Labels section of Section 2.7). Partly for that reason, partly because they are focused on their quotidian work as opposed to fantasies of success, and partly because they are focused on internal rewards (Section 2.4), the prolific tend to see their writing not as some kind of holy mission but their "work," "craft," or even "job".

> *Stephen King*: "Don't wait for the muse ... This isn't the Ouija board or the spirit-world we're talking about here, but just another job like laying pipe or driving long-haul trucks. Your job is to make sure the muse knows where you're going to be every day from nine 'til noon or seven 'til three."

> *Anthony Trollope*: "Let [other writers'] work be to them as is his common work to the common laborer. No gigantic efforts will then be necessary. He need tie no wet towels round his brow, nor sit for thirty hours at his desk without moving,—as men have sat, or said that they have sat."

(I love the skepticism at the end of Trollope's statement, which I think is entirely justified when reading grandiose statements about writing.) Ironically, it's the nongrandiose attitude that frees writers to consistently experience the glory and transcendence that grandiosity promises but only rarely, if ever, delivers.

The final problem with grandiosity is that it causes perfectionists to distrust and devalue work and success when they come too easily. "If it came easily, then it couldn't have been any good" is their motto. I can't imagine a more self-defeating attitude.

The idea that grandiosity fuels perfectionism always shocks perfectionists, who tend to think their problem is low self-esteem. But it's grandiosity that causes the shame and low self-esteem by constantly setting goals and conditions the writer can't possibly live up to.

Section 2.3 Perfectionists Prioritize Product Over Process

In *The War of Art*, Steven Pressfield describes the end of his writing sessions thusly:

I wrap for the day. Copy whatever I've done to disk and stash the disk in the glove compartment of my truck in case there's a fire and I have to run for it. I power down ... How many pages have I produced? I don't care. Are they any good? I don't even think about it. All that matters is I've put in my time and hit it with all I've got.

Prolific writers tend to trust themselves and the writing process, knowing that the latter will take them where they need to go. Even that poster boy for quality and *le mot juste*, Flaubert, said, "Success must be a consequence and never a goal," meaning that it should arise organically from the creative process.

Perfectionists, in contrast, focus obsessively on (1) the quality and quantity of their output and (2) the external reward or result they hope to reap (Section 2.4)—all measured grandiosely, of course. Focusing on product is a way of trying to control the outcome, a common and understandable response to fear. If you're terrified that you'll fail, and that the consequences of failure will be disastrous, you'll naturally want to do everything you can to avoid that fate. (It's also a trauma symptom; see Section 2.9.)

Of course, some writers do use word counts and other metrics to gauge productivity, but you should only do this after having overcome your perfectionism. Otherwise, you'll just set unrealistic word-count goals and bash yourself for failing to meet them. And even those writers who do set goals devote most of their attention, while writing, to the creative demands of the work itself (Section 2.16).

Section 2.4 Perfectionists Over-Rely on External Rewards and Measures of Success

Perfectionists tend to dwell on questions like these: *Will my book sell quickly? Will it sell a million copies? Will it earn me a million dollars? Will it receive a wonderful review from the* Times*?* The reality is that very few books achieve those levels of success, and success at that level is often a crapshoot, anyway. (You could write a fabulous book and it might not sell. Or it could sell, but get dreadful reviews from clueless reviewers.) So these preoccupations are not just grandiose distractions, but dangerous in that they set you up for likely huge disappointment.

Please note that I have nothing against ambitious goals—in fact, I'm all for them. The problem is when you set them without planning for them, or without being willing to make the necessary investments and sacrifices, or you are unrealistic in your expectations (for instance, by pretending that there's not a large luck component to success). Someone determined to write a bestseller, for instance, can greatly increase his odds of doing so by writing to a popular formula, doing shrewd networking, and investing a lot in marketing and promotion. Whether you're willing to do those things or not—and I'm not saying they're bad, although most people who abstractly want to write best-sellers turn out not to want to do them—you need to get clear on not only your motives and goals, but your strategy (Section 8.6).

Another problem with ambitious goals is that even when you do everything right, there's a good chance you'll fall short. (That's why they're "ambitious.") And if you're prey to another perfectionist trait, overidentification with your work (Section 2.6), that can be devastating. But it you approach ambitious goals nonperfectionistically then you'll probably achieve plenty—and have lots of fun doing it—even if you don't achieve stratospheric heights of success.

Most of us, perfectionist or not, love stories of improbable or outrageous success, like J.K. Rowling rising from welfare to billionairedom. But to make your happiness and self-esteem dependent on such an outcome—or even a far lesser one, or any external reward or outcome at all, really—is risky in the extreme. Far better to do what most prolific writers do and enjoy the external rewards when they come, but derive most of your satisfaction from the act of writing and the creativity-centered lifestyle you build around it.

Section 2.5 Perfectionists Deprecate the Ordinary Processes of Creativity and Career-Building

Perfectionists are all about the easy win. They think they should be able to write easily and build successful careers easily. When a perfectionist hears Anne Lamott's famous dictum that almost all writing projects begin with a "shitty first draft," he nods and says, "Of course—that only makes sense." But when you ask him to describe such a draft, he inevitably describes something already organized and polished, and that just needs a few tweaks here and there.

Perfectionists' idea of shitty first drafts is the same as other writers' almost-final drafts!

A blocked graduate student once told me, "I never thought the idea of drafts applied to me." As is often the case with perfectionist delusions, hers was built on a grain of truth: she had, as an undergraduate, been able to write papers in a single sitting. (She wasn't actually eschewing drafts so much as blowing through them quickly.) When she got to grad school, however, the assignments got more complex and her process was inadequate. This is a common problem, actually, yet few graduate programs seem to help students with it, or even recognize that it exists.

Epically blocked humorist Fran Lebowitz also deprecates drafts, deriding them as "waste paper."[1] She says she does nearly all her revisions in her head and then writes out a final. Most writers would find that process profoundly antiproductive—which it obviously has been for her. In Section 5.2, I discuss how prolificness is achieved, counterintuitively, by writing not fewer drafts, but more.

Whether they realize it or not, many perfectionists grandiosely believe excellent writing should flow from their fingertips. And even if they admit they need to write drafts, they tend to grossly underestimate the number it takes to get to the final. (The correct answer is "as many as it takes.") And, as if all this weren't bad enough, here's an example of the kind of standard they tend to hold their finished products to: "If I couldn't write about debtors' prisons with Dickens's authority, I failed. If I couldn't outwit Jane Austen, I failed. If I couldn't philosophize like Bellow, I failed."

Perfectionists also deprecate the resources and preparation needed to write, and to succeed as a writer (Chapters 3–8), and they love stories of spectacular success that confirm their perfectionist, grandiose biases. (And, as discussed in Section 2.8, the media are only too happy to oblige.) Here's Brenda Ueland, from *If You Want to Write*:

> We writers are the most lily-livered of all craftsmen. We expect more, for the most peewee efforts, than any other people. A gifted young woman writes a poem. It is rejected. She does

---

[1] Thomas Beller, "Interview with Fran Lebowitz," Mr. Beller's Neighborhood (blog), October 11, 2002 (mrbellersneighborhood.com/2002/10/interview-with-fran-lebowitz).

not write another perhaps for two years, perhaps all her life. Think of the patience and love that a tap-dancer or vaudeville acrobat puts into his work. Think of how many times Kreisler has practiced trills. If you will write as many words as Kreisler has practiced trills I prophesy that you will win the Nobel Prize in ten years.

In his book *Outliers*, Malcolm Gladwell provides examples ranging from chess players to Olympic athletes to The Beatles to substantiate his claim that it takes around 10,000 hours of dedicated practice to achieve world-class mastery of a complex skill. And that's just to succeed technically. To build a career around your talent requires entire other skillsets, including the abilities to strategize and plan; manage time, money and other resources; and market and sell. Perfectionists tend to elide all that with their obsessive fetish about talent as the key determinant of success (Section 2.7).

Section 2.6 Perfectionists Overidentify with Their Work

One of the worst torments of procrastination is that many people do it only around a goal they care deeply about. In other areas of their lives—day jobs, community work, family responsibilities, etc.—they are dynamos. Many blocked writers are even writing dynamos—on pieces other than the one they most want to be writing. They'll write emails, work reports, or letters to the editor galore, while their novel or thesis goes a-wasting.

We already know part of what's going on: the procrastinators are using the other tasks to mimic productive work so that they can feel less aware of, and guilty about, not working on their main project. But why should they so strongly need to procrastinate in the first place?

In Section 1.1, I discussed how procrastination is grounded in a craving to escape from perfectionism-induced fear. Most of that fear arises because perfectionists overidentify with their work, meaning that they see it as an extension of, and reflection on, their deepest soul. When a work fails—and, remember: for a perfectionist, failure is not just inevitable, but constant—a perfectionist feels that he himself is a miserable failure.

Perfectionism reduces your entire existence and value to your writing—and, often, just one aspect of your writing (Section 2.7). "If I can't write, then who am I?" the perfectionist asks—and his answer, unlike that of a psychologically healthy person, will be "nothing," because perfectionism values all your non-writing attributes and accomplishments at approximately zero.

Because perfectionists reduce their entire value to their writing, any "failure" becomes a kind of ego death or annihilation—and that, in turn, engenders not merely a fear of failure, but a terror of it.

Can you remember the last time you felt truly afraid or terrified? We tend to confuse fear with less intense emotions like aversion, but it's actually far more horrible and disabling than that. When we're afraid, our priority is to return to safety, and the three most characteristic responses to fear—flight, fight, freeze—are intended to help us do that. Not coincidentally, they match the most common manifestations of procrastination:

Flight: doing something else other than your writing—or writing something other than what you had planned to.

Fight: adopting a combative relationship with your writing, as in "Why should I be stuck inside writing on such a nice day when everyone else is outside having fun?" (Because fear impairs our ability to problem solve, it never occurs to the combative writer that she could take her laptop outside and write.)

Freeze: a sense of helplessness or hopelessness; an inability to act.

It's mainly the perfectionism-fueled terror that knocks perfectionists off their "path" and prevents them from returning to it.

So those are the six defining behaviors of perfectionism—each both a symptom of and catalyst for the problem. To make matters worse, there are a whole host of other attitudes and behaviors that also characterize perfectionism, which I discuss in the next section. Many, I suspect, will be familiar.

Section 2.7 Perfectionism's Toolkit

Invidious Comparisons. Perfectionists love comparisons. They'll compare themselves to living writers, dead writers, rich writers, poor (and, thus, "noble") writers, non-writers who make a lot of money, non-writers who seem to be having more fun, etc.

And they'll compare themselves on any point, including writing quantity, writing "quality," worthiness of topic, purity of mission, income, audience, the size of the house they live in, the speed of the car they drive, the glamorousness of the parties they attend, etc.

And they'll *always* come out on the losing end of any comparison—because the point of a perfectionist comparison is not to yield useful insight, but to serve as yet another club to bash yourself over the head with to try to coerce yourself into more productivity.

Perfectionist comparisons are *always* invalid, and sometimes crazy. A perfectionist with a day job will compare her productivity to that of a friend without one, and somehow conclude she should be able to match her friend's output. (Often, with a weak rationale, e.g., "My job isn't that hard.") Or, a perfectionist will compare the size of his audience to that of another writer, ignoring the fact that the other writer writes in a more popular genre and does more marketing. Or, he'll compare himself to a writer who got published more quickly, ignoring the fact that that writer specifically chose to take a workshop with a well-connected teacher known for helping her students get published.

Another common comparison is with some illusory or uncommon level of peak performance. "I should be able to write three hours every morning before work," not just because (a) "three hours isn't much," (b) "Anthony Trollope did it," and (c) "my job is easy," but (d) because "once in a while I can actually do that." Instead of measuring yourself against an impossible or exceptional productivity standard, measure yourself against a reasonable one while meanwhile working to uncover, and duplicate, the reasons for your occasionally higher productivity. (Maybe the roommates were out and so the apartment was quiet—and so, maybe you'll rearrange your day job schedule so that you're home more when the roommates are out, or look for a quiet place outside the apartment to write.)

Dichotomous Thinking. Either/or, black-or-white, "dichotomous" thinking is a hallmark of perfectionism—and also of trauma, by the way (Section 2.9). A perfectionist tends to see her projects—and, by extension, herself—either as a total success or total failure, which again reinforces a terror of failure. Here's a fine example of dichotomous thinking from Gail Godwin's novel about a struggling painter, *Violet Clay*:

> What if Violet Clay wasn't to be one of the shining ones after all? But: no. I hadn't yet reached that point of resignation where I surrendered the image of my greatest self. If and when that day came, I might as well be dead.

The eponymous heroine dichotomously envisions only two fates: glory or death. (This brief excerpt also ingeniously manages to incorporate several other perfectionist traits, including grandiosity, over-identification with the work, and over-reliance on external rewards.)

Dichotomization means that even many successes will be classified as failures, simply because they were not total, amazing, 100% successes according to perfectionist criteria—an attitude that, all by itself, will be hugely demotivating (Section 2.12).

Negativity/Cynicism. Many perfectionists have a strong negative tendency that causes them to devalue not only themselves and their work, but everyone and everything around them. At its worst, this negativity devolves into cynicism, or a wholesale distrust of your own and others' motives.

Along with clouding your vision, negativity also prevents you from seeking help, either because you see your situation as hopeless, or don't think others will respond. And, in fact, negativity often does repel others—and particularly the kinds of successful and grounded people you need as mentors.

A writer who finishes a manuscript should be celebrating its completion, not bemoaning its deficiencies. You can note the deficiencies and make a plan for future improvement, but you shouldn't be dwelling on them or bashing yourself for them. (And, just in case you didn't catch this, only a perfectionist would expect a manuscript to have zero deficiencies.)

Someone who publishes a book should be celebrating that milestone, not bemoaning the fact that the publisher wasn't his first choice.

Someone who succeeds even partially in the face of significant obstacles should give herself huge credit for that. (And all successes are partial, by the way.) And someone who utterly fails in the face of significant obstacles should still give herself huge credit for trying.

Someone who planned to write ten pages but only writes one

should still be proud and happy about that one page (and set more reasonable goals in the future).

And someone who works for five minutes on a manuscript they haven't been able to face for months or years—or, who even just opens the document—should also be proud. Learning to recognize and celebrate your successes is a powerful technique for overcoming perfectionism and procrastination (Section 2.11).

Rigidity. Perfectionists often persist in trying the same ineffective solutions, sometimes for years or decades. There are lots of reasons for this, but the main one is that repeatedly trying an ineffectively solution is, in itself, a fine form of procrastination. Also:

Perfectionists usually misdiagnose their problem (as laziness, etc., instead of fear), and so they don't have a clue as to how to solve it.

Perfectionist psychology inclines strongly toward one "solution": coercion. So, in the face of a problem, the perfectionist is unlikely to come up with anything better than, "Just cope, dammit." And, finally,

Rigidity is a trauma symptom (Section 2.9).

If you have trouble writing in a certain setting—say, because it's too quiet and you feel isolated, or too noisy and you can't concentrate—the thing to do is to pack up your gear and try writing somewhere else. A perfectionist, however, is likely to stay put, teeth gritted, and say, "I should be able to write here, dammit, and I'm going to sit here until I do." And so, his time and energy are wasted on a fruitless struggle.

It's actually amazing how simply changing your setting or procedure (e.g., switching from on-screen editing to editing on paper) can boost productivity—and this probably has less to do with the change itself than with the empowered feeling that led the writer to make it. Empowerment leads to productivity.

Conversely, "chaining yourself" to a specific location, procedure, or part of the project (Section 5.4) sends a powerful message of disempowerment, which creates fear that can, in turn, lead to yet *more* disempowerment, and an urgent need to escape via procrastination.

Labeling and Hyperbole. Perfectionists, being drawn to reductiveness, dichotomization, and rigidity, love labels. But the labels they use are almost always harmful in that they either denigrate the writer or increase the pressure she feels around her work. Examples of good labeling would be to call writing "my job," and the particular piece of writing you're working on an "experiment" or "early draft," since those labels tend to ease your fears around your writing. But most of the labels perfectionists use increase their fears, and are thus antiproductive, including those that deem your project to be "hard," "important," "my life's mission," or "the great American novel," or those that deem the writing process itself to be some kind of epic struggle or holy mission (Section 2.2).

True, some projects are more important than others. But that shouldn't matter *while you're writing*. Prolific writers learn to lose themselves nonjudgmentally in their work, trusting that their skills, their community, and the writing process itself will get them where they need to go. Process over product, in other words (Section 2.3).

I've already discussed how harmful it is to label yourself "lazy," "uncommitted," etc., but writers never fail to surprise me with their inventive ways of putting themselves down. One writer told me he was afraid of producing works that "polluted" the cultural sphere. What that implied was truly awful: that if he doesn't write well, he's a kind of garbage or blight.

As discussed in Section 1.1, our reasons for procrastinating are always valid—but that doesn't stop perfectionists from labeling their reasons as "excuses," "complaints," "whines," or "being high maintenance." Don't do this—and also keep in mind that oppressors often use this kind of labeling as a control tactic. (It's also often sexist.)

Hand in hand with labeling goes hyperbole. Formulations such as "The project was a total disaster," "I'm a total loser," and "It's going to take a million hours to edit this thing" are not helpful, whereas clarity of expression is. "It's going to take ten or fifteen hours to edit this thing" is a nonperfectionist statement because it is nonjudgmental and grounded in fact.

Fran Lebowitz refers to her inner critic as a "Nazi general," a comic but ultimately self-defeating hyperbolic formulation.

Make no mistake: labels create a powerful expectation. Only use those that support your success. (See Chapter 6 for a larger discussion of labels related to writers and writing.)

Of course I know that calling someone a "procrastinator" or "perfectionist" is, in itself, a harmful form of labeling. As I explain in the vocabulary and text note, I use these labels in this book only for clarity. In conversations and teaching I try to avoid using them, although I will use words like "perfectionist" and "antiproductive" to nonjudgmentally characterize someone's behavior.

Shortsightedness. Perfectionists tend to elevate their current project to supreme importance, so that finishing it becomes a matter of life or death. Tom Grimes in *Mentor*: "I staked my future on this book. I either wrote it and succeeded, or I failed to and was finished." This is the opposite of the prolific viewpoint, which tends to see the current project, no matter how large or ambitious, as a way station along the journey of one's writing career and life. (Grimes later writes that "limiting myself to [the book's] fate was deeply foolish.")

Another example of shortsightedness was a woman who, in one of my classes, reported that she had had a busy week and hadn't written much— "only ten or fifteen minutes a day." When I asked her how much she had written in the months before she had started the class, she grinned and admitted, "Nothing—so I guess ten minutes is huge."

She was right. You need to take both the long view and the broad view, which also happen to be the wise views.

Fetishes. Many perfectionists obsess on a specific aspect of writing that they feel themselves to be hopelessly deficient in, such as "authenticity," "originality," or "profundity." When you talk to them about their writing, they bring it up over and over again.

Sometimes the fetish is that "I can't do [dialogue or plot or characters, etc.]," or that "I should be doing [longer works or more intellectual work or more commercial work, etc.]." Any highly charged self-critique is probably a fetish, and a fetish is always pointless and destructive. (And probably rooted in a traumatic rejection; see Section 7.1.)

Credentials (e.g., a lack of a Master of Fine Arts or other degree) are another common fetish. Who cares? You may need an MFA to teach (or would, if there were any good teaching jobs; see Section A.8), but other than that, degrees are meaningless and, in my view, a peculiarly 20th-century concern.

Talent is probably the biggest fetish of all. There are probably hundreds of quotes out there on how talent is meaningless compared with hard work, preparedness, persistence, etc., but I'll just give you two:

Stephen King: "Talent is cheaper than table salt. What separates the talented individual from the successful one is a lot of hard work." And,

Erica Jong: "Everyone has talent. What's rare is the courage to follow it to the dark places where it leads."

Unconsciousness. Perfectionists tend to be unaware of their writing processes—they operate on autopilot. Prolific writers, in contrast, tend to be conscious writers. This is not to say that they don't lose themselves luxuriantly in their work—they would not deprive themselves of such a pleasure! But they are aware of their processes and techniques, and what works for them and what doesn't, and they use this information to make conscious decisions that support their productivity and success.

Pathologizing. Each of these statements—

- "My first draft [or timed writing exercise] is pretty rough."
- "I really need people to support me when I write."
- "It took me forever to write that." Or,
- "I was sick and so I got started late and didn't really do a great job."

—describes an ordinary episode in a writing session or writing career. First drafts ARE supposed to be "rough"! Most writers DO need a lot of support—not because they're weak but because writing is difficult (Chapters 3 and 6). Some pieces DO take forever. (Although "forever" is a hyperbolic label that should be avoided. See how the perfectionism sneaks in?) And sometimes you DO get sick and it affects your productivity. Prolific writers experience these events all the time, but hardly notice them, and certainly don't bash themselves for them.

Perfectionists, however, cite these and similar normal (and inevitable) occurrences as evidence of how unfit they are for a writing vocation.

Blind spots. Perfectionism is fundamentally delusional, so I guess it shouldn't be surprising that, in classes, it commonly happens that, a few minutes after reviewing the list of perfectionist symptoms, someone will come out with a blatantly perfectionist statement that they don't recognize as such. Remember: Any harsh judgment, dichotomization, negative reductive labeling, fetish, etc., is probably perfectionist.

Sometimes a student will say, "I actually don't mind my perfectionism," or, "I don't think perfectionism is all bad." They are confusing perfectionism with having high standards. *Perfectionism is not about setting high standards: it's about setting unrealistic or unachievable standards and then punishing yourself harshly for failing to meet them.* It is a form of delusional thinking that is always antiproductive!

So that, in a rather large nutshell, is perfectionism's repertoire. Pretty extensive, isn't it? It is hard to overestimate perfectionism's impact on our lives since it tends to distort our thinking at a fundamental level. Someone will be telling me about their writing, or another difficult challenge, and my half of the conversation will go: "That's perfectionist ... That's perfectionist ... That's perfectionist, too ... And, wow, that's *really* perfectionist." Perfectionism, as I mentioned at the very beginning of this chapter, is not a behavior or habit but a toxic filter that can grow to pervade every aspect of our thinking and behavior.

Fortunately, however, there's an equally powerful repertoire of behaviors we can use to overcome it! I'll get to those shortly—I know you're waiting for it—but first let's do a quick overview of the common causes of perfectionism. It's important that you recognize them so you can defend yourself against them.

Section 2.8 Perfectionism's Origins I: Social and Cultural Causes

I've already mentioned a prime source of perfectionism: **the media** (Section 2.2). The media are soaked in perfectionism, which means we basically swim in an ocean of perfectionism our entire lives.

Dramatic narratives of stupendous success achieved under adverse conditions, including "rags to riches," "overnight success," "accidental success," "self-made success," and "teenage billionaire" stories are, overwhelmingly, perfectionist bunk. If you can find a story that talks honestly about how someone achieved their success, including the role that family connections and luck played, and the compromises and sacrifices he and others made (in the latter case, often not entirely willingly), that might be an exception—but these truthfully told success stories are so rare as to not be worth your time to look. (You can get real stories of success from your colleagues and mentors.)

Perfectionism is also ubiquitous because it sells products. If I can convince you that your clothes are unfashionable, your house unclean, and your kids subpar, I can sell you products that supposedly solve these supposed problems.

Perfectionism also sneaks into our media through advertising slogans ("no pain, no gain"), movie clichés ("they all lived happily ever after"), and television shows that depict easy living or easy success (most sitcoms).

You must be vigilant about not buying into any of the media's perfectionist fantasies even a little. Be aware, though, that society acts on us not simply through overt perfectionist messages, but also by creating a perfectionist context fundamentally hostile to creativity—see Section 6.7 for more on that.

We also get perfectionism from our **parents and other relatives**, who say things like, "Is this the best you can do?" "Why just a B?" "Why can't you do as well as your sister?" "It's not about trying, it's about succeeding." "It's easy! What's your problem?" And, "If you don't get into the Ivy League [or become a doctor or lawyer], you're letting the whole family down." These are the kinds of statements that turn up years or decades later in people's self-abusive litanies, in addition to the many nonperfectionist misguided or outright abusive messages many parents convey, including "You'll never amount to anything," "Who do you think you are, wanting to be a writer?" and "Girls can't do math."

Many procrastinators grew up in neglectful or abusive households and learned to survive as children by hiding (figuratively or literally; see Section 6.1). Invisibility is a great strategy for a kid who doesn't have a lot of other options, but it's a terrible strategy for adults, including writers who need to be able to show their work and interact within professional communities. Chapter 6 is all about how you can overcome the strong tendency toward invisibility and isolation that many procrastinators have.

Bosses are often perfectionist, especially those who expect us to produce in chaotic, badly managed workplaces or without adequate resources, and those who see us as "resources" to be exploited rather than human beings with full lives. ("It's too bad your kid is sick, but I still need you to come in today.") Like all oppressors, they inevitably blame the victim, and therefore many people carry around a burden of shame for work "failures" that were either not failures or not their fault.

Teachers are a prime source of perfectionism. Along with saying the kinds of dumb, perfectionist things parents say, or expecting results that conflict with their own poor performance, like some bosses, teachers also often deliver the kinds of toxic rejections that lead to trauma and blocks (see below, and Chapter 7). There are a lot of bad teachers out there, unfortunately, and at all levels—and students can often quote me verbatim harsh or callous remarks that a teacher made years or decades earlier.

I particularly regret to say that there are many, many bad *writing* teachers out there, in part because many writers teach only to make money and have no real love or affinity for teaching (Section A.8).

Below is a list of teacher malfeasances; it's long not because I want to pick on teachers, but because I don't want you to blame yourself if you have been victimized by a teacher who behaved in any of the ways listed. I strongly believe that, except in unusual circumstances, learning failures and fiascos are never the student's fault. Students come to their teachers with legitimate needs, expectations, and dependencies, and are also relatively powerless. Teaching is not an easy job—and many teachers are, of course, themselves disempowered by their institutions or other forces—but that doesn't excuse unprofessionalism. Although an oppressive teacher will be quick to blame the student in case of problems, the student should never believe that.

> **Teacher malfeasances:** harshness (attacking); bias (against you, your subject matter, your style); rigidity and dogmatism (only one way to succeed or make progress); pickiness (lack of proportion; attacking); fatalism (about you or your work); overgeneralization from one work; jealousy; competitiveness; unresponsiveness; criticalness (of you, your life, and/or your values); unpredictability; erraticness; lack of compassion, empathy, or kindness; playing favorites (with or against you); coming on to you inappropriately (in friendship or sexually); stealing your work; not admitting his/her own mistakes or limitations; admitting problems but not apologizing, atoning, or rectifying; lack of preparedness or other unprofessionalism; dishonesty; denial of truth about writing process or careers; obfuscation or mystification; aggressiveness; condescension; patronizing attitude; inadequateness (intellectually or otherwise); lack of time for you; laxity; uncaringness.

"**Innate perfectionism**." People often ask whether someone could be "born perfectionist." It's true that some kids are born with a more critical or judgmental temperament than others—any parent knows that. So it would be fair to say that some kids have a *propensity* for perfectionism. But compassionate parenting and teaching can help kids avoid perfectionism. Remember that criticality itself is not perfectionism: perfectionism is when you set unreasonable standards and punish yourself harshly for failing to meet them, are grandiose, emphasize product over process, etc. Criticality itself, in the sense of being able to make meaningful distinctions, is a good thing.

Unfortunately, perfectionism is so pervasive that most kids wind up having their perfectionist tendencies reinforced.

Section 2.9 Perfectionism's Origins II: Trauma and "Situational Perfectionism"

Trauma is what psychologists call the collection of psychological and physiological changes that can arise from incidents of profound helplessness in the face of threat. You may be familiar with post-traumatic stress disorder (PTSD), which happens to victims of war, violent crime, or natural disaster; its symptoms include intellectual or emotional rigidity (inflexibility), dichotomous (black-and-white) thinking, and attempts at control.

Notice how those behaviors also characterize perfectionism. In fact, I've learned that **many cases of writer's block are really a kind of trauma catalyzed by a traumatic rejection or criticism (Section 7.1)**. The way I learned this was that I would be discussing a cause of perfectionism in class—say, bad teaching or a callous rejection—and a student would say something like, "I just realized that something like that happened to me, and I never finished a work after that." Or, "I never submitted anything after that." Or never workshopped a piece again, wrote fiction again, etc. This happened over and over again until I realized that traumatic incidents were very common causes of blocks.

Maybe you can look back at your writing history and find a similar traumatic catalyst for your underproductivity.

It's important to realize that what makes a rejection traumatic is not simply what is said, but its context (Section 7.2). Relatively mild criticism from a writer whom we revere can be much more devastating than horrible criticism from a clueless relative. Also, rejection will tend to be felt more keenly by those who overidentify with their work or are otherwise perfectionist.

If you've suffered from professional (or other) trauma, you should see a therapist or other specialist.

Many events will cause your perfectionism to spike, and when that happens I call it **"situational perfectionism."** A harsh rejection or criticism will do it, of course, but so, paradoxically, will a success, if it causes you to raise the bar for future achievement or focus on external rewards. Here's how one particular writer reacted to the unexpected success of her first published novel: "For the first time ever in my life, I got writer's block. The stakes seemed to have gone up a lot, and I attracted a lot of publicity in Britain for which I was utterly unprepared."[2]

The famous "second novel problem" is classic situational perfectionism, as is the situation when a precociously successful young writer shuts down after getting seriously critiqued or rejected for the first time. To make matters worse for that second group, their early success means they typically never got the essential lessons in coping that the rest of us got perforce—a problem J.K. Rowling addressed in her brilliant 2008 Harvard commencement address, "The Fringe Benefits of Failure, and the Importance of Imagination."[3] There is also usually an element of blindsiding to these types of rejections, which only makes things worse (Section 7.2).

Another common type of situational perfectionism is when someone who's been blocked starts writing reliably, but then gets cocky and expects too-fast improvement. They'll use the timer (Section 2.14) reliably for ten minutes a day, for instance, and then all of a sudden decide they're "cured" and set it for thirty minutes—thus triggering perfectionist anxiety. (Devious procrastination will actually militate for you to do this.) That's why the timer should never be increased more than around 25% every week.

---

[2] Margaret Weir, "Of Magic and Single Motherhood: Bestselling Author J.K. Rowling is Still Trying to Fathom the Instant Fame That Came with Her First Children's Novel," Salon, March 31, 1999 (www.salon.com/life/feature/1999/03/cov_31featureb.html).

[3] Rowling, J.K., "The Fringe Benefits of Failure and the Importance of Imagination," (Harvard Commencement Address), June 5, 2008, (harvardmagazine.com/commencement/the-fringe-benefits-failure-the-importance-imagination).

And yet another example of situational perfectionism is when you have made a financial investment in your writing, such as a new computer, redecorated office, babysitter, or class or conference, and are now telling yourself you *must* write so that the money isn't wasted. Ditto for a time investment, such as taking a leave from your job or switching to part-time work.

A particularly dangerous time for situational perfectionism is just after you've finished a class or workshop, or graduated from a program. Suddenly, you're much less supported than you were—no writing community, deadlines, mentorship, etc.—but also under pressure to not only maintain your productivity but recoup your educational investment. There's also a natural tendency, after a workshop, to feel ready—or wish we were ready—to begin a more ambitious work.

In general, **transitions and re-entries (e.g., from vacation to "real life") are tough,** and we tend to lose productivity during them. As noted in Section 2.5, the transition from undergraduate to graduate school is often especially tough, in part because of the poor job many graduate programs do in preparing their new students for what's to come.

As with all cases of perfectionism, your rationalizations for your situational perfectionism will probably be compelling. But you need to see through them and categorically reject all forms of perfectionism.

The Solutions to Perfectionism and Procrastination

Section 2.10 Cultivate a Mindset of Compassionate Objectivity

The major solutions to perfectionism and procrastination are:

1. Cultivate a Mindset of Compassionate Objectivity
2. Develop the Habit of Abundant Rewards and No Punishments
3. Arrive at a More Mature Understanding of Failure and Success
4. Use the Three Productivity Behaviors
5. Build Your Capacity for Fearless Writing via Timed Writing Exercises
6. Choose the Right Project
7. Learn to Balance the Creative and Non-Creative Aspects of Your Career

There are also some minor techniques.

Compassionate objectivity (CO) is the foundational technique. It's a mindset where you combine:

Compassion, meaning you view yourself and your work with abundant empathy and understanding, with

Objectivity, meaning you see things accurately, with all their nuance and complexity. In place of perfectionism's reductive, rigid, and punishing worldview, CO offers nuance, flexibility, empathy, and true love and respect. The compassionately objective (CO) person sees through perfectionism's illusions and understands the realities about herself and her work. She knows to:

> Set achievable goals and be compassionate about any failures or mistakes
>
> Be realistic and grounded, as opposed to grandiose
>
> Emphasize process almost entirely over product
>
> Rely on internal rewards
>
> Work within the realities of creativity and career-building, and
>
> Not identify with her work. (She especially knows this one.)

The CO person also eschews invidious comparisons, dichotomization, rigidity, unhelpful labels, hyperbole, negativity, shortsightedness, fetishes, unconsciousness, pathologizing, and blind spots.

Don't confuse CO with "permissiveness," "self-indulgence," "being a Pollyanna," "letting yourself off the hook," or "giving yourself a pass." It isn't any of those things. CO calls it like it is—and with much more accuracy than perfectionism. CO people forgo unproductive blame and shame, but that doesn't mean they don't take responsibility.

Perfectionists tend to see CO as permissiveness because they see everything through a harsh, judgmental lens—and they dread permissiveness because they feel that constant harshness is the only thing keeping them from devolving into useless, unproductive monsters. It's such a sad, difficult mindset, and so unnecessary: I promise you that if you use the techniques in this book you won't devolve, but evolve.

In the end, CO is simply wisdom. The CO person knows how to be truly productive, and she also knows the costs of delusion. She knows, for example, that:

- Everyone operates under constraints of time, money, and skills. She judges a result against her own capacities and resources instead of an unrealistic ideal.
- She doesn't have to fix all the problems with a piece of writing right now—she'll have plenty of opportunity to fix them later. She also knows she shouldn't expect to fix them "all" anyway, since that's a perfectionist goal.
- Even if this writing project ultimately falls short, she'll have plenty of other chances to succeed.
- She can't perform superhuman feats, such as suddenly writing twenty pages in a day when her previous record is ten. She also knows she's not a robot who can work 24/7, or when ill or seriously troubled.
- She's not precognitive. Therefore, she won't second-guess or punish herself for having made reasonable choices that didn't work out as well as planned.

Finally, she knows she's not just a writer but a human being, and that she needs to take care of the broad range of her human needs (health, safety, material comfort, relationships, etc.), not just because that's the sane and humane thing to do, but because ignoring those needs is antiproductive. She also knows that progress in other areas of her life will support her writing success—and that, conversely, her writing success will feed her success in other important areas.

The CO person also knows important stuff about "failure" and "success" that I'll discuss in Section 2.12.

The fundamental work of overcoming perfectionism is that of "switching" your mindset from perfectionism to CO. There's no magic to doing this: you just catch yourself thinking perfectionistically (i.e., the self-abusive litany) and GENTLY interrupt and correct yourself:

Instead of: "I can't believe I'm behind on submitting my chapter to my thesis advisor. Whatever made me think I was a scholar? I'm just a fraud. I haven't written anything in two months—and what I wrote before that is crap. And look at Mary—she's a *real* scholar. She's already submitted five chapters, and hers are all great. I'm just lazy, that's all."

The CO person thinks (and maybe journals, for extra impact and clarity): "Okay, let's calm down. I actually have done some writing in the last two months. It wasn't very much, and honestly it wasn't very good, but there's a big difference between that **and not writing anything.** The big problem is that I've been stuck on my analysis ... I guess I'll submit what I have to my advisor so he at least knows I'm working. And I'll talk to him and my other mentors about the analysis. As for Mary, well, her partner supports them both, so she gets to stay home and write all day. I still have my teaching job and we also have the kids—and if I can get three hours in of writing a day, I'm lucky. I guess I'll talk to my partner to see if I can cut down on my work hours for a while, and also to see if he'll do more of the housework and childcare. But mostly, I'll stop comparing myself to her because when I do it drives me crazy."

Note how in the CO response the writer isn't letting herself off the hook: she admits that her writing hasn't been very good. It is possible to acknowledge mistakes without taking on a mantle of shame—and you must absolutely learn to do so. Notice also how a shame-free examination of the causes of her underproductivity enables her to easily problem-solve.

Here's another example of substituting CO for perfectionism:

Instead of: "Even though I'm sick, I should still be able carry out my normal schedule and commitments, including writing. I'm not that sick, anyway: I'm just using a few sniffles as an excuse for being lazy." (A formulation that is not only self-contradictory—are you sick or not sick, which is it?—but will lead to a poor workday, resentment, a lingering illness, and perhaps infecting others.)

The CO person thinks: "I'm sick, and I'm going to spend the day focused on getting better. I'm going back to bed and will take some Vitamin C. Oh, and there's no food in the house, so I will call Frank and ask him to bring me some."

And a third example:

Instead of (after dropping a dish): "Oh, what a klutz I am."

The CO person thinks: "Oh well, I dropped a dish. It's no big deal—I'll just be more careful in the future." (Practicing CO in other areas of your life will help you be more CO in your writing.)

At first, these self-corrections may feel awkward and even contrived, but keep practicing and eventually CO will replace perfectionism as your reflex response to underperformance. Just don't try to immediately correct every tiny instance of perfectionism, or berate yourself harshly when you slip—that's perfectionism! Just focus on building the new habit gradually.

Students have described the CO voice as that of the "good grandparent" or "wise teacher." These adult metaphors are no accident: CO, unlike terrified and regressed perfectionism, is a mature viewpoint. The more you replace perfectionist thoughts and feelings with CO ones, the less fear and the more confidence you will feel around your writing—and writing will become, first, easier, and then a joy.

Section 2.11 Develop a Habit of Abundant Rewards and No Punishments

Every time you substitute CO for perfectionism, and any time you experience *any* success at all in your writing or in other areas, you need to acknowledge that success and reward yourself.

Every time.

Without fail.

And reward yourself lavishly.

The habit of recognizing and lavishly rewarding success is one of your strongest techniques for overcoming perfectionism. It is actually the opposite of what perfectionists do, which is to relentlessly devalue their successes and punish themselves.

"Acknowledge and reward" helps you do four very important things:

1. Recognize your success—something that, as discussed in the "dichotomizing" section of Section 2.7, perfectionists have trouble doing.

2. Celebrate your success, which is a more emphatic form of recognition that also reinforces the successful behavior. It also helps "fix" the success in your memory, so that you can call on it when needed: "Oh, I'm struggling now because I got distracted by that phone call. But I got a distracting phone call last week and was able to recover and keep writing. So I guess I'll just start writing now and see what happens."

3. Heal the burden of shame and guilt you are probably carrying around from years of underproductivity, and harsh perfectionist attempts to correct it.

4. Build your confidence and hope, two powerful precursors to productivity.

It's particularly important that you learn to recognize and reward partial, small or even trivial-seeming successes, for three reasons:

1. As a perfectionist, you are probably routinely undervaluing your successes, and so they are probably all more significant than you realize.

2. *All* successes are partial. There's no such thing as a perfect writing session or perfect piece of writing.

3. There's also really no such thing as a "big success," since all big successes are really compilations of small ones. In a sense, Tolstoy didn't write *War and Peace*: he wrote a huge number of paragraphs, pages, and chapters that added up to *War and Peace*—and before he began that project he succeeded at other writing projects, and at intellectual and life challenges that readied him to take on the big one.

How to Do Rewards

The practice of "Rewards," as I call it, has three parts: a tangible reward, a celebration, and an activity reward.

The **tangible reward** could be a cookie, bubble bath, or DVD: whatever you like. (For heaven's sake, don't judge your choice!) Gold stars—yes, the kind that elementary schoolteachers use—or some other physical tracking of your achievement (see Section 5.9) is another terrific physical reward.

The **celebration** involves taking some time to feel honest pride and satisfaction at your achievement. It's actually the most important part of Rewards because it's the part where you most directly challenge perfectionism.

Taking a few seconds to feel proud sounds easy enough, but for perfectionists the temptation to gloss over one's accomplishments can be huge, and the idea of rewarding oneself for partial productivity can seem a dangerous form of self-indulgence. If you feel an urge to skip this part of Rewards, it is especially important that you not do so.

Please note that by "proper pride" I'm *not* talking about the giddy "I'm king of the world!" feeling perfectionists tend to feel on those rare occasions when they think they've written well. That's a clear sign of overidentification with the work, and is almost inevitably followed by an equivalent "crash" the next time things don't go so well. Honest pride and satisfaction are what prolific writers look forward to after a good day's work. (There may be a time for giddiness—say, when the manuscript is finished or the book sells—but this isn't it.)

And, of course, don't expect perfectionism to give up without a fight: it will almost certainly pop up with a litany crafted just for the occasion: "You wrote a paragraph and now you're celebrating? How pathetic! How do you ever expect to finish your novel writing a paragraph at a time?"

***Never listen to the perfectionist voice, a.k.a. the voice of the oppressor.* The best way to respond to it is to dialogue with it via journaling, while assuming the role of a CO adult:**

> Perfectionism (in disgust, but also terror): You wrote a paragraph and now you're celebrating? How pathetic!
> CO (with honest curiosity): Oh, so you think it's ridiculous to celebrate? Why is that?
> Perfectionism: Well, it's just a paragraph!
> CO: So you don't think it's a long enough passage to be worth celebrating?

Perfectionism: Of course not—and how do you expect to finish your novel?

CO: I'll get to that in a minute. But, first, isn't a paragraph a meaningful achievement after weeks of not writing at all?

Perfectionism: Errr ... maybe.

CO: And am I hurting anyone when I celebrate?

Perfectionism: Well, no, I guess not. (Then, with sudden franticness) But, but, but—if you celebrate, then you might get the idea that a paragraph is enough! And it really isn't! We'll never get the novel done a paragraph at a time! And then everyone will know we're losers!

CO (with extra compassion): I understand your fear—and you're absolutely right: a paragraph really isn't that much writing compared with an entire novel. This was only a first step, though. I promise you that I'll be working as hard as I can to boost our productivity to a rate we both think reasonable.

Perfectionism (relieved): Really?

CO: Yes, but we can't rush it, or we'll go back to writing nothing.

Perfectionism: I guess you're right. But, you know, I really do want to rush it. We've lost so much time already.

CO: I know—I kind of want to rush it, too. But we tried that approach for years, didn't we? And it never worked. So, let's just try this other way for a while.

Perfectionism (not entirely convinced, but now willing to go along with it): I guess you're right.

CO: OK, so let's try celebrating and see what happens.

What is likely to happen is that the writer will feel good—great, maybe—and more confident and inspired around her writing.

Dialoging compassionately with the oppressor should help alleviate its fears and rigid antipathy to CO, Rewards, and the other solutions discussed.

Finally, it's a good idea to have an **activity reward**, both to amplify the celebration and help your body recover from all the sitting and writing. This could be a stretch or a happy dance.

Always Reward Lavishly—meaning, don't stint on time or money. Lavish Rewards not only feel great and are healing, they strongly reinforce the activity you're Rewarding. Take the same time and energy you've put into bullying yourself, and reroute it into equally intense pride and satisfaction. Eventually, you probably can skip the tangible and activity rewards, but never give up on the celebration. **The goal is to evolve a mindset where you see your work as a continuous series of successes—some big, but most little or even tiny—and automatically celebrate, if only briefly, each one, so that you're in an almost continual state of pride. (This is probably similar to the state many of us remember from when we were children and used to effortlessly create.) Then writing will become a joy, and nothing will hold you back.**

It's great to involve others in your Rewards. All writers should have critique partners and alpha readers (Section 3.11) with whom they can share their writing victories, including those that might seem weird or trivial to "civilians." And if you've got kids around who you can do your happy dance with, that's great! They'll reinforce your celebration, and you'll be modeling CO for them. My favorite Rewards story, however, involves a writer who also runs a dog daycare out of her home, and so is constantly surrounded by adoring canines. (Lucky woman!) I urged her to get the dogs involved in her Rewards, and now whenever she does her happy dance, the dogs join in and sometimes sing!

At the same time: NO PUNISHMENTS. If, for some reason, you don't meet your goals, just ignore that except to learn from the experience so you can try to do better next time. When you start the next writing session, do so with a clean emotional slate that's primed for Rewards.

Section 2.12 Compassionate Objectivity as an Antidote to Fear of Failure and Success

Years ago, I was fortunate to hear one of my heroes, former world chess champion and current Russian democracy activist Garry Kasparov, discuss important lessons he had learned from chess. Here's how he began his talk: "I have won hundreds of chess games, and lost thousands. You have to have the courage to fail."

The courage to fail. What an amazing phrase—and coming from a hypercompetitive chess champion it takes on a special meaning.

Kasparov probably hates failure more than just about anyone—in fact, as his use of the word "courage" implies, he probably fears it—but he had to develop a tolerance for it to reach his goals. That he chose to begin his talk with this point only underscores its importance.

Perfectionists are terrified of failure for all the reasons mentioned earlier, including that they define it too broadly, punish themselves harshly for it, identify too strongly with it so that it becomes a kind of ego-death, and are shortsightedly focused on the immediate.

To a CO person, however, failure is not just inevitable, but an essential element of any ambitious path, and probably our most potent route to learning and growth. In other words, if you're not failing at least some of the time, you're probably not pushing yourself enough or taking enough risks. Herman Melville called the willingness to fail "the true test of greatness." Samuel Beckett famously said, "Go on failing. Go on. Only next time, try to fail better." And Winston Churchill, who apart from his statesmanship also wrote and painted prolifically, famously defined success as arising from "the ability to go from one failure to another with no loss of enthusiasm."

Needless to say, CO people also don't overreact to success for the same reasons (non-identification with the work, taking the long view) that they don't overreact to failure. They also understand that pleasurable as success is, it isn't nirvana, and that it introduces its own stresses and complications. (If you sell your book, you have to worry about building your audience—or writing the next one.) Success can also bring a sense of loss, as Joan Bolker eloquently writes in *Writing Your Dissertation in Fifteen Minutes a Day*:

> How do we deal with the fact that there is sadness as well as joy about each major step we take forward—including finishing a doctoral degree? You may expect that you will feel only relief and pleasure when you earn your degree, so you may be startled by feelings of loss and sadness. Maybe you will grieve that a major stage of your life is over, or perhaps you will mourn the important people who are not alive to witness your triumph, or maybe you'll confront the gap between the dissertation you've actually written and the one you imagined you would write ... Every major life change destroys the equilibrium of our lives and our self-image and leaves behind a portion of an old self.

I'm guessing that, for many people, a sense of impending loss is a major, unrecognized barrier keeping them from taking their next step. CO people therefore work not just to succeed, but to prepare themselves emotionally and logistically for success—say, by consulting others who are already there and creating processes and infrastructures before they are needed. Someone who will need to market her novel, for instance, could (and should) create a marketing plan, and gather the resources needed to complete it, well before the actual publication date (Chapter 8.6).

CO people also realize that there is no such thing as a pure failure or success: that most failures contain some element of success (at least, as a learning experience), and most successes an element of failure or compromise. They also realize that **failure and success are not huge, show-stopping, life-defining events but merely transient states that one moves into and out of throughout one's career.**

Section 2.13 Use the Three Productivity Behaviors

The three productivity behaviors are: (1) showing up exactly on time, (2) doing exactly what you are supposed to be doing, and (3) doing it uninterruptedly (except for small breaks) for long periods of time. The "showing up exactly on time" presupposes that you have done your time management (Chapter 4) and have a time budget and schedule. The "doing it for long periods of time," a.k.a. endurance, can be achieved via timed exercises (see next section).

These behaviors support a mindset of accountability. You're scheduled to write at ten o'clock, so at ten your butt is in the chair and your fingers dancing away at the keyboard. **What you really want to do is glide over to your chair, sit down, and start writing, all in a sort of calm Zen state without anxiety, drama, or anticipation.** Eventually, you'll probably be able to anticipate your work pleasurably, but right now there's too great a risk that the anticipation will lead to unreasonable expectations for success.

It is also helpful to practice the behaviors on activities other than writing. Practice doing the dishes at precisely 7 p.m., or getting the mail at exactly 2 p.m., or calling your folks right at 3:30 p.m. Or, practice boosting your endurance (in small increments; see next chapter!) while exercising or meditating. All this is not just beneficial in its own right; it will build your capacity to use the behaviors when writing.

Practice these behaviors on only two or three activities at a time, resisting the perfectionist temptation to try to change everything at once. Only when you can reliably do a behavior on time and with focus should you start practicing on another. And don't forget to use abundant Rewards every time you even attempt to use the behaviors (the result doesn't matter). And remember: *Never* any shame, blame, guilt, or other punishments.

Section 2.14 Build Your Capacity for Fearless Writing via Timed Writing Exercises

The work of becoming prolific consists largely of managing your moment-by-moment writing experience to maintain a CO rather than a perfectionist attitude, and to easily solve problems as they come up (Section 1.2). You're in the midst of writing something, and feel some perfectionist terror—or physical discomfort or another obstacle or trigger—and instead of trying to coerce yourself to write through it (a response that, in the past, has elicited panic), you take prompt steps to keep yourself calm and address the problem so that you can resume writing as quickly as possible. (In Section 5.4, I discuss how you can learn to "write past the wall" of minor distractions, but for someone in the early stages of tackling perfectionism, it's probably best to stop writing and focus on coping.)

Recalling the illustration, in Section 1.2, that showed the difference between procrastinators and the prolific, this is the technique that will help you shift from an easily-derailed (c) to a "minorly delayed" (b) or even a "steady as she goes" (a).

Hopefully by now you've "journaled out" your spaghetti snarl (Section 1.5), so that you're aware of the many strands of your disempowerment and underproductivity. Hopefully, you've also been working to overcome or eradicate your obstacles, and to get less triggered (Section 1.1.)

Also, hopefully, you will soon read the rest of the chapters of this book and identify yet more strands and more techniques for resolving them.

These steps should have already eased some of your fears around your writing.

To cope with the remainder, and to strengthen yourself for coping with future fears, practice building your capacity to write fearlessly.

Get a timer—such as the large stopwatch available at online-stopwatch.com or any kitchen timer—and set it for five minutes.

Then start it, and begin writing on your desired project, in a low-stress, low-expectation, "free-writing" kind of way (Section 5.2). **Your goal is to put in your time (finish your interval) while maintaining a non-judgmental focus on the writing itself, as opposed to any outcome you hope for it.** You are especially not aiming to "write something good"—and shouldn't judge your writing at all. (Remember: "process trumps product," and recall Steven Pressfield's remark: "How many pages have I produced? I don't care. Are they any good? I don't even think about it.")

Don't feel you have to write on the "next" part of your project, but choose whichever part seems easiest and/or the most fun. A key mistake of underproductive writers is to treat their projects linearly, e.g.: "I must finish section 1 before moving onto section 2, section 3, etc." Prolific writers, in contrast, see their works as landscapes and hop on over to whichever part of the terrain they feel like working on (Section 5.4). If you can't think of anything to write *in* your project, then write *about* it: note-taking, organizing, outlining, and editing are all okay. No research, though: you need to be writing, not reading, during this time.

Also, **no pondering**, particularly at the beginning of writing sessions. Pondering isn't writing. If you're stuck, either write about the problem, or leave a blank and start writing on another part of the project. This is especially true for the beginnings of writing sessions; some people—and, especially, many graduate students—like to have a "big think" before getting started, but they should just start writing, and let the writing catalyze their thinking. As Natalie Goldberg famously instructed in *Writing Down the Bones*, "Keep your hand moving."

If, while writing, you feel the litany starting up, or any fear or anxiety at all, have your CO persona gently remind your inner bully (who, remember, is scared and trying to protect you), that it's okay; this is just a little test; no one's being hurt, etc. Then try to keep writing. If necessary, switch to journaling, outlining, editing, or an easier passage.

When the timer dings, then stop and ... extra points if you've guessed it ... Rewards!

Okay—that's it for today. You set aside your project and go about enjoying your day, hopefully remembering at intervals to feel proud about your accomplishment.

Then, tomorrow, you do your five minutes again.

If you don't make it through the entire five minutes, that's okay and NO PUNISHMENTS. In fact: Rewards for trying! Try again tomorrow, setting the timer for two or three minutes, or even thirty seconds. Don't worry, you'll catch up.

Only after you can *easily and consistently* handle five minutes of non-fearful, non-judgmental writing should you increase the timer to eight minutes, and then ten minutes, fifteen, twenty, etc. A general rule of thumb is to spend at least a week at an interval before increasing it, and to never increase it more than 25% at a time.

This simple exercise was described by a student as "incredibly powerful," and it is. Do you want to write eight to ten hours a day? You can get there using timed exercises—and faster than you might imagine, provided you maintain your compassionate objectivity.

Two additional points:

1. My suggested starting interval of five minutes is good for many seriously blocked writers. If you can accomplish it easily, however, feel free to start with a larger one.

2. It's okay to do more than one timed exercise in a day, but beware of perfectionist grandiosity and overidentification with your work. If after doing two or three intervals you start to get that giddy "I'm queen of the world!" feeling, stop and ground yourself emotionally.

It's particularly important, when doing multiple intervals, not to push it. It's okay to round a writing day off with a final smaller interval—the icing on the cupcake, as it were—but any intervals you start, do your best to complete.

Section 2.15 Choose the Right Project(s)

Your choice of writing project is always important, but even more so when overcoming perfectionism. Underproductive writers tend to either: (a) obdurately commit to an over-ambitious project (I call that "the Ahab syndrome," and they often do, in fact, go down with the ship), or (b) can't commit to any project.

These seemingly disparate problems are really opposite sides of the same perfectionist coin in that both sets of writers are wedded to a vision of an "ideal" project compared with which all others seem lacking. The non-committers are probably also looking for a "magic" project that will somehow help them stay motivated, and they're probably also starting new projects as a way of procrastinating on old ones. Committers and non-committers alike are also shortsightedly over-focusing on the current writing project (Section 2.7).

Perfectionists also tend to overcomplicate their projects, partly because they are suspicious of work and success when they come too easily (Section 2.2), and partly as a way of delaying completion and the feared next steps of the project. Graduate students are particularly prone to "ballooning" up their theses, particularly in the absence of good supervision. (In *Writing Your Dissertation in Fifteen Minutes a Day*, Joan Bolker invokes a hypothetical diligent advisor asking a student, "Do you really want to take on all of Henry James's novels in your thesis?")

Here are some guidelines for keeping everything in balance:

1) **Choose the smallest, simplest project you can.** That's essential because it maximizes the chances you'll actually finish—and finishing is crucial, not just as a goal in its own right, but because it teaches you essential lessons (e.g., on perseverance and problem-solving) that you won't otherwise learn. And it's not until you've actually finished the work, of course, that you will learn the lessons on submitting your work, dealing with publishers, and dealing with your audience.

Once you've finished your simple project, you can then tackle a slightly more ambitious one, and then a slightly more ambitious one after that, etc., all the way up to your own version of *War and Peace*, if you want. (You can actually see this progression in the *Harry Potter* series, with the first books being relatively short, the last ones massive, and a big leap in size and scope—and presumably, J.K. Rowling's confidence and capacity—between books three and four.) But if you start out writing a *War and Peace* equivalent and don't finish it, your whole career can be short-circuited.

Your inner perfectionist is likely to be fiercely critical of a decision to start small, calling up some of her deadliest arsenal, including "trite," trivial," "unambitious," "pathetic," or even "a waste of time." You can, in fact, measure the effectiveness of your strategy by the vehemence of her attack: the stronger it is, the more directly you are tackling your perfectionism. So: (a) congratulations! (b) dialogue intensively with the perfectionist to help alleviate her fears, and (c) stay the course.

Conversely, watch out for wily perfectionism when it says "Okay, you've chosen an easy project, so the writing should be a snap."

2) **Rework your project so it's even simpler.** To further counter-act the tendency toward over-complication, actively work to simplify your already-simple project. Eliminate inessential subplots, subthemes, secondary characters, and other elements, especially if they hugely complicate the project.

If you're unsure whether something should go or be left in, con-sult your critique partners, alpha readers, and mentors—but when in doubt, take it out.

3) **Keep your focus tight**. While writing, forget that you're work-ing on a "book," and just focus on the chapter, section, page, paragraph, or sentence. In *Bird by Bird*, Anne Lamott metaphorically suggests viewing your work through a "one inch picture frame," which trans-lates to focusing on "one small scene, one memory, one exchange."

4) **Choose the right goal**. I used to say that the main goal for any writing project was simply "to finish," and that's still true. Other goals—for instance, quality or impact (i.e., selling the book)—need to be subordinate (Section 2.16). Recently, however, I spoke with a graduate student who had had the misfortune of working with an abusive thesis advisor. Against the odds, she had persevered and fin-ished her research; now, she had a job waiting as soon as she finished and defended her thesis.

I asked her what her goal for the thesis was, and she wisely said, "to finish." (Hardly anyone says that.)

"There's a better goal," I said. "It's to get the hell out." (You do want to get the hell out of an abusive situation.) That focused her thinking remarkably. Now, instead of talking about "editing" in gen-eral terms, she started to discuss page counts and the specific content changes that would most likely get her thesis quickly approved.

In a way, the goal of all writing projects should be to "get the hell out." You don't simply want to finish; you want to finish as quickly and easily as possible (without undue stress or pressure, of course) so that you can move on to the next project—or, the rest of your life. Perfectionist people, when I tell them this, think I'm saying they should compromise on quality, but I'm not: I'm talking about working efficiently and not succumbing to either perfectionism or the grandiose idea that for a work to be good, it must be the product of an arduous struggle.

Section 2.16 Moving Forward: Your Post-Perfectionism Writing Career

As you begin to overcome your perfectionism, you can anticipate moving through four career stages:

> Stage 1: You focus on just your writing process (more specifically, on overcoming perfectionism while writing);
>
> Stage 2: You focus on process + your creative goals for the overall project;
>
> Stage 3: You focus on process + creative goals + your external (commercial, academic, or other) goals for the project; and,
>
> Stage 4: You focus on process + creative goals + external goals + your overall career goals.

Stage 1 is probably where you are right now, and it's the foundation for all future success—so don't rush it. Dialogue with any perfectionist worries that your progress is too slow or that you're too far from your goal.

After you can reliably write nonperfectionistically for half an hour or more, it's time to tackle **Stage 2**. Here, you expand your focus beyond the moment-by-moment experience of writing, and out to your overall creative goals for the piece.

So, while most of your consciousness remains focused on the experience and process of writing, some part is asking and answering critical questions (critical in the artistic, not blaming, sense) about what you're writing, and making decisions about what to write based on the answers to those questions. Some of those questions might be:

Would my character be likely to react this way? Would he speak that way? Does it make sense that he lives in the city?

Or: Does this scene have dramatic tension? How well does it integrate into the plot? Is there too much exposition? How can I turn that into action?

Don't ponder the questions! Explore them in writing. As mentioned earlier, your writing time should be spent writing, not pondering; pondering can also easily lead to procrastination.

If the idea of balancing the immediate and larger goals of the piece seems daunting, it shouldn't. We do it routinely in many areas of our lives:

A cook has to mentally juggle the short-term imperative of not burning the sauce with the longer-term ones of getting the table set, checking on the dessert in the oven, and figuring out what's up with the Smiths, those rascals who never RSVP'd.

A parent whose toddler is clamoring for a candy bar has to balance the short-term benefits of giving him one with the larger goal of encouraging him to eat healthily. (Parenting is full of these short-term/ long-term balancing acts.)

Businesspeople are routinely advised to not let their jobs interfere with their careers—meaning you want to make decisions that further your immediate success, but not at the expense of your long-term prospects.

Back to writing. Even in Stages 2 through 4, most of your focus should remain on your process. (Process always trumps product!) If you're writing something formulaic, or according to specification, then the external concerns might be more prominent, but even then your aim is to stay mostly immersed in a nonperfectionist creative process. Those other concerns will "visit" your consciousness once in a while, but only as needed. They will never dominate.

And just because you're at Stage 2 doesn't mean you stop doing timed writing, by the way. Actually, you never stop doing it; it's just that the timer gets set to larger and larger intervals. (After you start counting in hours, your "timer" may simply become your clock.)

If you're one of those people who just wants to write and doesn't care at all about being published, then you can remain happily in Stage 2. But if you do want to be published (in any format, or for any audience), then you'll want to move on to Stage 3.

If you ever find yourself becoming frightened or overwhelmed while writing in Stage 2—and it will happen—return promptly to

Stage 1. Don't return to Stage 2 until you once more feel comfortable and nonperfectionist about your writing.

During **Stage 3**, you focus not just on the creative process and your creative goals, but your "external" goals for the project. So you start asking questions such as: "Is this what my editor is expecting?" "Will it be approved by my thesis committee?" "Will it sell?" "How will my audience like it?" And so on.

Because focusing on external goals can invite perfectionism or distort the creative process, many writers choose to ignore them till late in the writing project. In a *Writer's Digest* interview,[4] novelist Anne Tyler said, "I've learned that it is best not to think about readers while I'm writing. I just try to sink into the world I'm describing. But at the very end, of course, I have to think about readers. I read my final draft pretending I'm someone else, just to make sure that what I've written makes sense from outside."

If you're one of those people who is content with occasional publication, or who isn't counting on a significant monetary reward from his writing, then you can remain at Stage 3. If you want a full-fledged writing career, or to earn significant money from your writing, then you'll want to move on to Stage 4.

If you ever find yourself becoming frightened or overwhelmed while writing in Stage 3—and it will happen—promptly return to Stage 2 or 1. Don't return to Stage 3 until you feel totally comfortably doing so.

Stage 4. Now you focus not just on process, creative goals, and external goals, but your career goals and strategy. Maybe you seek fame and fortune, or tenure, or enough income from your writing so that you can quit your day job.

At Stage 4, you're treating your writing like a business or profession and thinking about things like revenue, profit, marketing, and sales (Section 8.7). (If you're an academic, substitute career strategy, tenure, and job openings.) However, the same rule applies about maintaining most of your focus on your creative process while writing.

If you ever find yourself becoming frightened or overwhelmed while writing in Stage 4—and it will happen—promptly return to Stage 3, 2, or 1. Don't return to Stage 4 until you feel totally comfortably doing so.

---

[4] Jessica Strawser, "Anne Tyler's Tips on Writing Strong (yet Flawed) Characters," *Writer's Digest*, September 8, 2009 (www.writersdigest.com/article/anne-tyler-tips/).

Another way to think of the stages is using the path metaphor from Section 1.6. As you move on to each new stage, you let more and more people onto your path: in Stage 2, an editor; in Stage 3, your readers; and in Stage 4, professional partners, and perhaps a wider audience. As you work to replace perfectionism with compassionate objectivity, and to provide more resources for yourself, you'll get more and more adept at balancing seemingly opposing demands, including art and commerce, without getting overwhelmed or derailed. And you'll probably also soften around topics you are now rigid about, such as "success = selling out" (Section 6.7), and won't demand immediate, or definitive, answers to tough questions.

In other words, you will have replaced all the harsh and delusional perfectionist voices that previously gummed up your writing process with kind, inspiring, and realistic ones that spur you on to productivity and success.

Section 2.17 Anticipate Plateaus and Backsliding

Emotional growth and capacity building, which is what we're aiming for here, don't occur in a straight line, like this:

But rather in a curve, like this:

You'll have "good" days and "bad" days (defined relative to your own standard for writing productivity), and perhaps also good and bad weeks, months, and maybe years. You'll also have plateaus and backsliding. A plateau is where you stay at the same level of productivity for a while; backsliding is when your productivity drops. Sometimes they happen because the work itself is tough (in which case, it might not be an actual plateau or backslide, but only tough work), other times because of personal problems or other distractions.

On challenging days, scale back your ambitions—drastically, if necessary—to the point where you no longer feel fear. Your inner bully will probably appear right on schedule to scorn you as lazy, etc., which is how you'll know you're using an effective strategy. *Always ignore that voice.* I promise you that the shortest route back to maximum productivity is to work patiently within your human limitations so that you have a chance to regain your confidence and focus.

If your priorities change so that you no longer want to write, or if life gets stressful enough so that you can't write, by all means take a sabbatical. You can return to writing later, and probably will do so with even more energy and ideas and commitment as a consequence of having respected your needs.

Section 2.18 Other Antiperfectionist Techniques

1) Create a Lifestyle That Supports Your Writing. It's hard to be productive in the midst of chaos, or when struggling with an ongoing difficult personal or family situation. Some writers manage to shut everything else out and just write, but (even assuming you agree with that approach) most of us can't compartmentalize so effectively. We need to follow Flaubert's famous dictum to "Be regular and orderly in your life like a bourgeois, so that you may be violent and original in your work."

In *On Writing: A Memoir of the Craft*, Stephen King writes: "When I'm asked for 'the secret of my success'... I sometimes say there are two: I stayed physically healthy ... and I stayed married ... The combination of a healthy body and a stable relationship with a self-reliant woman who takes zero shit from me or anyone else has made the continuity of my working life possible."

Take prompt steps to resolve, or at least ameliorate, health, personal, and relationship problems as well as emotional problems such as depression and anxiety. Remember that procrastination can attack healing endeavors every bit as eagerly as it does your writing, and in particular is likely to strike at the beginning of the project. So, do what you can to get over the initial hump, and see a doctor, therapist, or other professional.

2) Create a Supportive Community. I write extensively about community throughout this book, and devote Chapters 6, 7, and 8 largely to it. Community's importance cannot be overstated—in fact, it could well be the determining factor in your success.

Community doesn't just provide colleagues and mentors; it provides a powerful expectation. **It's hard, if not impossible, to succeed if people around you are telling you you can't.** Or if they're expecting you to sacrifice your goals in favor of theirs. Or if they are threatened by your success. Or if they are ignorant about the mechanisms of success and vocally obstinate in their ignorance.

Writing is such a challenging vocation, in fact, that the absence of hostility isn't enough: you need active support. Prolific people are assiduous in seeking out supporters and equally assiduous in minimizing contact with those who might undermine them, even if the "underminers" happen to be related. This may not be easy, but the prolific, in common with most successful people, tend to clearly understand the implications of their choices—in this case, the prospect of a life of bitter under-accomplishment—and it's that clarity that gives them the courage to act.

3) *Get an Instructive Hobby.* Many writers have hobbies or other creative outlets in which they are much more productive than their writing, or even wholly unblocked. Every writer should have one, and should practice working out her productivity and perfectionism issues in that realm as well. A student once told of a quilting teacher she had who chirpily told a class, "If no one's bleeding, we're doing great!" That's a great antiperfectionist lesson.

My hobby is hiking, and every time I do it I viscerally re-experience the truth that progress is made one step at a time. Also, I learn important lessons in overcoming fear and asking for help.

4) *For Radical Productivity, Follow the Advice in the Book— Radically.* After you can reliably write nonperfectionistically, you free yourself to write easily (without major barriers), and then almost effortlessly (without any barriers to speak of). At this point, writing becomes enthralling and even joyful. Even the "difficult" (in the intellectual or emotional sense) parts of the work become much easier. In fact, you'll come to see that "easy" and "difficult" are largely arbitrary labels, and that there's much less difference between the supposedly easy and difficult parts of your projects than you now think.

The state of creativity without barriers is what psychologist Mihaly Csikszentmihályi famously called "flow." In flow, you're deeply engrossed in your work and time flies.

Perfectionists fight their creativity every step of the way, while paradoxically waiting and hoping and praying for flow to arrive. Compassionately objective writers, in contrast, develop work habits and attitudes that invite flow in, and so they experience flow many or even most of the times they write.

In flow, it's no problem to write for four, six, or even eight hours at a stretch. (With breaks, of course.) In contrast, to a perfectionist even six minutes—or thirty seconds—of writing can seem an eternity.

Do you hunger to write four or more hours at a stretch? Then *radically* embrace compassionate objectivity, and *radically* manage your time and other resources (Chapters 3 and 4), and *radically* optimize your writing process (Chapter 5). Also, *radically* come out as a writer (Chapter 6), *radically* deal with rejection (Chapter 7), and develop a *radically* empowered career path (Chapter 8). Just remember: You can't rush the process or cut corners especially at the beginning.

And remember that it is all founded on compassionate objectivity and short timed writing exercises.

Overcoming perfectionism is a key step toward becoming prolific, but for best results you need to write in an environment and context in which you have all the resources you need to create in abundance. That's the subject of Chapter 3.

Chapter 3

Coping with
Resource Constraints

"Oh, Time, Strength, Cash, and Patience!"
—Herman Melville, *Moby-Dick*

Section 3.1 So You Want to Run a Marathon...

I n classes we do an exercise where I tell the students, "Hey, everyone, I've decided to run a marathon tomorrow. Why not? It's just running- -a natural activity. And I've got a pair of sneakers." Everyone laughs at this obviously naïve statement. "Okay, so what do I need to run a marathon?"

The list we come up with runs something like this:

List of Resources to Run a Marathon

Material Resources	Psychological Resources	Community Resources
Running shoes	Dedication	Supportive family
Running clothes	Focus	Supportive boss and coworkers
Watch	Ability to "run past wall"	Coach/mentor/trainer
Water/water carrier	Self knowledge: ability to analyze	Running buddy
Music (MP3 player)	and improve performance	Friends
Reflectors (if training at night)	Self-forgiveness/resilience	Running community
Place to practice	Ability to tolerate discomfort	Supportive crowd (during race)
Proper nutrition before	Perseverance	Medical, nutritional,
and during race	Ability to stay attached to goal	psychological, and
Training plan and software	Ability to prioritize and to	other professionals
Maps/mapping software	sacrifice lesser priorities (e.g.,	
Vaseline	to create time for this goal)	
Heart-rate monitor	Devotion to self-care (basic nutrition,	
Sunscreen	rest, mental, and physical health)	
Hair band	Luck	
	Clarity and strength of purpose	
	Belief in self, the goal, the process, etc.	
	"Runner's identity"	

71

Wow, that's a long list for "just running." That's because, obviously, a marathon isn't just running, but a kind of serious or "professional" running, and professionalism is more demanding than a usual involvement.

Same goes for your writing. If your aim is small—say, the occasional grocery list or thank you note—then you can probably do it without much preparation or many resources. (Although plenty of people have trouble writing thank you notes!) But if your aim is to produce substantive works, or a serious body of work, then you need to prepare like a professional. And you need professional-caliber tools and other resources.

Before we list those tools and resources, let's look at some of the other lessons we derive from the marathoner's exercise.

Section 3.2 More Lessons from the Marathoners

(1) *Ambitious endeavors require **many** resources.* In the case of running (and writing, as you'll see), there are dozens of requirements, and many of them have "sub-requirements."

(2) *Guessing at the requirements for an ambitious activity isn't enough—you must consult experts.* Whenever I do the exercise, I ask any runners in the room to refrain from answering until the non-runners have had their chance. The non-runners typically come up with a list that's half (or less) complete. Then the runners chime in, and typically add a bunch of stuff that the non-runners hadn't even thought of.

In fact, you need to consult several experts. I've never had a class come up with anything near a complete list, and that includes classes with actual marathoners. Also, do an online search. It was online that I learned that Vaseline was a requirement for marathon training. (It prevents chafing.) No one in class has ever mentioned it, but the moment I mention it the runners all say, "Oh, yeah—you REALLY need that."

(3) *There are three categories of requirements: Material, Psychological, and Community.* In class I don't mention these categories until after we complete our list but just write down whatever answers people call out. Most people initially focus on the material needs and I have to prompt them to consider that there might be others. Again, the runners tend to do better than the non-runners, but

even the runners must be prompted to come up with reasonably complete lists of non-material needs.

This blind spot around our psychological and community needs is a serious impediment to our success not just in vocations like running and writing, but throughout our general lives. It's also an impediment to societies that want to better themselves. Fortunately, in recent decades we've seen increased acceptance of therapy and other tools for helping people meet their psychological needs, and we've also seen renewed interest in community.

(4) *Money is a huge blind spot.* My students rarely mention it, and yet you need it to buy everything in the Material Resources column, and also things like transportation to races, race entry fees, running club dues, and sports doctor visits. Money also lets you "buy" time for practicing and running races by allowing you to take time off from your job, work part-time instead of full-time, or hire help to cover your household responsibilities.

Why is money such a blind spot? Perhaps because it's a "secondary" resource, used to procure others. Or perhaps my students are comparing running with a more obviously expensive sport, like skiing or golf. (Just the same way you might compare "cheap" writing to "expensive" painting or sculpting.) But I also think many people are ambivalent about money in general, and the role it plays in success.

(5) *The more resources you provide for yourself, the better your odds of success. And with every resource you lack your odds diminish.* The relationship between resources and success is direct and strong for reasons I'll explain in Section 3.4.

(6) *It's not enough to provide a resource; you must optimize it.* Setting aside twenty hours a week for your practice runs is a good start, but they should be at times when you're energetic and motivated. If they're not—if you're practicing when you're drained or distracted—you won't benefit nearly as much.

That said, it's important to be adaptable. If mornings are your ideal time to practice, you should work to hold most of your practices in the mornings. But if a morning isn't available, it's usually better to practice at midday than skip practice entirely.

(7) *Although there may be resources you yourself don't need, there are no trivial resources.* The lack of a simple hair-band, for instance, could create not just a physical distraction but an actual danger if your sweaty hair gets in your eyes.

(8) ***Luck is crucial.*** The first time I did this exercise a student who was a marathoner said, "You could have all those other resources, but without luck you still won't finish the race." What a revelation! And of course she was right: if the weather is bad, or you have a cold, or you sprain your ankle, you probably won't finish.

Luck goes in the Psychological column because (1) it's the "residue of design" (i.e., planning), as Milton said,[1] and (2) psychological research has shown you can actually "create" luck via an optimistic attitude that encourages you to persevere and discover opportunity where someone pessimistic might not.[2] In Chapter 8, I talk about strategies for minimizing the role of luck in your success, but luck will always be a factor and good luck is always helpful.

(9) **Belief in self and process, a strongly held purpose or mission, and/or a "runner's identity" are crucial because they create a context that helps you focus on your goal and make good decisions.** These qualities lead to a mindset that says, "I am a runner, and therefore I will run today." Or, "I am a runner, and therefore I will invest in top-quality running shoes." This is similar to the "writing comes first" dictum many writers use to make sure the writing gets done despite life's many responsibilities and distractions.

Section 3.3 Resources for Ambitious Writing

Like running, writing is an activity that requires few resources if you're going to do it casually, but a lot more if you're going to do it seriously. William Faulkner, who notwithstanding his literary and other virtues was a font of perfectionist grandiosity, famously said in his Paris Review interview, "My own experience has been that the tools I need for my trade are paper, tobacco, food, and a little whiskey." I'm pretty sure that that wasn't, in fact, the complete list—he forgot, at the very least, a writing instrument—but, in any case, most writers need a lot more than that to write prolifically.

---

[1]He actually said, "Luck is the residue of opportunity and design," and was later famously quoted by philosophical baseball player Branch Rickey.

[2]Richard Wiseman, "Psychology of Luck" (blog), n.d. (www.richardwiseman.com/research/psychologyluck.html).

List of Resources for Sustained/Ambitious Writing

Material Resources	Psychological Resources	Community Resources
Writing space/room	Dedication	Supportive family
Computer (with Internet, for research, Web, emails)	Focus	Supportive boss and coworkers
	Ability to "write past wall"	
Computer (without Internet, for writing)	Self knowledge: ability to analyze and improve performance	Coach/mentor/trainer
		Critique partner(s)
Computer printer and other peripherals	Self-forgiveness/resilience	Friends
Ergonomic furniture	Ability to tolerate discomfort	Writing community
Reference books	Perseverance	Audience
Software—planners, outliners, note-takers, progress tracking, etc.	Ability to stay attached to goal	Medical, nutritional, psychological, and other professionals
	Ability to prioritize and to sacrifice lesser priorities (e.g., to create time for this goal)	
Money		
Comfortable clothes	Devotion to self care (basic nutrition, rest, mental, and physical health)	
	Luck	
	Clarity and strength of purpose	
	Belief in self, the goal, the process, etc.	
	"Writer's identity"	

Your list will probably be somewhat different from those of other writers.

The same lessons from the running list apply to this one:

1. Ambitious writing requires many resources.
2. Guessing at the requirements isn't enough—consult experts.
3. Don't devalue non-material resources.
4. Don't forget money.
5. The more resources you provide for yourself, the better your chances of success.
6. Optimize.
7. There are no trivial resources.
8. Don't overlook the role of luck.
9. An organizing vision/identity is crucial.

It's interesting how much the Psychological and Community lists overlap those for runners; perhaps all ambitious endeavors require much the same resources in these areas.

The Material list is very different, however, and much shorter. We writers are lucky in having fewer material requirements than those in many other fields. That's not the same as having no requirements, however, and it's also not to say that the requirements we do have aren't essential. The fact that writing has few material requirements often confuses naïve writers and others into thinking writing is easy. As I discuss in Section 6.4, it's not—and, anyway, as discussed in Section 2.7, "easy" and "hard" are antiproductive labels.

Section 3.4 What the Prolific Know

The prolific know that the thing to do with resources is provide them for yourself in abundance. Don't waste time asking "Do I really need this?" or "Can I get along without that?" Yes, you can equip yourself to the point of waste and self-indulgence, but most underproductive writers are so far from crossing that line that they don't even have to worry.

The prolific equip themselves abundantly because they are focused on their goals and have a clear sense of their priorities. They also understand, consciously or intuitively, the nine rules above. And they understand that even an expensive-seeming purchase is a good investment if it yields an important result—and they don't define "important" narrowly. A perfectionist might define "selling my book" as the only worthwhile outcome for a conference he's attending, but a compassionately objective person can identify many others, including learning valuable information and meeting a potential critique partner.

The prolific are also prepared to "waste money" in the service of an important endeavor; for instance, to spend it on a conference that turns out not to be useful. That's because, as discussed in Section 2.10, they don't expect themselves to be precognitive or infallible.

And the prolific also watch out for the situational perfectionism that can follow a major investment (Section 2.9).

The prolific also know that every time you provide a resource for yourself, you boost your productivity not only by improving your writing conditions but by validating yourself as a writer. "This is who I am, and this is what is important to me," you proclaim, not only to others but yourself,

Be this writer...

...not this one.

thus working to overcome the barriers of bias and internalized oppression (Chapter 6). Resourcing yourself is also an intrinsically empowering act and can help heal the disempowerment fundamental to procrastination.

Depriving yourself of resources, in contrast, not only stalls you logistically but sends a message of shame and disempowerment. One writer told me how in the midst of spending $50 on her kids' school supplies she agonized over whether to buy a $5 pack of pencils for herself, and ultimately decided not to. As you can imagine, the deprivation felt bad. Later, however, she returned to the store, bought her pencils, and then felt great—and wrote a bunch.

Section 3.5 Generous Writers vs. Snobs and Obfuscators

Writers, like others, tend to be fascinated by the work habits, techniques, and tools of their more successful colleagues. John Gardner wrote, in *On Becoming a Novelist*, "The single question most often asked during question-and-answer periods in university auditoriums and classrooms is: 'Do you write with a pen, a typewriter, or what?'" (This was in 1983, so computers weren't part of the dialogue.)

Fortunately, many successful writers are generous with that kind of information. The *Paris Review* interviews are a treasure trove, as is *The Guardian* series on Writers' Rooms[3] and Rules for Writers.[4]

Here's Steven Pressfield in *The War of Art*:

> I get up, take a shower, have breakfast, I read the paper, brush my teeth. If I have phone calls to make, I make them. I've got my coffee now. I put on my lucky work boots and stitch up the lucky laces that my niece Meredith gave me. I head back to my office, crank up the computer. My lucky hooded sweatshirt is draped over the chair ... It's about ten-thirty now. I sit down and plunge in. When I start making typos, I know I'm getting tired. That's four hours or so. I've hit the point of diminishing returns. I wrap for the day. Copy whatever I've done to disk and stash the disk in the glove compartment of my truck in case there's a fire and I have to run for it. I power down. It's three, three-thirty. The office is closed.

---

[3]"Writers' Room" series, *The Guardian*, various dates (www.guardian.co.uk/books/series/writersrooms).

[4]"Rules for Writers" series, *The Guardian*, various dates (www.guardian.co.uk/books/series/rules-for-writers).

And here's an excerpt from science fiction writer Cory Doctorow's 3,000-word description of his writing tools:

> Laptop: Thinkpad X200. This is the next-to-most-recent version of Lenovo's ThinkPad X-series, their lightweight travel notebooks. The X200 is fast enough that it never feels slow, and like all ThinkPads, is remarkably rugged and easy to do small maintenance chores upon. I bought mine in the UK but I prefer a US keyboard; I ordered one of these separately and did the swap in 20 seconds flat without every having done it before. I bought my own 500GB hard drive and 4GB of RAM separately (manufacturers always gouge on hard drives and memory) and installed them in about five minutes. Lenovo bought the ThinkPad line from IBM in 2005, but IBM still has the maintenance contract, through its IBM Global Services division. For $100 or so a year, I was able to buy an on-site/next-day hardware replacement warranty that means that when anything goes wrong with the laptop hardware, IBM sends a technician out to me the next day, with all the necessary replacement parts, no matter where I am in the world. I've been using ThinkPads since 2006 and have had occasion to use this maintenance contract three times, and all three times I was favorably impressed (lest you think three servicings in four years is an indicator of poor hardware quality, consider that every other brand of computer I've carried for any length of time became fatally wounded in less than a year).[5]

Doctorow is a self-described geek; he also does a lot of traveling, and so has equipment needs beyond those of most writers. (The next paragraph is all about his choice of computer *battery*!) You don't have to get as immersed in the technical details of your equipment as he does, but I quoted this lengthy excerpt to give you an idea of the importance some writers attach to their tools.

---

[5]Cory Doctorow, "What I Do," Locus Online, July 3, 2010 (www.locusmag.com/Perspectives/ 2010/07/cory-doctorow-what-i-do/).

Pragmatic descriptions such as the above are antiperfectionist and ungrandiose: they generously support other writers' productivity. Not all writers respond so helpfully, however. Some blather on about talent and how you either have it or don't, while others trot out the clichéd "apply ass to chair" maxim. Not all of these writers are ill intentioned; some are genuinely ignorant of the mechanics of their own work and success. Some, however, do scorn pragmatic questions, and I call them "snobs and obfuscators." If you ever run into one, don't take it to heart but simply take your question to someone wiser.

The current king of non-snobs is probably J.A. Konrath, whose ebook, *The Newbie's Guide to Publishing*, is a collection of hundreds of blog posts that delve deep into the habits and psyche of a professional writer. If you're reading this book, you probably want to buy that one.

The remaining sections of this chapter provide **general** advice and strategies related to the material and community resources needed by prolific writers. (The psychological resources are covered throughout the rest of the book.) Everyone's needs differ, so you should see what works for you.

Section 3.6 Your Hardware and Software

The key concept here is **not to settle**. A generic computer and word processing system are fine, but there are specialized tools that will help make you even more productive.

You should have **two computers**: one just for writing, with no Internet connectivity, games, multimedia, or other distractions on it; and another for the Internet and distractions. A free or cheap used computer should work for writing, so long as it is reliable.

Especially when working to overcome procrastination, you shouldn't have any Internet connectivity in your workplace. None. Nada. Zero. I know that sounds draconian, but I'm in good company when I say it. From *The Guardian*'s Rules for Writers series:

> "Work on a computer that is disconnected from the Internet."
> —Zadie Smith

"It's doubtful that anyone with an Internet connection at his workplace is writing good fiction."
—Jonathan Franzen.

Let's face it: The Internet is a huge tempter for any writer. Perfectionists try to force themselves to write despite its constant tempting, almost always failing, while prolific writers don't waste time (and jeopardize their success) trying, but simply pull the plug. Even programs like Freedom[6] that let you temporarily disable your Internet connectivity are only half a solution, since you still have to decide when to disable it and for what duration—and then you actually have to start the program AND continuously refrain from "cheating" by rebooting. Each of these decisions provides an opportunity for that duplicitous "thief of time" procrastination to do its work.

Later on, perhaps, you'll be able to write on an Internet-enabled computer. I currently do, and on days I feel distracted I simply unplug the cable and throw it across the room. (I have WiFi for guests, but I don't have the password so it's not a potential distraction. Most of the time, in fact, I forget I have it.)

Beyond all this, how well are your computer, Internet, printer, etc. working? I shouldn't even have to say this, but if your equipment is flaky, fix or replace it immediately. Prolific writers never tolerate flaky equipment, but underproductive ones do, all the time.

Keep an eye out for **novel hardware** that might be useful. Some prolific writers use the Renaissance Learning NEO for first drafts and note-taking, since the tiny screen discourages editing. And many academics and others use pen-scanners to record and digitize passages from source materials. By the time you read this, there will be other interesting writing hardware out there, and the best way to learn about it is to talk with other writers.

If you write on a laptop outside the home, by all means buy an extra battery so that you can double your time between charges.

Many prolific writers will need to move to an **ergonomic keyboard** at some point. Be wiser than I was, and buy it *before* your wrists start hurting.

Clocks and timers really help with time management (see Chapter 4), so buy as many as you want. And if your project involves a lot of

---

[6]Freedom (productivity software) website (macfreedom.com).

research, invest lavishly in all the folders, binders, and other organizing tools you need to get it all in great order. Don't settle!

On to software...

Check out "artisanal" **word processors** such as Scrivener, Nisus Writer, Ulysses, and WriteRoom that incorporate efficient user interfaces with robust writer-friendly add-ons such as outliners, indexers, and project organizers. Academic writers should check out Nota Bene and EasyBib, which are specialized for handling citations, or LaTeX, which offers superior formatting for scientific and other documents. And playwrights and screenwriters will want to look at Final Draft or Movie Magic.

Whatever word processor you use, optimize it. Customize your toolbars so that your most-used commands (like word count or indexing) are easily accessed, and build up your Autocorrect list so you have shortcuts for common words or phrases (e.g., "ssp" for *The Seven Secrets of the Prolific*). Each time you use one of these features you might only save a few seconds, but those seconds add up.

I discuss emails from a time management/prioritization/boundaries standpoint in Section 4.9, and so will stick to the technological issues here. If you're emailing via your Web browser, consider moving to a dedicated email program such as Eudora, Evolution, or Thunderbird. Although it's possible to be productive with browser-based software, offline programs have many productivity features; plus being offline often enhances productivity (see above). This is especially true if you're planning to do serious marketing and sales (Section 8.8).

In your email program, use filters so that different emails are automatically sorted into different folders upon receipt or sending. Also, use autoresponders to respond automatically to incoming emails based on the subject line, and signatures to quickly insert frequently repeated text at the bottoms of outgoing emails. I have set up ten signatures in my email program so that if anyone emails me about coaching, workshops, or videos I can send a detailed reply with just a couple of mouse clicks. (Besides saving time, this also ensures consistency of message.)

Writers tend to have a lot of subscriptions to news sites, blogs, etc., so you should manage those through a newsreader or RSS feed program. Your email program and/or browser probably incorporates one.

To build an audience for your writing, you'll need a **website** and **mailing list/newsletter program**. It's a huge waste of time to do these yourself, and the result is likely to be disappointing. (Hint: You need technology AND design AND marketing skills to do them right.) Find a Web designer who has worked with other writers.

Many email programs come with a built-in **calendar, to-do lists, note-takers, and other productivity tools**; if yours doesn't, there are plenty of free or cheap programs that handle these tasks. **Personal finance software** such as Quicken or bookkeeping software such as QuickBooks will also save you a lot of time, and is particularly important if you are running a business (see Section 8.7). And **paying bills online** not only saves time but protects you from identity theft.

An easy way to **back up** your writing and other crucial data files is to email them to yourself after each writing session: this saves copies both in your email program and on your email server. (Make sure both your program and the server are set to indefinitely save emails, and I'm assuming the server is offsite.) This technique also helpfully maintains a chronological record so you can revert to an older version if you wish.

You can theoretically back up your entire disk onto a thumb drive, but a better technique is to use a service such as Mozy or Carbonite that automatically backs up your disk via the Internet. These services also maintain archives so that if your system gets hit with a virus or otherwise corrupted you can revert to an earlier version.

Viruses are a huge risk to Windows users in particular, and they should be diligent in using and maintaining **antiviral software**. Everyone should use an email service that automatically scans incoming messages for viruses (most of the popular ones do) and set their browser to avoid connections to sites that host viruses, trojans, and other "malware."

I'm a huge fan of **free/libre/open source software (FLOSS)**, which is software whose code is available for inspection and change by anyone. Its transparency is protective of our civil rights (because it makes it hard for governments or others to sneak code in that spies on us, controls our PCs, etc.), and most FLOSS also has the more prosaic advantages of being available for free over the Internet and of never requiring registrations and mandatory upgrades. FLOSS programs tend to run really well, and on cheap hardware. (Cory Doctorow, the geek/writer mentioned earlier, loves FLOSS too.) I use the Ubuntu GNU/Linux operating system, Oracle's OpenOffice office suite, Novell's Evolution email program, and Mozilla's Firefox browser, but there are also other choices. FLOSS programs sometimes lack "advanced" features (meaning features you probably don't use anyway) found in commercial/proprietary programs, and you often have to convert your document files to share them with Windows and Mac users, but for me these drawbacks are minor. Just make sure, before switching over, that any software you're wedded to—e.g., your artisanal word processor—will run on GNU/Linux.

When it's time for a new computer, I buy a cheap one and pay a GNU/Linux expert $50 to install the latest software from a disk. Less than an hour later I'm good to go.

Finally, because prolific writers understand the critical importance of their computer systems and Web marketing, and because they value their time too highly to work inefficiently, they **hire abundant professional computer help**. If you absolutely can't afford to hire someone, try bartering via timebanks.org or less formally via an ad on Craigslist.

Section 3.7 Your Writing Space and Furniture

Years ago, I attended a problem-solving workshop where one of the exercises was to work in teams to put together small jigsaw puzzles. The puzzles were on tables set up behind curtains along the edges of the room—a claustrophobic setting and also a dark one, since the only light came from over the tops of the curtains. During the exercise, a few teams dragged their tables out into the well-lit main part of the room (no one had told us we couldn't) or commandeered one of the floor lamps that were "coincidentally" scattered around the room (ditto). But most chose to struggle along doing their puzzles literally in the dark.

This experience vividly illustrated a key difference between productive and underproductive people: **productive people tend to take charge of their physical environment, while underproductive ones tend to "suffer in silence" with suboptimal conditions.** Many writers, for instance, wind up in dreary basements or cluttered guest bedrooms along with the treadmill and last season's wardrobe. Along with the inconvenience, imagine the message that working in such a place sends to yourself and others about your writing.

Don't settle for that! Claim the best space you can for your writing—displacing treadmill and guests (who can sleep on the living room couch, or a hotel for that matter)—and then work to optimize it around your needs. Install shelves or soundproofing or whatever else you need, and redecorate it so it's a more congenial setting for your craft.

Gail Godwin's novel *Violet Clay* provides a vivid illustration. At its beginning, Violet's deprecation of her art is embodied in her apartment, in which only a small corner has been allotted to her painting. At the end, after she has fully embraced her artistic identity and mission, the situation has been reversed, and she's transformed the cottage she's living in into a full-blown artist's studio, with only a small corner reserved for her living space.

If you work best outside the home, don't settle for a mediocre writing space if a little cash will get you a better one. One of the most glorious places I've ever written in was the Boston Athenaeum, a venerable private library that elegantly combines Whartonian luxury and elegance with spacious writing cubicles and state-of-the-art WiFi and other amenities. Membership was just $230 a year, an incredible bargain given not just the facilities but the ability to check books out for three months at a time and to write surrounded by serious authors (some famous) doing the same. It was truly a writer's heaven on Earth.

Less opulent, perhaps, but equally functional are the writers' centers[7] or freelance business centers where you can also rent a desk (with access to WiFi, copiers, etc.) for a reasonable fee. Or, if you're writing in coffee shops, (1) find one frequented by other writers, as the company will help keep you motivated, and (2) tip the baristas generously, both out of principle and to gain a willing helper who will, say, keep an eye on your laptop when you use the bathroom.

If, through all this, a little voice in your head says, "It's a shame to waste money like this," dialogue compassionately with it to find out why, exactly, it feels that investing money in your writing is a waste—and to help it understand otherwise. True, you might not have $230 a year for a writing space—although in that case be sure to ask about a scholarship—but it's also true that many who do have money make the self-defeating choice not to invest in their writing.

I am not deprecating public libraries, by the way—they are terrific and important and valuable in all kinds of ways. Some are more writer-friendly than others, however. Comfortable furniture, easily accessible WiFi, and the community of others also immersed in writing

---

[7]Ginny Wiehardt, "Writers' Rooms: Spaces for Urban Writers," About.com Fiction Writing section (blog), n.d. (fictionwriting.about.com/od/startingtowrite/tp/urbanspaces.htm).

or scholarship all contribute significantly to productivity—and not all libraries meet those conditions.

Beyond the space, make sure your furniture is comfortable and ergonomic. Carpal tunnel syndrome, backaches, and eyestrain are real hazards, and so you should take prevention seriously.

Now, on to your community needs. I talk about community throughout the book, and especially in Section 2.18 and Chapters 6–8, but here are some specifics you should look for when deciding whom to involve in your writing, and how to involve them.

Section 3.8 Your Family

A truly supportive family supports you not just with words, but actions. When you articulate your writing-related needs—be they for time, space, privacy, or a new computer—they do their best to help. Someone who says he supports your writing but still expects you to handle all the housework, cooking, childcare, etc., is not being supportive. Nor is someone who expects you to sacrifice your writing to a rigorous day job when the household could function, albeit perhaps less luxuriously, with you working an easier one that pays less.

It's *your* job, however, to articulate your needs. Too many writers don't, either because they are conflicted about their writing (Section 6.5) or assume they'll get no help. (There could also obviously be larger family issues.) Nearly every writer I know who has asked family, friends, bosses, or others for help, however, has gotten it, and often in excess of what they expected. Lots of times, people are eager to help us, but don't know how until we tell them.

One of the most important things writers can do for themselves is ask for help. Not only is the result often beneficent, but the act itself is empowering, regardless of the outcome. I love it when I get an email from someone asking to talk over a difficult problem and then, shortly afterwards, another saying, "Never mind, I figured it out." The very act of asking for help, which probably entailed overcoming some shame and guilt, empowered the asker enough to enable problem solving.

The wrong way to ask for help is to say, "You guys are all slobs, and I'm sick of it! From now on everyone cleans!" The right way is to involve all interested parties in **cooperative problem solving**, which I discuss in Section 4.11.

Some people have the unfortunate habit of showing love and support via criticism or nagging (e.g., "Did you write today?" asked over and over). This, obviously, is also not helpful. If someone you know does that, tell them (1) how grateful you are for their support, (2) how their communication style is affecting you, and (3) what *specifically* they could say or do to provide better support. They will probably be grateful.

If your family is unsupportive, family therapy might help, or individual therapy might help you cope. If these don't work, you will probably need to minimize contact with your family. Some writers move thousands of miles away from unsupportive families (often to communities more generally supportive of their identities and goals), and/or cut off all contact. Some divorce unsupportive spouses. These steps might sound draconian, but prolific writers (and other successful people) won't hesitate to employ them as a last resort because they clearly see the consequences—to not just their writing but their life—of passivity in the face of oppression. They won't tolerate it, and neither should you.

Section 3.9 Mentors and Writers' Communities

Mentors are so vital that the presence or lack of them will probably determine your success. If I see someone who is well-mentored, I can assume he is integrated into a productive and professional community, is able to ask for help, and is able to take advice, all of which point to a successful outcome for his efforts. If I see someone who is under-mentored, conversely, I assume he is isolated, unable to ask for help, and/or unable to follow advice, and I am less optimistic. In fact, I've never met anyone underproductive who wasn't also under-mentored.

A mentor is either a writer whose success you wish to emulate ("success" defined, as always, according to your own values), or someone who can teach you a specific important skill, such as compassionate objectivity, networking, or organizing a book tour. You want mentors not just for your professional life, but your personal life, including for marriage, parenting, aging, health and fitness, personal finance, property ownership, and community work.

Along with information, wisdom, and perspective, mentors

also provide vital contacts. Many writers get traditionally published after a mentor says, "I love your current work—is it okay if I send it to my editor?"

Underproductive people tend to believe mentors are few and far between, but the truth is they're everywhere:

Most of us reflexively turn to more successful people as mentors, but our "lateral" colleagues and subordinates also have much to teach us.

We tend to look toward older people as mentors, but mentors come in all ages. Some of my most important mentors are half my age, and even small children can mentor joyful, nonperfectionist creativity.

And we tend to look at humans as mentors, but nonhumans can be great mentors. I learn relational skills and pure joy from my dogs every day.[8]

Even a plant or a rock could be a mentor, I guess, because in the end it's less about who the mentor is and more about how open you are to learning and insight. The world is filled with lessons.

Avoid perfectionist, harsh, or capricious mentors no matter how brilliant, important, connected, or otherwise potentially beneficial: the risk of toxic rejection is too great (Section 7.3). At most, seek out such a person for a few answers to specific questions, be prepared for possible mistreatment, and be prepared to flee at the earliest sign of it.

The easiest way to find mentors (the adult, human, professional kind) is to participate in organizations filled with them, such as these:

The *local chapters of professional groups* such as Romance Writers of America, Science Fiction Writers of America, or Mystery Writers of America. I'm partial to these because they tend to be not only focused on professional development and publication but welcoming of newcomers and beginners. You'll also meet financially successful writers, which is always enlightening and inspiring.

Even if you don't see your work as fitting entirely within a genre, if it's got strong romance, science fiction, or mystery elements, try attending a meeting.

Community writing programs or centers, such as Boston's Grub Street Writers, the New York Writers Workshop, or Minneapolis' The Loft. These can be great, too, for the same reasons as the professional groups, and they typically serve a wider range of writers.

---

[8]Here's another dog-as-mentor story: Dana Jennings, "Life Lessons from the Family Dog," Well (*New York Times* blog) , March 31, 2009 (well.blogs.nytimes.com/2009/03/31/life-lessons-from-the-family-dog/).

Colleges and universities often host writing workshops that are open to the public, as do some ***literary landmarks***. (See B.J. Welborn's book *Traveling Literary America* for a list of the latter in the United States.)

In the absence of the above options, contact a local writer whom you admire and ask if there's an informal ***local or regional writers group*** you could join. Or ask at a local bookstore.

You can also find mentors at:

Content groups. If you write on a specific topic, such as anatomy, architecture, or apes, there are probably professional organizations or hobbyist groups that meet locally on it.

Community groups. If you're active in a community organization, be alert to potential mentors, especially in areas related to marketing, sales, and accounting (Chapter 8). A basic tenet of networking is that you never know whom someone knows, so be alert to the possibility that someone in your group has a contact in media or another helpful field.

Only join groups that are welcoming, professionally run (i.e., focused on goals, even if the main goal is not publication), and compassionately objective. When you find one, participate actively. Joining the membership committee, organizing an event, or writing for the newsletter are all terrific ways to meet potential mentors.

Don't join groups that are cliquish or unwelcoming, or where writers are sorted into "castes" (e.g., published versus non-published). The best groups are egalitarian, with the more successful writers recognizing that they're on the same basic path as the less successful ones, only somewhat further ahead. Also avoid groups that are perfectionist or competitive. Remember that remaining in a bad group for even a short while can undermine you.

Online groups can be fantastic, but they are no substitute for joining an in-person group. Many prolific writers travel fifty or more miles to their local group's monthly meetings, which gives you an idea of how much they value them.

Special note for graduate students: Because universities often fail to deliver on their mentorship promises (see Appendix), and because they can be such hotbeds of hypercompetitiveness and perfectionism, some students supplement their schooling with participation in one of the groups I just listed. That's a fantastic idea.

Section 3.10 How to Work With Mentors

Don't be shy. Remember that, in general, people love to give advice and support, even to strangers. (In the classic *How to Win Friends and Influence People*, Dale Carnegie says that our deepest need is to feel important.) Savvy people also know that mentoring is one of the best ways to develop their own skills and strengths, and many also feel a moral imperative to "give back" for mentoring and other assistance they themselves received.

At the same time, mentors tend to be busy people who get asked for help a lot, sometimes by people who are not serious or focused. When approaching a potential mentor, therefore, make sure he knows you are one of the serious ones by making a focused, personalized and time-bounded request, such as: "I loved your biography of Cervantes, and especially your emphasis on his intellectual influences. I'm working on a novel on the life of Lope de Vega[9] and am having trouble sorting out his religious and other influences. Would it be okay if I called you about this? I just need five or ten minutes of your time."

Note that the asker does not ask the listener to "be my mentor." What you're asking for is a favor, not a relationship; if the relationship is destined to develop, it will. (In fact, you may never need to use the word "mentor.")

When calling or meeting with a mentor, be prompt, prepared, and professional. Your conversation will be a kind of audition, during which the mentor will be deciding whether to continue the relationship beyond this interaction. If you're professional, he probably will want it to continue.

Don't go past the agreed-on time—although if the mentor is enjoying the conversation he might, which is fine. In your discussion, focus on problem-solving as opposed to how frustrated or miserable the problem is making you feel. (Save that part of the discussion for your friends and critique partners; see next section.) And sometime during the discussion, be sure to ask, "Do you know anyone else who could advise me on this?" This will help you build your mentor network. Also:

Send a thank-you note. Thank-you notes are not just polite; they're a powerful affirmation to your mentor and a powerful reminder

---

[9]A super-prolific writer, by the way. According to Wikipedia, "He is attributed some 3,000 sonnets, 3 novels, 4 novellas, 9 epic poems, and about 1,800 plays ... at least 80 of his plays are considered masterpieces."

of your professionalism. They take only a few minutes to write, so I'm constantly amazed at how many people neglect them. (Saying a quick "thank you" at the end of a conversation is NOT enough.) An email is fine, although a paper note is classy. (One of Carolyn See's chief recommendations in *Making a Literary Life* is to get some professional stationery and use it to write "charming notes" to people with whom you want to be in professional contact.)

Stay in touch. If you contact your mentors only when you need help they will feel used. Instead, contact them every few months just to let them know how things are going, and especially to share good news. Don't forget to ask how they are doing!

Reciprocate. Mentors appreciate, and often expect, return value. It can be hard to see what you can offer a more successful mentor, but most appreciate receiving useful articles or other information, or offers of help when their own schedule gets crowded.

And, finally…

Mentor! Yes, YOU should be a mentor. First, because it's good to give back, and second, because mentoring fosters your own growth and success.

Think you don't know enough to be a mentor? Think again: I've never met anyone who didn't have valuable wisdom or experience to impart.

Learn to recognize mentor relationships that aren't working. This could either be because the person isn't a competent mentor, or the two of you aren't a good fit. In his review of Tom Grimes's *Mentor*, *New York Times* reviewer Dwight Garner opined that the "blind allegiance and bursting enthusiasm" of Grimes's mentor Frank Conroy "probably hurt more than helped,"[10] and I agree. Based on Grimes's account, Conroy also apparently failed to maintain healthy boundaries with his student/protégé, so that their relationship devolved first into an uneasy form of friendship, and then a father/son dynamic in which Grimes felt a "crippling dependency." It is irresponsible for a teacher to encourage that kind of dynamic, since, dependency issues aside, it also often short circuits learning and career development—which is exactly what happened to Grimes. Contrast his experience with Jay Cantor's as a student of Bernard Malamud at Harvard: "It

---

[10]Dwight Garner, "A Writer's Prayer, Halfway Answered," *New York Times*, August 3, 2010 (www.nytimes.com/2010/08/04/books/04book.html).

wasn't love at first sight, mostly because he wasn't looking for love from us, but for admiration and understanding, and even then, only in small doses that wouldn't knock a person off balance." (From *Mentors, Muses & Monsters*, edited by Elizabeth Benedict.)

Sometimes mentor relationships just go stale, or a protégé outgrows a mentor. These situations aren't anyone's fault, or even anything to feel bad about: people do grow and change, after all. Hopefully, you'll be able to gradually evolve the "mentor" into a "colleague" with whom you will remain productively in touch.

Section 3.11 Critique Partners, Workshoppers, Alpha Readers, Beta Readers, and Your Audience

Beyond mentors, most prolific writers rely on "concentric circles" of support starting with critique partners and expanding out to an engaged audience. Please note that the descriptions below are generalizations—not everyone will fall neatly into one category, and not everyone in a category will provide the same help. Be flexible in your expectations.

You call your **critique partner** (a.k.a., critique buddy) when you're having a tough writing day, had a tough rejection (or a wonderful acceptance!), or for help with a writing- or publishing-related problem. You also commit to sending her work on deadline—and she kindly but firmly calls you on it if you're late. And, finally, you send her work to review.

Being a critique partner is a serious commitment. Typically, two simpatico writers will fill this role for each other, and communicate frequently—in some cases, daily.

Please note that while some critique partners (and workshoppers, etc.) can act as mentors, many mentors do not want to be critique partners. "Important" mentors are often more interested in helping you strategize, plan, and problem-solve than in providing detailed manuscript critiques or emotional support. (They may also not be suited for those tasks.) Teachers, of course, have an obligation to span both roles, but often don't.

Workshoppers provide manuscript critiques and problem-solving in a classroom-type setting. Workshops typically provide less individualized emotional support and problem-solving than critique partners, although what support they do provide can be invaluable. The tenor and usefulness of a workshop is usually determined by the teacher or leader, and writers who find a good one often stick with him for years.

Workshops are also common places where people find critique partners.

Most writers have a small group of **"alpha readers"** who are the first people they show their work to after their critique buddies and workshoppers. These could be other writers or "civilians." A diverse alpha reader pool is a huge asset, particularly for writers aspiring to a large audience: it's illuminating—and, sometimes, career-saving—to have your work critiqued from various age, gender, religious, ethnic, national, regional, and other viewpoints. I once was saved from sending out a manuscript with an ethnic slur in it when someone older read it. The slur wasn't in common use among my generation, but it leaped out at anyone older.

You probably don't want too many alphas—around ten is a good number—and you should only choose people whom you trust not just to give good feedback but to keep your manuscript confidential. In workshops, it's usually explicitly stated that manuscripts are confidential; you need to explicitly tell your alphas the same thing, and maybe print your copyright and confidentiality information on each page.

Think carefully before using family members as critique partners or alpha readers. In many cases, they aren't qualified, and in others—say, if your manuscript is about your family, or touches on controversial themes—the critique partner or alpha reader role conflicts with the family role. In general, if your family isn't fully sympathetic to your work, if they give too-harsh criticism, showing them early drafts is counterproductive.

Beta Readers: Some writers, after making the revisions suggested by their alpha readers, send their manuscript to a much bigger pool of **beta readers**. Again, aim for diversity, and at this point it might make sense to include some sympathetic and savvy family members.

Needless to say, everyone in *all* of the above categories should be (1) enthusiastic about your work and (2) capable of giving constructive criticism.

Finally, we come to your **audience**. It's hard to write when you don't have one, or can't envision one, so you need to create one for yourself using marketing and sales (Section 8.8). The idea that audiences happen spontaneously, say in response to "excellent" or "timely" work, is perfectionist (Section 2.5): most audiences are built over years and decades.

One of the joys of authorship is being able to touch people emotionally and intellectually. Especially now in the Internet age, many of those whom you touch will be motivated to contact you, which is overall a good thing. Some may become part of your alpha or beta teams, while others can help with marketing and sales. Treat your audience members with courtesy and appreciation, respond at least briefly to their notes, and add them (after asking permission) to your mailing list.

If you get to the point where reader correspondence becomes burdensome, take that as a sign of success. (It means you're inspiring a lot of people, and it's a good problem to have!) See Section 4.8 for help with establishing boundaries and Section 4.9 for tips on dealing with email overload.

The negative side of the Internet is that it's also easier for people to send abusive messages. Ignore those unless they contain a threat or are otherwise scary, in which case you should call the police.

Section 3.12 Other Key Community Members

Day Job Boss and Coworkers. As discussed in Section 4.6, a key difference between prolific and underproductive writers is that the former manage their day job in such a way as to minimize its impact on their writing. Typically, this means working part-time, and on a schedule that reserves your most energetic and alert hours for your writing.

This is yet another situation where you must (a) articulate your needs and (b) collaboratively problem-solve, and in order to do those steps you must first come out to yourself and others as a writer (Section 6.6).

I've twice gotten day-job bosses to give me the schedule I wanted: once gaining a three-day workweek that left four days a week for writing and home life, and another time gaining an afternoons-only workweek that left mornings free for writing. I've also coached other writers on how to do it, and without exception they've received more support and cooperation than they anticipated. Many people, it turns out, are happy to help us pursue our dream.

So don't assume your boss won't be flexible on your schedule. If, however, he is—or if you're even afraid to bring up the topic of your need of a new schedule—it's time to look for another job. Visit www.

hillaryrettig.com and download my free ebook *It's Not You, It's Your Strategy* for tips on how to look for a job effectively.

Yes, looking for another job is hugely unpleasant. But if the alternative is never having quality time to write, then staying where you are should not be an option.

Agents and Editors. In Chapter 8, I advocate for self-publishing as a strategy for avoiding the kinds of unequal and/or exploitative business relationships endemic to publishing. If you choose not to follow this advice, be careful to only work with agents, editors, and others who are compassionately objective and have a basic sense of fairness and egalitarianism. Although this advice may seem idealistic, it's actually highly pragmatic: most successful writers, along with successful people in every field, know that unequal partnerships tend not to succeed.

It takes a special kind of agent or editor to not succumb to a sense of superiority or entitlement when sitting at the "top" of an inequitable system, but they're out there. You'll know you're in a healthy and productive business partnership if it embodies most or all of the qualities of empowered careers described in Section 8.5.

Chapter 4

Liberating Yourself from Time Constraints

"Being in a hurry decreased [helping behavior] ... ethics becomes a luxury as the speed of our daily lives increases."
—John M. Darley and C. Daniel Batson,
"'From Jerusalem to Jericho': A study of situational and dispositional variables in helping behavior." In: *Readings About the Social Animal*, 7th Ed. (Elliot Aronson, ed.), New York: Freeman, 1995.

Section 4.1 The Crucial Importance of Time Management

In 1973, social psychologists John Darley and Daniel Batson asked forty students at the Princeton Theological Seminary to write and record a sermon. Half were given the topic of career planning for seminary students. The other half were asked to sermonize about the Good Samaritan parable in which a priest and an aristocrat ("Levite") callously ignore a wounded and suffering man on the street, while a humble Samaritan stops to help.

After the students had prepared their sermons, some were told that they had plenty of time to get to the nearby building where they would be recording, some were told that they were right on time, and some were told they were late and had to hurry.

Here's the diabolical part: as each seminarian walked (or ran, in the case of the late ones) to give his sermon, he encountered a confederate of the experimenters who was lying on the ground, coughing and moaning in obvious distress.

He was being confronted with the Good Samaritan scenario in real life.

I'll let Darley and Batson describe the result:

> Subjects in a hurry were likely to offer less help than were subjects not in a hurry. Whether the subject was going to give a speech on the parable of the Good Samaritan or not did not significantly affect his helping behavior.

And (as if that weren't bad enough):

> Indeed, on several occasions, a seminary student going to give his talk on the parable of the Good Samaritan literally stepped over the victim as he hurried on his way!

The experimenters concluded that "ethics becomes a luxury as the speed of our daily lives increases." In fact, it's not just our ethical capacity that diminishes when we're rushed; many important capacities do, including our abilities to think, judge, decide, focus, remember, and relate. Moment by moment, when we're rushed, we're simply not the people we're capable of being.

A related problem is that many rushed people don't get enough sleep—and fatigue also degrades our capacities, often in dangerous ways. Sleep-deprived people have more car accidents[1], and they also get sick more often.[2]

The antidote for all this rushing around is time management, a practice that is particularly important for writers not just because writing often represents an additional major commitment on top of an already-busy life, but because creativity requires a freedom of mind and spirit that is hard to achieve in the midst of a crowded schedule. Put

---

[1] DrowsyDriving.org, a Website of the National Sleep Foundation, n.d. (drowsydriving.org/about/facts-and-stats/).

[2] Penelope A. Bryant, John Trinder and Nigel Curtis, "Sick and Tired: Does Sleep Have a Vital Role in the Immune System?," *Nature Reviews Immunology* 4, 457-467, June 2004 (www.nature.com/nri/journal/v4/n6/abs/nri1369.html).

another way: writers need lavish time not only to write, but to think, and experience, and feel.

What Time Management Is and Isn't

Because there's a lot of misinformation about, and confusion around, the concept of time management, it's important to define just what it is and isn't. Time management isn't about working around the clock, or at some otherwise perfectionist defined level of "maximum" productivity: it's actually the opposite of that. The goal of time management is to align, as much as possible, your actions with your values. Time management mandates that you get honest about who you are and what's important to you, and then to make choices based on that assessment, and not out of guilt, shame, obligation or convention. It is strictly grounded in reality, and forces you to acknowledge basic facts, such as that you have limited time, energy and other resources, and can't be in two places at once.

Time management is a tool for creating peace, success, joy, and impact. A good time manager is likely to be busy, but not crazy or stressed. She[3] shows up for meetings on time or early, and is well prepared. She completes her work on time, and to a high degree of quality. She has plenty of time for her relationships, health, relaxation, and fun—and also to invest in others, including wounded strangers.

She feels great about herself and her work—and, because of this, she is a natural leader who attracts and influences others.

The hardest parts of time management are the accountability, and the need to make tough choices as to how your time will be invested—but in the end, these will seem like small prices to pay for the benefits.

---

[3]In this section, I dispense with the alternating gender pronouns and use only the feminine, since even in many "egalitarian" households women are still disproportionately responsible for childcare and housework, and thus face a stronger time-management challenge. Also, women often have more trouble than men with the techniques discussed in this section, including prioritizing their own needs.

SILVER BAY PUBLIC LIBRARY

Section 4.2 The Five Foundational Principles of Time Management

The practice of time management is not difficult: you budget and track your time as you would any valuable limited resource. It's the philosophy underlying the practice that you need to understand, because once you do, the practice becomes easier—and almost automatic. That philosophy can be summed up in five basic principles:

1.   Time is the most valuable resource.
2.   Always seek to invest time, not spend it.
3.   The things you invest quality time in are the things you will improve at or succeed at, and the things you don't are the things you won't.
4.   The purpose of time management isn't to stuff as much as possible into your schedule, but to remove as much as possible from your schedule so you have time to get the important stuff done to a high degree of quality, and with as little stress as possible.
5.   There is no such thing as unmanaged time. If you don't manage your own time, others will be happy to manage it for you.

Let's take those one at a time.

Section 4.3 Time-Management Principle #1: Time is the Most Valuable Resource

Picture two people trying to get fit:

One spends thousands on a fancy health club membership, fancy exercise clothes, and a top-of-the-line racing bike, but never gets around to using them.

The other spends $75 on a good pair of running shoes, and maybe $20 on a second-hand set of weights, and uses them for an hour or more each day.

Who will get fit? Obviously, the one who invests time rather than money.

Or, imagine a parent who hardly spends any time with her children, but tries to compensate with expensive gifts, versus one who can offer few gifts but lots of quality time. Who is likely to have the better relationship with her children? The latter, obviously.

Time, as it turns out, does not equal money; it's far more valuable than money, because it can create values that money can't. And the principle that time is the most valuable resource is by far the most important of the five principles because it is the one that has the most fundamental impact on our behavior. People who value their time highly behave very differently from those who don't:

They are intolerant of wasting time. Wherever they go, whatever they do, there's a little voice in their head asking: Was that a good use of my time? Could I have done it in less time? Could I have delegated it? How could I do it more effectively or efficiently in the future? In other words, they are **optimizers** who work strenuously to eliminate even small inefficiencies from their schedules. They do this because they know that (1) the trivial savings can add up, (2) trivia often take longer than planned, and often lead to more trivia, and (3) even trivial activities can add stress or distract from more important endeavors.

Please note that the optimizing voice is always gentle and helpful, never harsh or punitive. Harsh corrections are the voice of the oppressor: perfectionism.

They value small amounts of time. They see even a five-minute gap between meetings as valuable time during which they can make a call, send an email, or review their notes—or do some calming stretches or meditation. (Recall how a lot of procrastination begins in the body; Section 1.9). In contrast, people who do not value time highly see not just minutes, but hours, days, weeks, months, and even years as expendable on low-value "busy work," "time wasting," and projects outside their mission.

They invest time and money in time management. They buy organizers, timers, clocks, watches, and other tools. They read books related to time management. And they actually use all these tools, as well as the techniques discussed throughout this chapter.

They don't do a lot of housework, chores, busywork, or maintenance, and they don't overgive. See Sections 4.4 and 4.8.

They tend to have shorter business meetings and conversations. At work, they're polite and friendly, but not big on small talk or running off on tangents. At meetings, they stick to the point. Also, they don't visit someone when they can call, don't call when they can email, and don't manually answer emails that they can set their email program to answer automatically (see below). Obviously, you can take this too far and "over-optimize" to the point of ineffectiveness, but many people, for fear of seeming rude or other reasons, have a hard time limiting unproductive conversations.

They invest in technology and automation. They use signatures, autoresponders, how-to lists, reminders, and other tools to streamline their work (Section 3.6). They also invest in technology that aids their functioning in other areas of their lives, such as top-quality household appliances and housecleaning tools and supplies.

They avoid personal and professional drama. Drama is profoundly antiproductive and often leads to bad outcomes, so productive people are selective about whom they get involved with, personally and professionally, and what types of interactions they tolerate. And, finally,

They are resilient in the face of criticism. They don't give in, or even feel particularly bad, when they've made a principled decision regarding their time use, and someone says, "What do you mean, you can't you help me with my project?" or "Why can't you go out tonight? You're no fun any more!" or even, "If you loved me, you'd do ___." They know that they are really not selfish or killjoys or unloving, but self-directed and mission-focused. They also know that those who truly support them and their goals will understand and support their time-management efforts.

Let's face it: there are plenty of selfish people in the world, plenty of exploiters. But most of the people who seek out my coaching and workshops, and presumably you (since you are reading this book), have the opposite problem: over-giving (Section 4.8), or the too-frequent sacrificing of your mission and needs to others'. That's a much nobler problem, but still a problem. **That's why I tell people that if ,after you start managing your time, people start complaining, congratulations! It means you're doing it right.**

To develop more resilience, work to build your compassionate objectivity (Section 2.10) and to overcome any internalized oppression (Chapter 6).

Section 4.4 Time-Management Principle #2: Always Strive to Invest, Not Spend, Time

An investment is something that accrues value over time. An expense is something that loses value.

You're probably familiar with financial investments including the stock market and real estate. Pretty much everything else is an expense, including cars, cell phones, clothes, food, and entertainment. Sure, we may need some of those things, but they are still expenses, and personal finance gurus advise us to spend as little as possible on them.

The division between investments and expenses is not always clear, since some expenses are actually investments in the non-financial realm. It costs money to eat healthily and stay in shape, for instance, but that's money you should invest. Also, some people's lives are so enhanced by music, travel, or other "expenses" that those expenses are more properly thought of as investments. (The corollary is that one person's investment can be another's expense.) Regardless of their benefits, however, these activities remain financial expenses, so you still have to exercise restraint.

It works exactly the same way with time: you want investments, not expenses. The common time investment categories are: health and fitness, healing and recovery, personal growth and development, education, planning and management, relationships, community/civic work, creativity, any kind of serious vocation or hobby, and what I call "replenishing recreation" (see below). These all yield a profound return in terms of productivity and happiness, and you should be allocating as much time as possible to them. This means, of course, that you should be allocating as *little* time as possible to everything else, including a day job you do primarily for the income, cleaning and other household chores, and tasks outside your mission.

Most investments are fun, by the way—and when an investment isn't, it's often because we're being perfectionist about it. Many people struggle with money management, for instance, but approached the right way it is interesting and engaging, and definitely empowering. The solution, when you can't get motivated do something you absolutely must do, is to (1) work to overcome your perfectionism and internalized oppression around it, using the techniques in this book, (2) go deeper into it, so that it becomes an interesting intellectual challenge instead of a tedious chore, (3) reframe it as empowerment (which all investments really are), and (4) do it with the help of a supportive community. Even the least enjoyable investments, such as dealing with a chronic health problem, become much more palatable with these steps.

As with money, the line between time expenses and investments is not always clear. **In general, if you truly enjoy doing something and/or find it rewarding, then it's probably an investment.** If, however, you're just doing it just because you have to (e.g., a day job), or to "kill time" (television), or because it's the conventional thing to do (housework), or because you're afraid of what others might think or say if you don't do it (committee work you don't really care about, or a visit to unpleasant relatives, or, yeah, housework), then it's probably an expense, and you should work strenuously to eliminate it from your schedule.

Recreation is a special case. It's hard to talk about someone's recreational choices without sounding judgmental, but there are important differences between what I call "replenishing" and "escapist" recreation. Replenishing recreation is typically active and/or engaging. It typically connects you with others, the environment, and/or even parts of your personality you don't ordinarily get to connect with. It often supports your other investments (e.g., your health or writing or relationships), and leaves you happy and fulfilled. Examples include sports, socializing, art, crafts, and many outdoor activities like hiking or gardening.

Replenishing recreation is an investment, and when we do our time budgets in Section 4.7, I'm going to recommend you include plenty of it.

In contrast to replenishing recreation, escapist recreation such as television, Web-surfing, and videogaming tends to leave us bored or depleted. It also tends to be passive, solitary (even if you're in a room with others, you're engaged not with them so much as with the television or PC), and not supportive of your investments—in fact, it's often detrimental to them. Here's Stephen King (from *On Writing*) on television:

> TV ... really is about the last thing an aspiring writer needs. If you feel you must have the news analyst blowhards on CNN while you exercise, or the stock market blowhards on MSNBC, or the sports blowhards on ESPN, it's time for you to question how serious you really are about becoming a writer. You must be prepared to do some serious turning inward toward

the life of the imagination, and that means, I'm afraid, that Geraldo, Keith Obermann, and Jay Leno must go. Reading takes time, and the glass teat takes too much of it.

Judith Wright, author of *The Soft Addiction Solution*, writes extensively about a large category of expenses she calls "soft addictions," which she defines as,

> ... [T]hose seemingly harmless habits like overshopping, overeating, watching too much TV, surfing the Internet, gossiping, procrastinating—that actually keep us from the life we want. Whether we realize it or not, our soft addictions cost us money, rob us of time, numb us from our feelings, mute our consciousness, and drain our energy.

Of course, many people resort to escapist recreation after long and exhausting days or weeks, when they feel they don't have the energy to be active or creative. In that case, escapist recreation is serving as a "band-aid" covering up serious problems with the person's lifestyle; also, it's correlated with depression and physical health problems.[4]

Escapist recreation is a clear expense—if not a clear danger—and so you want to minimize it. However, since we're not robots who can be programmed 100% but complex beings with complex needs, including the need for down time, in Section 4.7 I'm going to suggest one hour of escapism per day, although your own need may be for more or less than that. (As you move deeper into the realm of your investments, television and other escapist time-sinks are revealed for what they are—weak tea—and it becomes easier than you might now imagine to give them up.)

---

[4]Here are two scientific articles: Mark Hamer, Emmanuel Stamatakis, and Gita D. Mishra, "Television- and Screen-Based Activity and Mental Well-Being in Adults," *American Journal of Preventive Medicine*, vol. 38, issue 4, pp. 375-380, April 2010 (www.ajpmonline.org/article/S0749-3797%2810%2900010-3/abstract); Emmanuel Stamatakis, Mark Hamer and David W. Dunstan, "Screen-Based Entertainment Time, All-Cause Mortality, and Cardiovascular Events: Population-Based Study With Ongoing Mortality and Hospital Events Follow-Up," *Journal of the American College of Cardiology*, vol. 57, issue 3, pp. 292-299, January 18, 2011 (http://linkinghub.elsevier.com/retrieve/pii/S0735109710044657). And here's a general one: Emily Main, Too Much TV Can Make You Depressed, Rodale.com (blog), May 6, 2010 (health.yahoo.net/rodale/PVN/too-much-tv-can-make-you-depressed).

Helping others is another complex category. There are two general guidelines:

1. In an emergency, HELP. I *want* you to be the Good Samaritan, and if you do your time management, you'll be able to do it without sacrificing your mission.
2. In non-emergencies, **try as much as possible to help others *only* with their investments and *only* when you can do so by providing your high-value activities***:* **those which are congruent with your mission; leverage your strengths; and are impactful, i.e., they create change in the real world.**

Contributing your high-value activities to others' investments will ensure that you make a meaningful contribution—and probably enjoy doing it—while contributing low-value activities to others' expenses is a route to ineffectiveness, resentment, and burnout. Limiting the amount and type of non-emergency help you provide may sound narrow or even selfish—and some of the people you decline to help may even label your behavior as such!—but the reality is that the need for help in the world around us is vast, and your time, energy, and other resources are limited. You must be selective—and in being selective, you'll gain the skills and capacity that will allow you to become an even more powerful helper in the future (Section 4.8).

Section 4.5 The Other Time-Management Principles

Time-Management Principle #3: The things you invest quality time in are the things you will improve at or succeed at, and the things you don't are the things you won't.

If you invest a lot of quality time in your writing, you will probably end up an accomplished and successful writer. If you invest a lot of quality time in your health and fitness, you will probably end up healthy and fit.

In contrast, if you spend a lot of time doing a day job you don't care about except as an income source, or housework, or low-value favors for others, or video games, you will end up being successful at those low-value activities.

This principle may seem obvious or even banal, but I constantly run into people who pine to write a book, start a business, exercise, do community work, etc., but who never clear time for those activities.

Clearing time is the first step for any ambitious goal.

Many writers live by the axiom, **"Writing comes first."** It means that, no matter what else is happening in your day, writing is the priority. (Often, it means you literally do it first thing in the morning.) Many successful entrepreneurs, athletes, and others employ a similar mindset.

Time-Management Principle #4: Time management is not about jamming as much as possible *into* your schedule, but eliminating as much as possible *from* your schedule so that you have time to get the important stuff done to a high degree of quality and with as little stress as possible.

In American society we make a fetish of overwork. We may say we disapprove of workaholism (Section 4.9), but we mostly admire it. (And employers are happy to exploit it.) We speak admiringly of multitasking, which is not just a scam—since most of us can't transition between tasks without losing capacity—but often a highly rationalized form of procrastination in which you delay working on your hard stuff by working on easier (and, often, less important) stuff instead.

Poor Time Managers (PTMs; see next section) often fall for these dysfunctional attitudes about time, and this, often combined with perfectionism and a tendency toward over-giving (Section 4.8), mires them in a perpetual, stressful frenzy of activity that tends not to yield much.

Aspiring Time Managers (ATMs) may understand the folly of overgiving and underinvestment, but they don't take things as far they need to. They may trim and prune their schedules in a half-hearted way, creating a little time here and there, but not enough to yield much payback. (I often have to remind ATMs that "the goal isn't 'to be semi-stressed' or 'semi-exhausted.'")

In contrast to the PTMs and ATMs, **Good Time Managers** (GTMs) ruthlessly purge their schedules of as many expenses and low-value activities as possible. Their aim is to have *abundant* time to devote to their important priorities so as to maximize their chances of productivity, success, mastery, and joy.

Time-Management Principle #5: There is no such thing as unmanaged time: If you don't manage your own time, others will be happy to manage it for you.

The list of those who will step in and manage your time for you includes not just your family, friends, and coworkers, but neighbors, others in the community, and, of course, corporations who want you to buy and use their products. These people will have all kinds of motives—and some will genuinely care about you—but trust me: you do not want to be the person whose time everyone else is managing.

Section 4.6 The Dire Fate of the Poor Time Manager vs. the Joy and Fulfillment of the Good Time Manager

The PTM probably lacks an understanding of the above five principles, and therefore tends to make the kinds of conventional choices regarding her time use that will lead her to this lifestyle:

She works 40 hours or more a week at a job that provides an income but is not related to her mission. Maybe it's an "okay" job, or maybe she hates it—but, in any case, she would rather be doing something else. (Obviously, it is possible to have a full-time job doing what you love—in which case, no problem!—but many people don't, and certainly not many PTMs.)

Actually, she's probably on the job 45 hours, including her unpaid lunch break, and she's probably also commuting at least one hour a day.[5] So let's estimate her weekly day job expense at 50 hours. That represents 44.6% of the 112 hours she's awake in a week, assuming she's getting eight hours of sleep a night (which, as a PTM, she probably isn't).

I need to repeat that: *Almost half her waking hours are spent doing something she'd rather not be doing, and maybe hates.*

What a sad situation, and, over decades, a tragic one. What a terrible waste of a person's skills, passion, and life.

I hope the PTM isn't giving her workplace free hours, but sadly I know she might be—PTMs are often chronic overgivers (Section 4.8).

---

[5]The current U.S. commute is 24.5 minutes each way (usgovinfo.about.com/cd/censusandstatistics/a/commutetimes.htm). However, a PTM is likely to have a longer-than-average commute.

Our PTM probably spends most of her weekends shopping, cleaning, and doing yard work and other household chores. (If she's got kids, she's of course devoting many hours to them.) And she probably spends a lot of her evenings doing yet more chores, or in escapist recreation, since the average American now watches more than five(!) hours of TV a day.[6] And many indulge in equivalent hours of videogaming, Web-surfing, and other escapism.

What's missing from the PTM lifestyle of work, shopping, home maintenance, and escapism? If you answered "the investments," you're absolutely right. The PTM is probably not investing much of her time in relationships, health, fitness, self-care, planning and management, personal growth, vocation, community, or replenishing recreation.

Or, of course, her writing.

How does the PTM feel? Look around you and you can probably answer. So many people are stressed and unhappy. So many relationships are sterile or faltering. So many parents are too busy and fatigued to enjoy their kids. So many communities are withering from lack of participation.

So many missions are unrealized, so many passions unexplored, and so many books unwritten.

Now, let's look at the GTM. Like many of us, she probably started out working 40 hours a week. But assuming her job is not part of her mission, she has relentlessly worked to reduce its hours and impact on her life. And so she's probably working 30 hours a week, or 25, or even 20. This probably necessitates her living frugally, but that's a trade-off most GTMs will happily make based on Principle #1.

Frugality is a fundamental element of a successful, happy life. It's too big a topic to go into here, but there are plenty of resources on and off the Web devoted to it. Besides allowing you to manage your work schedule, frugality also allows you to shorten your commute (see below), and quit jobs where you are being mistreated, which is key to avoiding the kinds of toxic rejections that can lead to perfectionism (Section 7.1).

---

[6]"Americans Using TV and Internet Together 35% More Than A Year Ago," Nielsen Wire (blog), March 22, 2010 (blog.nielsen.com/nielsenwire/online_mobile/three-screen-report-q409/). And also: Adam Singer, "The Ultimate Lifehack: Gain Back 13.9% Or More Time," The Future Buzz (blog), February 3, 2011 (thefuturebuzz.com/2011/02/03/tv-viewing-trend/).

While I'm at it, if you can go car-free, that also yields a marvelous benefit in terms of both money and time savings.[7] (I haven't owned a car in years.)

Our GTM isn't content to reduce her day-job hours, however; she also works relentlessly to arrange her work schedule to (1) reserve her best times for her writing and other investments, and (2) minimize unproductive and stressful commute. Many mission-focused people work, for instance, three long days a week, or just mornings or afternoons, etc. They also work from home a lot.

If you're not a GTM yourself, all this might seem unlikely, particularly in a bad economy where the employers seem to be calling all the shots. But I promise you that all around you there are GTMs who are making it happen. They find good jobs where they do great work and are treated well, and where, either as part of the initial hiring negotiation or after they've proven their worth, they negotiate to work nontraditional hours that support their writing and other investments.[8] (Often, it takes multiple negotiations over a period of years—first, for Fridays off, then to work at home on Mondays, then to work 10–6 instead of 9–5 for a shorter commute, etc.) See Section 4.11 for an example of how such a negotiation could go; also, if you join the right communities (Section 3.9), you should meet people who have solved this problem and can learn from them.

If a GTM can't get a reasonable schedule from her current employer, she won't hesitate to find another one, because she knows that **the long-term consequences of not managing her time are far worse than the temporary inconveniences of managing it.** (For job search tips, download my free ebook *It's Not You, It's Your Strategy* from www.hillaryrettig.com.)

Let's be conservative and say that our GTM manages to whittle her day job down from 45 hours a week (five eight-hour days, plus an hour of unpaid lunch) to 31.5 hours (three ten-hour days, plus a half-hour of unpaid lunch). At the same time, her commute has shrunk

---

[7]Adam Singer, "Going Car-Free," The Future Buzz (blog), December 1, 2010 (thefuturebuzz.com/2010/12/01/going-car-free/); Adam Singer, "Reflections On 6 Months Without A Car," The Future Buzz (blog), May 23, 2011 (thefuturebuzz.com/2011/05/23/going-car-free-follow-up/).

[8]For a delightful example of how it works from the boss's perspective, see: Chris Ashworth, "My Competitive Advantage: I Hire Artists," ChrisAshworth.org (blog), June 24, 2010 (chrisashworth.org/blog/2010/06/24/my-competitive-advantage-i-hire-artists/).

from 5 to 4 hours. She's now spending 35.5 hours/week on her job instead of 50, for a savings of 14.5 hours a week.

Many people tell me, by the way, that they welcome their commute as a chance to be alone and relax. Some also tell me that they read or do paperwork during their commutes. That's all well and good, but don't forget that GTMs are optimizers (Section 4.3); if a GTM wants peaceful time alone, she'll seek it in a more effective and convenient setting than sitting in traffic or on a crowded bus.

Scrub the Housework. By getting her day job under control, the GTM has reclaimed 14.5 hours for her writing and other investments—a glorious act of self-liberation. Most people, when they take this step, wonder what the heck they ever waited for—it's so wonderful to live more fully in the realm of mission and investments. (You do have to watch out for situational perfectionism; see Section 2.9.)

The next big step our GTM can take is to minimize time spent on household maintenance and chores. As mentioned earlier, many people spend all weekend, and many evenings, on these gruesome tasks.

Although members of the Calvinist (perfectionist) "suffering is good for the soul" school may disagree, **there is absolutely no reason to do more than the bare minimum of activities that are, (a) not part of your mission, and (b) unpleasant.** These activities are not character-building—in fact, they're character-depleting—and you are not an "idealistic dreamer" or "frivolous" for wanting to live your life as close as possible to 100% in mission and joy; in fact, you're enlightened and pragmatic. The thing to do with tedium and unpleasantness is to work strenuously to minimize them.

As mentioned in Section 4.4, if you truly enjoy something, it's probably an investment, and so you should revel in it; for many people, that includes cooking or gardening. But I haven't yet met anyone who truly loves laundry or mopping, except, perhaps, as a vehicle for procrastination (Section 1.8).

The main techniques for minimizing household chores are to:

(1) *Live simply and in a small space.* Remember that everything you buy costs you twice: in the time and money you spent to purchase it, and the time and money you spend to maintain it. And large spaces cost more to clean, heat, etc.

(2) *Professionalize.* Use good tools and supplies (e.g., a good washer and dryer, or a high-powered vacuum cleaner to cope with animal hair). Also, invest in convenience—say, by having a sprayer-mop

in each high-traffic room. And also budget your time so that you work swiftly without killing yourself. (Something like, say, thirty minutes per room per week.)

(3) ***Delegate whatever you can***, not just to other family or household members but to professionals. Use a grocery-delivery service (or get meals delivered from local restaurants), drop your laundry off to be done, and hire cleaning and lawn-care services. And, finally,

(4) ***Lower your standards***. I'm not talking about living in a dirty house, or even a messy one. But there's a great gulf of non-perfectionism between a "dirty" house and the kinds of spotless paragons the media promotes in its endless quest to get you to feel inadequate and therefore compelled to consume (Section 2.8). Ignore them all, as well as any critics within your personal circle; instead, figure out your own level of comfort and cleanliness and aim for that.

People typically raise two objections when I suggest they adopt these techniques:

(a) *It's wrong to ask others to clean up after me.* Assuming we're talking about professionals (since you shouldn't feel bad about asking your family or roommates to do their part), then I strenuously disagree—and, more importantly, the people whom you will be asking will also strenuously disagree. People need jobs, and for some people a cleaning or laundry gig where they're treated respectfully and paid well is the ideal job.

I discuss other common objections to delegation—too much time to train, won't do as good a job as me, etc.—in Section 4.11.

(b) *Cleaning services, take out meals, etc., cost money, and I can't afford it. Besides, you said to be frugal.* It's true that some people can't afford to delegate, but it's also true that many who can afford it choose to spend their money elsewhere. (Recall Section 3.4 and how many underproductive people chronically under-resource themselves.) We can deduce from Principle #1 that using money to buy more time for investments is a sound choice.

Let's say that using these four techniques—simplicity, professionalism, delegation, and lowered standards—the writer has managed to whittle her household chores down from around twenty hours a week to eight.

And let's say that she allots only one hour a day (versus three) to television and other escapist activities.

She's now gained 14.5 + 12 + 14, or 40.5 hours a week for her "investments"—more than the equivalent of a full-time job! Think of all the writing, relationships, exercise, fun, and other investments she can now partake of—and how much more profoundly happy and satisfying and meaningful her life will be as a result.

Section 4.7 The Time-Management Process, Step 1: Budgeting

It's best if you move from PTM to GTM as part of an organized process, and with clearly defined goals. And so, after six chapters of "philosophy," we at last come to the time-management process itself, which consists of these five steps:

1. Budget your time based on the goals you have for each investment category (a.k.a., your "mission").[9]
2. Schedule your week based on the budget.
3. Follow the schedule and track your time use.
4. Tally your time use at the end of the week and compare with your budget. If necessary, revise the budget and schedule. Then repeat steps 3 and 4 the next week.
5. Watch yourself get more productive!

The first step, **budgeting**, is by far the hardest, because it's the one where you need to make tough choices. Regarding the 60% of seminarians who did not stop and help during the Good Samaritan study, Darley and Batson note:

> Why were the seminarians hurrying? Because the experimenter, whom the subject was helping, was depending on him to get to a particular place quickly. In other words, he was in conflict between stopping to help the victim and continuing on his way to help the experimenter. And this is often true of people in a hurry; they hurry because somebody depends on their being somewhere. Conflict, rather than callousness, can explain their failure to stop.

---

[9] I'm not a fan of mission statements because they tend to be vague and abstract. I'm also not a fan of the "track your current time use" advice some other time-management experts give, since in my view it simply ties you to old habits. Let's look to the future!

Budgeting is basically a way of resolving as many of the conflicts, and making as many of the difficult decisions, ahead of time, which is a far better strategy than making them on the fly. It consists of three easy-seeming steps which, in the end, turn out to be far from easy: (1) listing your investments, (2) allocating weekly time to each, and (3) making adjustments so that you stay within your 112-hour-a-week total.

Let's take them one at a time.

(1) *Make a list of all your investments,* including health and fitness, personal growth and development, education, planning and management, relationships, community work, creativity, replenishing recreation, and serious vocations. (It's okay to exclude a category that doesn't pertain to you, of course.)

(2) Next, break each investment down into its "sub-investments." If you are planning an ambitious writing career, for instance, you'll need to invest time not just in writing, but editing, marketing, sales, and business management (Section 8.7).

In Health and Fitness, your subs might include exercise, meditation, and appointments related to health and wellness.

In Relationships, your subs might include your spouse, each kid, your parents, other family members, and friends.

Once you've listed the sub-investments, you might have to drill down some more, to sub-subs. Under the "writing/marketing" sub, for instance, you might list blog updates, producing and mailing your e-newsletter, social media, and phone calls with mentors and other professional colleagues (Sections 3.10 and 3.11).

(3) **Next, allocate the *ideal* amount of time you'd want to invest on each investment (or sub or sub-sub) each week**. Ideally, you want to allocate time relative to the activity's importance to you, or its prominence in your mission.

When doing this work, I recommend ignoring investments or subs that occur infrequently or irregularly, because it gets too complicated to create a budget (and schedule; see Section 4.10) around them. During the weeks you have such a commitment, simply re-budget and reschedule everything to accommodate them, and then revert back to your "default" weekly budget and schedule the following week.

When you finish, you'll wind up with something like the chart on the next page. (Download a free budget template at www.hillaryrettig. com.)

Sample Time Budget for Someone With a Day Job and a Writing Vocation
Your categories and numbers will vary!

		Budget (Hours/Week)	% of 112 Hr Week (rounded)	Notes
Planning & Management	Time Management	0.5		after the work of budgeting is done; this is tracking time and reviewing the week
	Financial Management	0.5		
	Planning/ Journaling/ Meditation	2		
		3.0	1.56%	such a small time investment to keep your life organized!
Self-care	Exercise	6		includes travel and prep time – e.g., 3 45 minute aerobics classes plus 1.25 hours each for travel and prep.
	Appointment	2		therapy, medical, etc. Includes travel. For monthly or irregular events, I recommend simply subtracting time from other commitments on the weeks that they occur, rather than trying to build an elaborate scheme that accounts for them in advance.
		8	11.16%	
Day Job	Job	25		
	Commute	3		
		28	29.46%	if your day job is not an investment, do your best to reduce this number.
Writing	Writing	12		
	Marketing and Sales	10		as I'll discuss in Chapter 8, if you're trying to build a serious writing career, you will need to spend approximately half your "writing" time marketing and selling. Should break this category down even further, to "marketing," "sales," "email newsletter," "social media," "meetings," etc.
		22	17.86%	
Recreation: Relationships	Partner	11		1 date night, plus 1 fun afternoon, plus dinners home
	Friends	4		1 night out plus emails, texts, social media, etc.
	Family	2		includes a visit every couple of weeks interspersed with calls and emails
		17	15.18%	
Recreation: Other	Replenishing	4		solo hobby, creative work, etc.
	Escapist	7		no more than recommended; budget what you need.
		11	10.71%	
Community Work		3	3.57%	1 meeting a week, plus associated tasks; it's important to invest at least a little of your time in community because when we all do, life gets easier for all of us.
Maintenance	Housework/ Shopping	8		of course, I'd like to see this number lower!
	AM/PM Routines	10.5		dressing, showering, breakfast, getting ready for the day, ending the day, etc. .75 hours morning and evening, every day, but shorter if you can do so without getting stressed.
	Total	18.5	17.41%	
Total		111.5	100%	

Most people's "ideal" budget winds up at 150-200 hours per week—which clearly ain't gonna work. You've got 112 hours a week to work with, or maybe 119, if you can get by on seven hours of sleep a night. (Again, no cheating—going without needed sleep is antiproductive.) Which brings us to Step 4:

(4) *Cut back to 112 hours.* This is the hardest step in the entire time-management process because you will probably have to cut things important to you or others.

The easiest way to cut back is to eliminate entire investments— for now. If you're finishing a thesis or book, maybe now is not the time for you to be doing any community work. Or, if you're struggling with a serious personal or family problem, maybe now is not the time to finish your book.

Eliminating an entire investment not only frees up a lot of time but creates enormous relief—and relief is an excellent barometer of your true needs. Of course, if you're perfectionistically over-identifying with your writing or other work, you'll have trouble giving it up even temporarily. See the section on sabbaticals in Section 6.5.

Once you eliminate entire investments, see if you can prune some subs. Maybe you can't or won't quit your community work— fine, can you eliminate one committee? Or, if you don't want to stop working on your thesis, can you simplify it? (Something you should do anyway; see Section 2.15.) Are there projects or committees you can be excused from in your day job? Or friends or relatives whose company is less than gratifying, and whom you really wouldn't mind seeing less often—or not at all? (Section 3.8.)

Next, start pruning your time expenses to recoup valuable fractions of an hour. If it typically takes you two hours to get to your office in the morning after waking up, see if you can pare that down (*without* rushing around or omitting important tasks) by fifteen or thirty minutes. If a fifteen-minute yield seems trivial, recall Principle #1, and how people who value time properly prize small amounts of it. Fifteen minutes a day yields you an hour and forty-five minutes a week—or 91 hours a year! And you can probably make the cut relatively painlessly by doing one or more of the following: simplifying your breakfasts, not checking your email, turning off the TV (try radio instead!), letting the kids get themselves ready for school and/or make their own lunches, delegating companion animal care, or leaving for work earlier or later to shorten your commute.

Work to trim *all* time expenses as much as possible, without resorting to rushing around or adding stress. You can probably reclaim another five hours a week.

Here are some tips to assist you with your budgeting:

1) *Budget in fifteen-minute (1/4 hour) increments*, as per the above example.

2) *Expect to move from relatively easy decisions to really hard ones*—in fact, some of the hardest you'll make in your life. You'll probably wind up giving up activities that you enjoy, or that others value, or that make you feel important or special, or that are entrenched habits or vehicles for procrastination. You'll almost certainly be moving outside your comfort zone, and perhaps letting go of a grandiose attachment to being a super-worker or prodigious helper (see Sections 4.8 and 4.9). Make no mistake: these changes are all positive. But they can be hard to get through. Be extremely kind and patient with yourself throughout the budgeting process, and give yourself abundant Rewards (Section 2.11). Also, seek out abundant support.

3) *As per Principle #4, if you're not sure whether to include an investment or sub you should probably jettison it.* If you're questioning whether something is truly important, it probably isn't—and, often, when we can't decide, it's because we're self-censoring. Also, if you're only including a goal because you're "supposed to" (i.e., it's conventional) or someone is pressuring you to include it, get rid of it.

4) *Build in plenty of self-care, recreation, and planning and management time.* Also, allot generous travel and preparation time between activities. The time-budget must always be a realistic reflection of your human needs and constraints.

5) *Show your time budget to your mentors and get their feedback.* This is very important, as your mentors are your "reality check." Ask them whether they think you are allocating your time in a way that will help you achieve your goals.

Section 4.8 Be a Specialist/Don't Overgive

If you're having trouble reaching 112 hours—or if you've reached it, but aren't sure which activities in each investment category to focus on—there is a time-management technique so powerful that it's a kind of magic: specialization.

Perfectionists, of course, decry it: they think everyone should be able to do everything—and extremely well! Science fiction writer Robert Heinlein provided a famous example in his novel *Time Enough for Love*:

> A human being should be able to change a diaper, plan an invasion, butcher a hog, conn a ship, design a building, write a sonnet, balance accounts, build a wall, set a bone, comfort the dying, take orders, give orders, cooperate, act alone, solve equations, analyze a new problem, pitch manure, program a computer, cook a tasty meal, fight efficiently, die gallantly. Specialization is for insects.

Like most grandiose perfectionist harangues, it is not just dead wrong, but silly. And, anyway, he put those words in the mouth of a character who lives thousands of years and therefore has a luxury of time none of us has.

In fact, it's incredibly important that you do specialize—or, more specifically, **aim to spend as much of your time as possible doing your high-value activities:** those that are, as noted in Section 4.4, mission-focused, that leverage your strengths, and that create impact ot change. Doing this will:

- Get a great result;
- Build your expertise/mastery;
- Increase your effectiveness;
- Boost your productivity;
- Create fulfillment and joy (because we usually enjoy the things we're good at, and vice versa);
- Help others build *their* expertise, effectiveness, productivity, and joy (because you'll delegate your low-value activities to those for whom they are high-value);
- Build powerful communities through the delegation process; and
- Transform you into someone who leads and inspires others.

If you don't focus on your high-value activities, you'll not only lose all of those terrific benefits, but also get stressed, exhausted, and resentful. Writers who try to build their own website or fix their own computers (Section 3.6), for instance, typically spend way too long at these tasks, find them frustrating, and get a subpar result.

Of course, all this applies to your personal life, too. When you take Mom out for a fun meal or accompany her to a medical appointment, you're leveraging your strengths—your filial devotion and caring, and, if you're helping her choose a treatment, your analytical skills, and it's doubtful whether anyone except perhaps another sibling could make as meaningful a contribution. When you run her errands or mow her lawn, however, you're not only not leveraging your strengths but doing something others could do equally well or even better, and thus wasting your time.

You should specialize even in the area of replenishing recreation, to optimize the amount of recreation per hour invested. If you love to garden, but not the backbreaking work of tilling the soil, delegate that part of the project to someone else. If you love to rehabilitate antique wooden furniture, but not the messy, tedious, chemical-y part where you strip the old paint and finishes off, delegate that. Ah, the joys of a pre-tilled garden bed or clean wood surface to start with! (More on delegation in Section 4.11.)

Are you at ristk for over-specializing? I don't think so, because I'm not talking about becoming a hyper-specialized "geek" who can't function except in a limited sphere, but simply maintaining a strong focus on your high-value activities within *each* of your investment categories. Another way to think of this is that most PTMs are far too *un*specialized in their time use, so a little specialization is simply restoring the balance.

The need to specialize means that GTMs routinely reject non-emergency requests for help in low-value ways—and, thus, they save themselves from overgiving, or the chronic subordination of their needs and mission to others'. As mentioned in Section 4.3, overgiving is a nobler problem than selfishness or exploitativeness, but it's still a problem, especially as it is one of the prime mechanisms by which procrastination mimics productive work (Section 1.8).

Here's what happens when you overgive to your job, an activist campaign, a community group, a business venture, or other people:

(1) For starters, you don't get to live out your own mission. This almost guarantees bitterness and regret.

(2) You're probably exhausted, and possibly broke. This means your lifestyle is not sustainable—which means that all the projects and relationships you contribute importantly to are also not sustainable. (And if your contribution is not important, why are you giving at all?)

(3) Dangerously, you attract the wrong people—those seeking to exploit you, or evade responsibility or accountability, or both.

(4) You compromise your effectiveness and growth.

(5) In a worst-case scenario, you don't give your best effort to anyone or anything, either because you can't (because you're frantically busy and/or depleted), or won't (because you feel angry and exploited), or both. In failing to commit to multiple individual tasks or engagements, you are actually failing to commit to entire projects or relationships.

Overgiving is, in short, a potent form of self-sabotage.

Many overgivers are nice people, but many also have trouble saying no and standing up for their own needs (Section 4.11), and many are grandiose (Section 2.2). Their grandiosity manifests itself as:

- Wanting to be the hero or "savior," or to be perceived as indispensable, a "problem solver," a "go-to person," etc.;
- Believing you should be able to take on others' burdens or solve their problems for them;
- Believing you should be able to do that AND live out your own ambitious mission;
- Believing you can break the rules, for instance, by not earning enough money to sustain yourself, or chronically working too many hours a week.

Even though many grandiose people have a logical-sounding rationalization for their behavior—e.g., "I can sign up for all these committees because I'm well organized,"—grandiosity is always fundamentally delusional.

A brief word about **psychological "boundaries,"** a topic that, from a time-management standpoint at least, is rather simple. There are two things you need to know:

(1) **Boundaries aren't "between" you and the other person, but within you, in your heart and mind.** You need to make conscious decisions about what you'd like your relationship to a person (or group) to be, what and how much you are willing to give, and what and how much

you expect to receive in return. Once you make these decisions, life gets *much* easier, since you are now operating from principle instead of the exigencies of the moment. However, if you don't make them, or only do so half-heartedly (see Section 6.5), then your work and relationships are likely to suffer. And,

(2) **It is *your* responsibility to state your needs.** Too many writers don't, and not only do they cheat themselves of help, they cheat the other person of the opportunity to help. There could be many reasons for their reluctance, including shyness, internalized oppression (Chapter 6), or a fear that the request will be denied—and that fear might be justified. Still, it is imperative that you learn to state your needs for several reasons:

- They might actually get met. In fact, the writers I encourage to state their needs to family, bosses, and others almost always come back to tell me that the person not only complied, but was grateful to be asked.
- Perfectionist myths about "lone geniuses" aside, it's practically impossible to succeed at an ambitious goal without a strong, supportive community behind you. And,
- As discussed in Section 3.8, the act of asking for help is, itself, empowering.

The key to outstanding achievement is to be a specialist, surround yourself with other specialists of diverse types, and give and accept help liberally in the form of high-value activities within that group.

Section 4.9 Problems Related to Overgiving: Workaholism and Codependency; Email Overload; and Coping with Fame

Workaholism and Codependency. Working long hours could be the right choice if doing so (a) aligns with your mission; (b) doesn't cause you to sacrifice other important goals or values, such as your health or relationships; and (c) doesn't put you in the realm of deprivation, depletion, exhaustion, stalling out (Section 1.10), burnout, or compassion fatigue. In my experience, most overwork scenarios do *not* meet these requirements and therefore qualify as workaholism, an addictive habit of using work as an escape from life's pains and stresses. (For instance: "I feel sad and helpless at home because I'm alienated from my spouse, my kids are a trial, and things are chaotic. I might as well stay at work, where at least I'm appreciated and can shut the door and have some peace.")

Of course, workaholism is a fine vehicle for procrastination—not the least, because many employers and others will encourage you in it.

Codependency is a related, and often overlapping, problem: it's when you focus on someone else's problems as a way of avoiding your own. Often you'll see two codependents locked in a dysfunctional dyad—think of an alcoholic married to an overeater, or someone with a strong need for order working alongside someone perpetually disorganized. (In the human services realm, one often sees case managers overinvesting in clients who either can't or won't change.) A hallmark of codependency is that, no matter how much work you put into helping the other person, things never really improve, since: (a) the person is probably not ready to change—or may not even perceive themselves as having a problem, and (b) codependency is founded on the fallacy that you can control someone's behavior.

If you are locked in a workaholic or codependent situation there are books you can read to gain insight, but you will probably also need therapy—and, of course, time management will be an important tool for helping you regain life balance.

"Email overload" is a ubiquitous and serious problem that, believe it or not, is also rooted in overgiving. If you get just twenty emails a day and spend an average of three minutes on each, that's an hour a day spent just answering emails—an appalling chunk of time to go to what is probably mostly or totally a low-value activity.

I think the basic problem is that email is a weird hybrid medium that combines the formality and permanence of a letter with the casualness and transience of a phone call. The problem is therefore twofold: (1) we get lots of emails, and (2) we treat too many of them as if they were important (that's the overgiving). Then we and labor over them. (Texting, which severely limits your message length, basically solves this problem, although it introduces others.) Emailing is also an excellent mimic of productive work, and therefore often used as a vehicle for procrastination (Section 1.8).

Here are some techniques GTMs use to manage their emails:

(1) *Terse answers.* GTMs never write a long answer to an email when a short answer, or no answer, will do. They are quite comfortable replying with single words or short phrases, such as "Yes," or "Confirmed," or "Sorry—not a good fit right now." And, by the way, they understand and can live with the knowledge that some correspondents will be turned off by the terseness. But they know their true supporters will understand how busy they are and not mind—and also, they're probably associating with other productive people who are also emailing tersely.

I send many logistical emails with only a few words written right in the subject line, followed by (eom) for "end of message."

(2) *Use the phone.* GTMs know that conversation, or even voicemail, is often a better medium for conveying detailed and/or subtle messages that if you tried to email you would wind up laboring over and still not get right.

(3) *Technology.* GTMs make abundant use of email signatures and autoresponders to handle repetitive inquiries (Section 3.6), which not only saves time but assures that the right information is being conveyed.

(4) *Proactive management.* GTMs are also good at maintaining their mailing list memberships—especially at removing themselves from lists that no longer interest them. They often have multiple email accounts—say, one for family and friends, another for colleagues, and a third for blogs and mailing lists—with each getting different amounts of time and attention.

Fame. Hopefully, one day you'll get to the point where your writing commands a large audience. If so, you'll probably hear from many people who want to tell you what your work means to them, or who need a favor, or both.

In most of my classes for writers, there's at least one person who approached a well-known writer they admired only to be rudely or cruelly rebuffed. Sometimes, the hurt was enough to foment a block (Section 7.2), and of course such episodes do nothing for the famous writer's reputation. Fortunately, there have also been occasions where people approached a famous writer and were treated with kindness and decency. Those episodes affirm and inspire not only the person who was involved but the entire class when she tells us.

When someone writes or approaches you expressing admiration it's only good business sense, as well as common courtesy, to respond. But you don't have to do so at length—a few heartfelt words are fine. If you don't want an ongoing communication with the person, don't use language that implies that you do, such as "Stay in touch." As always, it's your job to communicate your needs.

If you get a lot of similar requests, like "How can I get published?" put your answer on your blog or the Q&A section of your website. This will take the burden off AND add traffic to your site—both great outcomes.

As for the requests for money, time, connections, or other assistance, it's of course your right, and often your obligation, to turn these down, but it's also your duty to do so with kindness and civility. This may be one of the few situations where a well-thought-out form letter might be appropriate, since the "form" reply itself conveys how busy you are and discourages follow-up.

Section 4.10 The Rest of the Time-Management Process

After you've finished your budgeting, you can move onto the rest of the time-management process, which is pretty straightforward:

Step #2: Create a Weekly Schedule. Take the time allocations you committed to in your time budget and fit them into a weekly schedule. Fill in the non-negotiables first and then the negotiables; also try, whenever possible, to schedule the same activities at the same times on the same days each week. In other words, set up **routines** that help eliminate guesswork around your schedule, and that also help you gear up, physically and mentally, for the scheduled activity. Stephen King, in *On Writing*, says, "Your schedule ... exists in order to habituate yourself, to make yourself ready to dream just as you make yourself ready to sleep by going to bed at roughly the same time each night and following the same ritual as you go." And Somerset Maugham wrote: "I write only when inspiration strikes. Fortunately it strikes every morning at nine o'clock sharp."

Starting at the same time each day saves you from uncertainty and hesitation, which are invitations to procrastination. As discussed in

Section 2.13, you want to calmly glide over to your desk and just start writing without hesitation, trepidation, expectation, or drama.

As mentioned earlier, don't bother trying to adjust your schedule to include the infrequent or irregular activities—just fit them in as they occur.

Step #3: Follow the Schedule and Track Your Time-Use. Try following your new schedule for a week. (I say "try" because you probably won't follow it exactly, or even closely. That's fine!) While you're doing that, track your time-use so that you can tell, at the end of the week, how close you came to sticking to the budget.

I suggest using a spreadsheet, which should be handy for most writers. Your time budget will be down the leftmost column, and the successive columns are Saturday, Sunday, Monday … all the way through to Friday. After that a Total column, so you can tally how much time you invested or spent in each activity over the week. Every time you work on a goal or task for fifteen minutes, add a checkmark in the box for it (e.g., in the "writing" box in the Tuesday column, or the "exercise" box in the Saturday column). It's important to track every fifteen minutes because if you use longer intervals you risk forgetting exactly how you used the time. (If you're away from your computer, print out the tracking form or simply keep notes in a pad.) Also, tallying every fifteen minutes helps keep you conscious and focused. If you get into the habit of asking yourself, "Am I doing what I'm supposed to be doing?" every fifteen minutes, there's a good chance you'll procrastinate less and start sticking to your schedule more.

Two more tips:

1) Track your "wake up" and "go to bed" times each day, because for maximum productivity you want to wake up and go to bed at about the same time every day. If your sleep schedule varies wildly, you're basically giving yourself jetlag—only without having had the fun of traveling.

2) It's important to record not just the time you spend on your investments, but on your expenses, including (especially) television, video games, and other escapism. You need to know precisely how much time you are spending on these activities—for most people, it's more than they think—in part so you will be more motivated to cut back.

Step #4: Tally Your Time and Review your Weekly Progress. At the end of the week, take your filled-in Tracking Form, and figure out (1) how much time you invested or spent on your various activities, and (2) how close those numbers came to your time budget.

Reflect on what worked and didn't work. Reward yourself for what you did right, but don't punish yourself for any areas in which you fell short. If necessary, refine the budget and schedule to align more with the realities of your life. Then, repeat steps 3-4.

Step #5: Watch Yourself Improve! If you follow this process you should automatically and probably dramatically improve, because, as it turns out, you don't need harsh correctives to improve your time use, but simply to get more conscious.

Perfectionists always think a harsh corrective is required, but if you're reading this book you are serious enough about your goals that gentle reminders—combined with the techniques I offer in this book—will probably be sufficient.

That's it! People often object that the process seems too onerous, but it's not. Budgeting and scheduling does, and should, take some time, but the tracking takes only about eight minutes a day, and the tallying and reflecting around half an hour a week—and it's a fascinating half hour.

Another common objection is that the process seems rigid and will make you robot-like. "What about spontaneity?" a student once asked. In truth, I'm not a huge fan of it. If your partner surprises you with a romantic weekend trip, it's okay to be spontaneous. (Or, of course, if there's an emergency.) But often spontaneity is merely procrastination wearing a playful mask.

Another common concern is, "Do I have to keep doing this forever?" The answer is no—unless you want to. Most people wind up tracking their time for two to four weeks, and are satisfied with the resulting productivity improvement, even if it's not all that they had initially hoped for. So they'll stop—but they may resume tracking later on when they're ready for another boost, or if they feel they've slipped. And, of course, it's also useful to budget and track anew whenever you experience a major life change.

A good "intermediate" approach after you've gotten your overall schedule under control is to only track the categories where you're likely to underinvest or overgive. For a while, I tracked only my writing, marketing, and exercising. (You probably won't be surprised to learn that I wasn't worried about over-giving in the area of housework.)

I think that what the objectors are really objecting to is the accountability that time management introduces—and I agree, accountability can be scary. But it's exactly what underproductive people need more of.

Section 4.11 Saying No, Delegation, and Cooperative Problem-Solving

Saying no, delegation, and cooperative problem-solving are essential time-management skills.

Many people say they "can't" **say no**—and many were taught to subordinate their needs to others'—but it's a skill you can, and must, learn. Practice on small requests first, then larger ones. Eventually, you'll not only get the hang of it, but you'll realize how great it feels to not get sucked into activities you'd rather not be part of.

There are ways to say no without having to directly say no, including to agree to do only a part of the project ("I'll help you with editing if you can find someone else to write a polished draft."), or to say you'll do it later ("I'm booked until July, but might have time to look at it then."). But sometimes you just have to say "No."

I've already discussed **delegation** relative to housework and other low-value activities. We tend to think of it as a hierarchical activity—something bosses do "to" subordinates—but it can be done non-hierarchically. Basically, you should aim to delegate all non-high-value activities to others for whom those activities are high value, and be generous in reciprocating with your own high-value support when needed. You want everyone involved to feel they've gotten a good value, but please note that that doesn't necessarily mean that everyone contributes equal money or hours. Particularly as you gain success, connections, influence, and mastery (the latter meaning you can work more efficiently), a relatively small time investment from you—even a letter or a phone call that helps someone get a great job—could be a fair exchange for many more hours invested on their part.[10]

As discussed earlier, this kind of delegation doesn't just help you

---

[10]There are those who would say that any inequality in time valuation is exploitation, but I think they're painting with too broad a brush. In many cases, the influential person is likely to be influential because of years of work *she* did that was free or underpaid.

gain time and reduce stress: it helps everyone involved build personal capacity, and also helps build community. You need to delegate responsibly, however, by generously supporting those to whom you delegate with information and other resources.

Don't forget to delegate small as well as big tasks. For one thing, most big tasks are really just a series of small ones. For another, the "small" stuff adds up. Don't run out for a quick shop if there's someone else who can run out instead. And if someone asks you for a favor (say, to write a letter of recommendation) but doesn't give you all the information you need (say, the recipient's full address), don't look it up yourself. Ask them to send it to you.

Many people are reluctant to delegate, or say they "can't," but this is an attitude you must get over. The common reasons for not delegating include: "It's easier for me to just do it myself." "No one will do as good a job as me." "It will take less time to do it myself." And my favorite: "I don't have time to delegate." But these always fail to hold water:

Yes, it may be easier for you to do it yourself—the first time. But not the second, third, or tenth time.

And yes, perhaps no one will do as good a job as you. But the question should not be whether the delegater will do the best possible job, but whether she will do a competent or acceptable job. **The goal of doing everything as well as possible should be subordinate to that of living your mission as fully as possible.**

Another popular reason people don't delegate is "I don't have anyone to delegate to." But this, too, is almost always wrong. You can delegate to immediate family, extended family, friends, coworkers, colleagues, neighbors, and basically anyone with whom you come in contact. *Help is abundant, and people, mostly, love to help.*

The successful people I know say no and delegate constantly—in fact, it's pretty much a reflex for them. The minute an activity crosses their path, they're figuring out (a) whether it's high-value, and (b) if it's not, how to get rid of it. Moreover, they know that most requests should be gotten rid of. If it happens to be an activity they feel they should keep, however, they're still figuring out which parts of it they can delegate to others.

A closely related skill to delegation is **cooperative problem-solving,** a process for problem-solving and conflict resolution that respects everyone involved. The steps are:

(1) *State the problem and how it makes you feel.* Example:

"Thanks very much for meeting with me, Boss. You know, I really do love working at XYZ Corp. I don't know if you know this, but for the last few years I've been working on a novel. I was making good progress for a while, but lately it's gotten tougher—it's just too hard to concentrate after a long day at work."

(2) *Propose a solution.* "I'm wondering whether I could switch my workday to noon to 8:30 p.m. [or a four day week, etc.] so I can have time to get the writing done in the morning."

(3) *State how the solution won't hurt things, and in fact will improve them for the person you're dealing with.* "I don't think the customers or my coworkers would mind, and it wouldn't affect my work performance. In fact, it means we would have someone on the phones later into the evening, which the West Coast customers would like."

(4) *Listen with great care and respect to the other person's response, and especially to their worries and concerns.*

The amazing thing is that, in many cases, the boss will say something like, "You're working on a novel? That's great! My kid's a writer! Let's give it a try." (If she starts asking well-meaning but awkward questions like "Why's it taking so long?" see Section 6.8.)

Or, she might simply say, "We could possibly do that, but I have a few concerns..."

(If you've got the kind of boss who will say, "Hell no—and don't bother me again with your personal problems," then, as discussed in Section 4.6, you need to find a new job.)

(5) *Try to incorporate the other person's concerns as much as possible.* "So it would be okay if I came in late on Monday, Tuesday, and Wednesday— but Thursday and Friday you'd prefer I maintain my current schedule. That would be fine." If you don't know how to address her concerns, it's okay to ask her for suggestions, or for time to think about the situation some more before talking to her again.

(6) *After you reach an accord, give recognition.* "Thank you so much—it's really amazing to work for an organization that cares about the whole person."

(7) *Confirm in writing.* "I'll just follow-up with a quick email to confirm the arrangement." This helps avoid miscommunication and reinforces the boss's decision. Keep the email short, simple, and non-bureaucratic; you're just summarizing the decision. And repeat your gratitude.

A variant of this process where you don't suggest a solution up front, but instead solicit suggestions from everyone involved, works very well in family or friend situations.[11] A student in one of my business classes spent all day in class, and then was supposed to go home and work on his business plan in the evenings. His five-year-old daughter had other ideas, however; she wanted him to spend his evenings playing with her. It was a difficult dilemma for him, and so one day he sat down with her and said, "You know, Daddy loves you very much and misses you all day. He really wants to play with you when he gets home, but he's also got homework to do, and when he doesn't do it, he feels bad. Can we think of anything we can do?" His five year old pondered for a few seconds—and then neatly solved the problem. "Let's do our homework together, Daddy," she said. And then she got her coloring book and crayons and sat next to him at the dining room table, happily coloring away while he did his writing—and every once in a while checking up on his progress.

I can't resist another kid story. One writer I know had a difficult time doing her college homework at night because her daughter was always asking for "one more bedtime story." Finally, they had a discussion in which Mommy said that even though she loved reading stories, she was sad that she wasn't getting her homework done. Her daughter listened carefully, and then suggested they limit themselves to one story per night on weekdays. Interestingly, it turned out that it was Mommy herself who sometimes wanted an extra story, in part to avoid facing her homework! (Can we all say it together? "Procrastination as a mimic of productive work.") But now her daughter had become an ally in her productivity, and whenever Mommy suggested an extra story, her daughter would remind her, "Mommy, aren't you supposed to be doing your homework?"

In the end, time management offers you the choice between productivity and underproductivity; success and disappointment; a calm, happy life and a stressed, unfulfilled one. PTMs and overgivers in particular tend to make one crucial mistake: they take in a lot of projects, tasks, favors, and information, but don't let enough back out by saying

---

[11] A great resource for all this is Adele Faber and Elaine Mazlish's classic parenting book *How to Talk so Kids Will Listen & Listen so Kids Will Talk* (Harper Collins, originally published in 1979). I recommend it to everyone, regardless of whether or not they have kids—it's a great tutorial on effective, compassionate communication.

no, delegating, and cooperative problem-solving. **The secret to profound productivity, success, and happiness is to let most of the stuff back out, retaining just the high-value activities for yourself.** You then become a conduit for ideas, information, and action, and have the time and energy not just to take care of yourself, but others—including the occasional needy stranger.

Chapter 5

Optimizing Your Writing Process

Captain Hook: "I must think!"
Mr. Smee: "What tempo, Captain?"
　　　　　—*Peter Pan* (1954 musical)

Section 5.1 Tempo and Your Need for Speed

Tempo is a musical term referring to the speed at which you play a piece. Wikipedia lists dozens of tempo markings from *largo* (funereally slow) to *vivace* ("Flight of the Bumble Bee" fast).

Tempo is also a valuable concept in productivity work because once we overcome perfectionism and start providing ourselves with abundant resources and time, the next challenge is to boost our rate of production—our tempo.

The benefit of increasing tempo can be spectacular: if you average 500 words a day and increase your output just ten percent (that's fifty words, folks, a mere two or three sentences), you'll write 18,250 more words a year: roughly a fifth of a book.

But we're not talking about ten percent; we're talking about doubling, trebling, or even quadrupling your output. Or maybe increasing it tenfold. These improvements are quite possible if you use these techniques:

1. Use a freewriting-based process for all your work, and do many drafts.
2. Develop a "smooth" writing process; minimize interruptions,
3. Write nonlinearly; leverage your project's easy parts.
4. Write backwards in the piece.
5. Show your work frequently; read it aloud.
6. Learn to write on the fly.
7. Achieve mastery.

There are also several minor techniques.

I describe all the techniques in this chapter.

Section 5.2 Use a Freewriting-Based Process for All Your Work, and Do Many Drafts

Freewriting is the unfiltered, uncensored, unedited, "stream-of-conscious" writing down of one's thoughts, feelings, and ideas. You may be familiar with it from journal-writing or creativity exercises. It tends to be:

- Private (not only do you not have to show your freewriting to anyone, you're often explicitly instructed not to);

- Raw (spelling, punctuation, and grammar aren't an issue, and you are often explicitly instructed to ignore them); and

- "Disposable" (because it's not supposed to lead to anything except, maybe, fun and insight).

Freewriting is the free-est, fastest, funnest writing most people ever do, which is why even self-described "blocked" students can do it in class exercises. **The major technique for increasing your tempo, therefore, is to free write *all* your writing, including your "serious stuff."** Here's how you do it:

Start with a "shitty first draft" a la Anne Lamott (Section 2.5). It can be of the entire piece you're working on, or a section of it.

Follow that with many shitty drafts, in each of which you correct a few *obvious* flaws of the former one. The drafts will still be filled with holes, mistakes, and grotesque aberrations of style or meaning. However, each will be somewhat less shitty than its predecessor.

When doing these drafts, aim for *speed*: correct the obvious errors and flaws, but don't get hung up on trying to solve the difficult ones.

As soon as you are comfortable doing so, show the work (or pieces of it) to your critique partners and alpha readers (Section 3.11) and get feedback. You'll probably also have a few intractable problems to discuss with them.

Keep revising and showing. Eventually, the drafts will cross the line into "non-shittiness," at which point you are within sight of your final draft.

Keep working the same way until you complete the final.

You're done! Now submit it.

If you follow this advice, you will probably wind up doing many more drafts than you're doing now. That's fine: a free writer can write ten drafts, or even twenty or thirty, in less time than it takes a "normal" (a.k.a., perfectionist) writer to write one or two. And, believe me, the free writer is having more fun.

Setting out to write many drafts is the opposite of what many people seek to do, which is to try to write as few as possible. (As discussed in Section 2.5, many perfectionists think the proper number of drafts is one.) The "limiters" think they've got the quickest process, but they're wrong because setting an arbitrarily low number of drafts causes you to struggle to perfect each one, which is not only an inefficient process but an invitation to perfectionism.

The limiters are also denying the incremental, nonlinear nature of creativity, in which change and improvement usually happen a little at a time, and unpredictably. A lot of creativity, in fact, happens via trial and error—and yet another reason freewriting works so well is that it lets you zip through "trials" (i.e., drafts) at maximum speed.

Can a freewriting-based process work even for complex or intellectually sophisticated work? Absolutely—because you're not suspending your intellect when you free write, you're unleashing it. Joan Bolker, author of *Writing Your Dissertation in Fifteen Minutes a Day*, strongly endorses freewriting, saying "it causes you less pain while you're doing it, and produces better writing."

Freewriting, in fact, solves a common problem graduate students (and some others) have when they write, which is that they

sit and wait for a "good idea" or "good sentence" to come before starting to write (see the "pondering" section of Section 2.14). Leaving aside the fact that their notion of a "good idea" is probably perfectionist, and hence unlikely to be achieved, this process is actually the opposite of what prolific writers do, which is to just start writing, and use the writing process to facilitate thinking.

Committing to a freewriting-based process for even your most serious projects represents the final frontier of your antiperfectionism work. It's actually antiperfectionism carried down to the micro level. Something's a little hard to write? Don't struggle with it! Just move on to another, easier section. Or, go back to the conceptualization, planning, or research stages of the project (Section 5.4).

When you back off, temporarily, from a tough piece of writing, you are actually giving it time to "marinate" in your mind—and just like with real marinades, it should soften and become easier to work with. Of course, if you buy into the perfectionist myth that creation is supposed to be an epic struggle, then not only will backing off seem like a defeat, but you will also view the freewriting process itself with suspicion simply because it's easy and fun. The voice of perfectionism, a.k.a., the oppressor, is a reliable compass for how *not* to think and behave.

Still doubting? Have others review your free-written passages, perhaps comparing them with others you've labored over. There's a good chance the free-written passages will be as good or even better than the "labored" ones, in part because grueling effort often produces a stilted result. (Joan Bolker: "From what I've seen, fast writing produces no worse results than slow writing does.") Even if it turns out that the labored piece has some superiority over the free-written one, you can probably easily adjust your freewriting process to achieve the same result—and still be far ahead in terms of productivity.

In class I often ask how many drafts people think it should take to get to the final.

Most people answer with a specific number between three and ten. The right answer is, "as many as it takes."

Section 5.3 Develop a Smooth Writing Process; Minimize Interruptions

Increasing your tempo also often entails replacing a "Swiss cheese" writing process filled with holes (pauses, hesitations, and interruptions) with a smoother one. Basically, you just sit down and write—and write. You don't stop to format the work, check your email, answer the phone (it should be shut off, anyhow), or get a snack. You just write.

You don't even stop to try to recall a word or fact; you just leave a space and move on. (This tactic obviously goes hand in hand with the "many drafts" one, above.) Memory is tricky, and you've probably had the experience of struggling to remember something, only to have it effortlessly pop into your mind later. So don't waste time trying to force it.

As for research, it's not part of the composition process, and it's also a common vehicle for procrastination, so save it for later. Leave a space in the manuscript to remind you of what you need to look up, or jot a quick note on a pad.

Section 5.4 Write Nonlinearly; Leverage Your Project's Easy Parts

Perfectionists tend to see their projects as long strings of words—and there's a natural tendency, when you have that viewpoint, to want to start at the beginning of a piece and write straight through till "The End."

Viewing your work from the meager and terrifying prospect of a point at the end of an endless string of words isn't helpful. It's far more productive to view it as a landscape that you're viewing from above, and whose topographic features include hard parts, easy parts, exposition parts, dialogue parts, parts involving Character A, parts involving Theme B, etc. Viewed like this, your project resembles an illustrated map, or maybe one of those miniature landscapes you see in museums, and it's now accessible to you in its totality.

And now you can use a visualization tool I call the "writercopter," a mental helicopter that can transport you to any place in your piece. The moment you feel you've taken a particular patch of writing as far as you can, hop onto your copter and take it to another section that looks enticing. Work there until you run dry, and then re-board and hop to another part.

What if no part looks appealing? Try writing *about* the piece, since

Prolific writers view their work as a landscape and have great fun using the "writercopter" to hop to whichever section they feel like working on next.

your alienation from it is probably rooted in the fact that you either need to think it through more or are trying to force it in the wrong direction (see Section 5.9). In the unlikely event that that doesn't help, set the piece aside and let it marinate while you work on something else.

Writing might sometimes be difficult, but it should never be unpleasant; if it is unpleasant—if you're feeling frustrated, bored or stuck—that's not an indication of any deficiency on your part, but simply the signal to move to another part of the project, or another project. While it's okay to practice "writing past the wall," i.e., sticking with a difficult section a bit longer than comfortable, don't perfectionistically dig in your heels and become an antagonist to yourself and your process.

The writercopter technique is similar to that used by the late, great, and famously prolific author Isaac Asimov, who wrote or edited more than 500 books:

> "What if you get a writer's block?" (That's a favorite question.) I say, "I don't ever get one precisely because I switch

from one task to another at will. If I'm tired of one project, I just switch to something else which, at the moment, interests me more." [From his memoir, *In Joy Still Felt.*]

Note Asimov's absolute sense of freedom and dominion (authority!) over his work—expressed not in grandiose terms, but the simple ability to do whatever he wants, whenever he wants. And, of course, the total lack of blame, shame, compulsion, and perfectionism.

Nonlinear writing obviously goes hand in hand with freewriting; using the techniques together should powerfully speed your writing. What's more, the process is accelerative, since the more easy parts of your project you finish, the easier the hard parts will get. (By writing "around" the hard parts, you're illuminating them and solving problems related to them.)

You can combine nonlinear writing with Anne Lamott's famous "one-inch picture frame" technique from *Bird by Bird* to get through even the toughest piece of writing. To combat overwhelm, Lamott reminds herself that:

> All I have to do is to write down as much as I can see through a one-inch picture frame ... All I'm going to do right now, for example, is write that one paragraph that sets the story in my hometown, in the late fifties, when the trains were still running.

I myself have gotten through very tough patches of writing (meaning, sections where I felt a lot of resistance to the writing—because the patches themselves are neither easy nor hard, but just writing) by switching back and forth between the difficult patch and an easier one, doing "one-inch picture frame"-sized pieces of the tough section and longer stretches of the easy one. The easy patches actually become a reward, in this context, which is in itself a lovely development: writing not as chore, but reward.

Take these techniques to their limit, as I assume Asimov did, and you develop a very light touch around your work. You're hopping everywhere in the writercopter, not in a distracted way but in a focused, effective way—and the writing is almost never a struggle, and the words just pile up.

The alternative is you struggle with grim determination to write the piece linearly. And so you write a page or two and ... wham! You're at a hard part and you stop dead. And because you don't know what else to do, you just keep throwing yourself against that wall—until procrastination steps in to "save" you from your predicament.

Tales of Space *and* Time

Besides seeing projects as complex in space, the prolific also see them as complex in time. While novice writers see writing as "just writing," the prolific see it as a process consisting of these or similar stages:

1. Conceptualization (a.k.a. note-taking or "noodling around")
2. Planning and outlining (a little more structured than above)
3. Research
4. First Draft
5. Revision(s)
6. Final Draft
7. Submission(s)
8. Cash the Check (for freelance and other writers who get paid)

Note how **the stage most people think comes first—First Draft—actually appears halfway down.** A major cause of underproductivity and blocks is that the writer omits, or skimps on, the earlier stages—which means she is trying to write something she doesn't sufficiently comprehend.

Trying to write a first draft without first spending adequate time on stages 1–3 is like planting a garden without preparing the soil, or building a house atop a shaky foundation: a risky proposition at best. Sure, once in a while a piece will just seem to write itself. But that's usually because we've either thought about it a lot or figured out a link between it and other topics we've thought a lot about. So the early stages were, in fact, done, only perhaps at a different time. (Also, the confidence that comes from writing something familiar helps us resist perfectionism.)

Obviously, the stages differ from project to project, and writer to writer. Some projects demand extensive research, others only a little. Some writers create detailed outlines, while others work from the seat of their pants (the famous "plotters" versus "pantsers" divide). And some writers do the stages mostly linearly, while others jazzily intermingle them. Whatever system works for you, and the particular project you're working on, is the right one.

It's helpful to remember that **most of us enjoy working on some stages more than others, and those are the stages we tend to get stuck on if we're prone to procrastination**. That's procrastination as a toxic mimic of productive work (Section 1.8), and it happens especially with first draft, research, and revision.

Conversely, many writers dislike, or are afraid of, certain stages and try to avoid them. These are, typically, the first draft and submission, as well as marketing and other business "chores."

You probably know if you're overworking or underworking a stage due to procrastination, but if you're unsure, ask your mentors. If the diagnosis is, indeed, procrastination, use timed exercises (Section 2.14) to overcome your fears.

Armed with the knowledge of the stages of a writing project, you can now use your writercopter to move not just through space (the landscape of your project), but time: more specifically, back to a prior stage whenever you're stuck. I recommend moving back to conceptualization, planning, outlining, or drafting, but *not* research because it is a frequent vehicle for procrastination.

Another important productivity technique is to **identify the easiest parts of your project so that, when all else fails, you can work on them**. When, during the writing of this book, I was severely distracted or demotivated, I worked on the bibliography.[1] Why not? It had to get done, and doing it empowered me and helped me get re-motivated as soon as possible.

You can do this temporally, too. The earliest and latest drafts of a project are usually the easiest, because the earliest ones tend to be free and fun (if you don't get perfectionist), and the later ones tend to have most of their elements in place, so that what you're doing is mainly line edits. So if you're working on multiple projects, or a project with multiple sections, all in different phases of completion, do "earlies" and "lates" when feeling distracted or otherwise unmotivated; save the tough middle drafts, where you're trying to make order out of chaos, for when you're feeling fresh and energetic.

---

[1] See www.hillaryrettig.com.

Section 5.5 Work Backwards in the Piece

There's a natural tendency to start each writing session by revisiting the beginning of your piece, which means that the beginning tends to get overworked. And then, if you've got a deadline (which you should, even if it's one you set yourself), you wind up rushing through the middle and end.

Although the writercopter can help, it itself is often biased toward landing at or near the beginning of a piece.

Correct for this tendency by devoting around half of your writing sessions to working backwards in the piece, meaning you start by writing or revising the last section, then move on to the section before that, and then the section before that, etc. Utilize freewriting, nonlinearity, the copter, and all your other tempo-building techniques, but use them while working backwards from The End.

Section 5.6 Show Your Work Frequently;
Read It Aloud

I know, I know: It can be *terrifying* to show your work, particularly when it's at an early stage. However, this is one of the single best things you can do to boost your productivity. It helps you:

1. Combat any shame you have about your work. Given that shame is a powerful catalyst of perfectionism and other barriers (Chapter 6), this is crucial.
2. Get advice (including on tough writing problems) that accelerates your progress.
3. Build an engaged audience who will later purchase and promote your writing (Section 8.8).

These are powerful benefits, and so you've really got to show your work—but, of course, be selective, since there's no use showing it to someone clueless or cruel. Choose your critique partners and alpha readers (Section 3.11) carefully.

Reading aloud, either to yourself or to others, is another powerful technique. When I do it, I usually find an excruciating number of painfully obvious errors that I somehow missed through twenty silent readings.

Section 5.7 Learn to Write on the Fly

This is where things get interesting. Minimize your perfectionism, resource yourself abundantly, and use the techniques described in this chapter, and writing will start to get *really* easy. You'll be able to start a writing session with a minimum of fuss, and achieve the inspired "flow" state almost effortlessly.

Soon, you'll find yourself starting to write at times and in places you never dreamed possible:

Fifteen minutes between meetings? Without even thinking about it, you whip out your laptop or notebook.

A thirty-minute train commute? You used to read or listen to music, but those activities now hold less appeal. Why settle for merely being distracted when you can become engaged and transported via your writing?

Family reunion with all kinds of *mishegos*? Writing is no longer an extra burden, but a refuge—just as it was, perhaps, when you were a kid.

Wow, do the pages pile up when you add in an extra fifteen minutes there, an extra half-hour here.

Section 5.8 Achieve (and Enjoy!) Mastery

You don't even have to work at the final major technique for increasing tempo. With time and experience, writing should become easier and your tempo should automatically increase. That's because you will have (a) learned a lot about the topics you like to write about, (b) optimized your writing process and techniques, and (c) accumulated most of your needed resources (material, psychological, community). Eventually, you'll probably be able to just sit down and almost effortlessly spin out competent, and sometimes excellent, writing. This is called mastery, and it's a terrific thing. You gain a little of it every time you write, actually, and can speed the process along by:

1. Getting a lot of training;
2. Working with lots of mentors (Section 3.11); and
3. Working as consciously as possible, and being alert to (and seeking out) opportunities to learn and grow.

Here, as elsewhere, a perfectionist is likely to try to erect barriers to success and happiness. If you think work is supposed to be an epic struggle and are suspicious of success when it comes "too easily," then you are likely to mistrust and fight mastery

Mastery is one of the great rewards of the productive life, and so you should learn to recognize, and celebrate, yours.

Section 5.9 Other Tempo-Building Techniques

Take Shorter Breaks and Focus Breaks on Relaxation and Recovery. Don't rush your breaks, but don't let them devolve into procrastination, either (see next tip). Keep them focused on relaxation and recovery actions such as stretching, meditation, a cup of tea, or a walk in the garden. Avoid information-centered activities such as email, reading (Web or paper), or television, which often don't represent a real break from mind-work, and which are also often vehicles for procrastination.

Time Your Breaks. When you're just overcoming perfectionism, you need long breaks—for instance, 24-hour breaks in between each five-to-ten-minute writing session—to recover from the work of managing perfectionist terror.

As you become prolific, your writing sessions should become longer and your breaks shorter. There was a time I kept two timers open on my computer desktop: one to time my writing periods and the other to time my breaks. I aimed to take no more than half an hour of accumulated breaks for every three hours I spent writing (3.5 hours total).

You know how time goes faster when you're having fun, and slower when you're not? Well, I can assure you that *no* time flies faster than break time. Because of procrastination's sneaky, stealthy nature, you can take a bathroom break and then read a few headlines—and wham! An hour's flown by.

It helps if you determine which activities suck up the most time. Reading blogs or social media is dangerous enough for me, but responding to a blog post or status update can derail a writing session more than anything, so I know to strenuously avoid those particular tempting activities. For you, the danger might lie in making phone calls, watching TV, or doing housework.

You should also time any "breaks" you take before starting work. One of the three productivity behaviors from Section 2.13 is to sit right down and write at your appointed time. Always aim to do that, but if you are compelled to do some housework or Web-surfing first, time that activity so you know exactly how much you're procrastinating.

Get enough sleep. Next to perfectionism itself, fatigue may be the top degrader of tempo. The prolific people I know prioritize getting a good night's sleep.

Use deadlines. Not as a whip, but as a productivity tool. Even if you don't have an actual deadline imposed by an outside authority, you should set your own; if your project is big, you should set many smaller sub-deadlines. Make sure all your deadlines are reasonable—modest, even—so as to prevent perfectionism. And make them meaningful by involving a critique partner and others (Section 3.12) who will hold you gently accountable.

Expand on recalcitrant stuff. If you're having trouble with a piece, try writing about it as expansively as possible. Often when we stall, it's because we're trying to force too much meaning into too small a space, or conflateing two or more points that need to be handled separately. (Sometimes what you thought was a small point really needs to be a chapter—or an entire book!) So let some light and air into the topic, and see where it wants to go.

Delete recalcitrant stuff. The other solution for recalcitrance is, paradoxically, to delete. If a section simply can't be made right, then try jettisoning what you've written and either rewriting it from scratch, or seeing if the piece works without it. (Which it does a lot of the time.)

Jettisoning is one of writing's great pleasures, so enjoy it. Ignore any perfectionist voices telling you, "You worked so hard and now you're deleting it! So much wasted time!" False starts, detours, and dead ends are ordinary parts of a healthy and uninhibited creative process.

Track your progress. If you write long or complex pieces, you will almost certainly need some way of tracking progress, not just to manage the project but to keep yourself motivated. When I wrote my book *The Lifelong Activist,* I used a spreadsheet to record daily and cumulative word counts and completed chapters. The spreadsheet contained both a colorful line graph, which helped me chart daily word counts, and a colorful cone chart to tally completed chapters. You can bet that the kindergartner in me got a thrill whenever the colorful graph and chart rose a notch.

When I started writing this book, I no longer felt the need to track daily word counts and chapters. So I simply tracked the chapters I completed.

Just do whatever works for you.

Add a physical component to your writing process. Some writers catalyze their productivity by creating multicolored plot diagrams or project plans; others by creating scrapbooks filled with pictures (from magazine ads and elsewhere) related to their characters and setting.

On a more prosaic level, I have often been amazed at how often, when I'm stuck, simply printing out the piece and laying the pages out on a big table, and then going at it old school with pencil, scissors, and glue stick (i.e., cutting and pasting), helps resolves things. (Part of that, of course, is that I get to see the whole piece at once, and not the few paragraphs that show on my screen.)

Slow down. I'll end this chapter on a paradoxical note. Building tempo is like any other writing goal: you must achieve it "accidentally" while focusing on your process and immersing yourself in your text. Flaubert's maxim about success being a consequence instead of a goal applies here, too.

So don't *focus* on speeding up; just work to deploy the techniques discussed in this section at a comfortable pace. If you do that faithfully, you'll be writing *vivacissimo* before you know it.

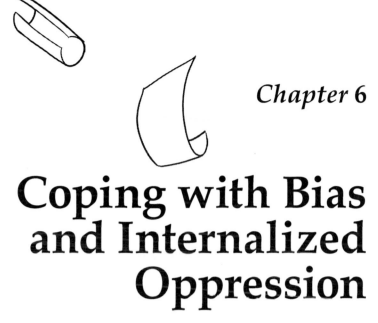

Chapter 6

Coping with Bias and Internalized Oppression

"Writing is a dog's life, but the only life worth living."
—Gustave Flaubert

Section 6.1 The Problem with Invisibility and Isolation

Procrastination makes you invisible and isolated. If you never finish your novel, you won't be seen by agents, editors, or your audience. If you never finish your thesis, you won't be seen by your committee, colleagues, and prospective hirers.

Invisibility and isolation are, in fact, key *strategies* and *goals* of procrastination:

They are *strategies* because community is essential to productivity and success (Sections 3.8–3.12), so if you're not seen, you probably won't finish your work or attain your other writing-related goals.

And they are *goals* because if you're not seen, you can't be judged—and, in particular, can't be judged a failure. Underproductivity may feel terrible, but recall that, for perfectionists, failure is a kind of ego death that feels far worse (Section 2.6).

Often, the craving for invisibility and isolation predates the procrastination habit. Many procrastinators grew up in critical or abusive families where they learned to survive by, as one writer put it, "flying under the radar." Once such children grow up, they still feel a strong desire to hide when threatened only now, not in the coat closet or remote corners of the backyard but via procrastination and underachievement.

To make matters worse, writing is about as self-revealing an activity as you'll find. Your thoughts, feelings, values, and visions are spread out nakedly on the page. This, of course, represents an extreme challenge for someone craving invisibility, and is a big reason why so many people procrastinate with their writing but not elsewhere.

Incidentally, it is also common—and antiproductive—to use writing, or a grandiose self-sacrificial vision of writing (see "Stalling Out," Section 1.10), as a way of making yourself invisible in other frightening realms, including:

- *Financial.* The writer may not want to be seen by decent employers—who he's afraid won't hire him—so consigns himself to a life of poverty and bad treatment in bad jobs. Or, he doesn't want to be seen by personal finance coaches and mentors, who might judge him a failure financially. Or the IRS, which literally has the power to penalize him.
- *Social.* The writer may not want to risk rejection by getting out and trying to socialize or date.
- *Health.* The writer may want to hide from frightening news not just about his health, but his health and fitness obligations (e.g., diet, exercise) by isolating himself from doctors, nutritionists, personal trainers, etc.

Of course, the deprivation in these key areas only further undermines your writing productivity. And so, once more we see that procrastination packs a multiple punch (Section 1.4), and perpetuates itself via a vicious cycle of procrastination leading to shame leading to isolation leading to yet more procrastination, etc.

Remember that your fears are always legitimate, even if procrastination is a suboptimal response to them (see Section 1.1). This is particularly true in the realm of finances, since money is a highly charged issue for many people, and the goal of earning a living often conflicts with that of living an authentic, creative life. However, the cost of not earning an adequate living is severe: in *Money Drunk, Money Sober,* Julia Cameron and Mark Bryan talk about "poverty addicts" who disempower themselves economically while justifying that disempowerment with the idea that poverty is somehow virtuous. (They published their book in 1993, when the economy was much stronger—these days, of course, one is far more likely to be poor without having any dysfunctional attitudes.)

I also believe that a desire to hide is a major factor in another common area of procrastination: weight loss. Weight is obviously another highly charged issue, and one around which people also make a lot of judgments and experience a lot of shame. You can apply the solutions in this book to money, weight, or any other area where you procrastinate.

Back to writing. Fearful writers don't just crave invisibility within their professional community; they often crave it within the communities of their family, friends, neighbors, and day-job colleagues. Each area of invisibility is a barrier to success, not just because you need those communities' support but because invisibility in any realm adds to your shame and fear.

So a primary task for any writer is to "come out." Yes, I mean that in the exact same way the queer community does—to reveal your true identity to yourself and others. I'm going to talk about ways to do that, but first let's discuss societal and other forces that encourage invisibility and isolation.

Section 6.2 How the Public (Including Your Family!) Sees Writers and Writing

In the writing classes I teach, we do an exercise where students list stereotypes about writers and writing. Here's a typical list:

Deluded **Unproductive** **Immature**
Arrogant **Undisciplined** **Violent** **Childish** Dreamer
Male—so no women need apply **Self-indulgent**
Philanderer Perverse **Selfish** Egomaniacal
Wife-beater **Affronter of authority** **Degenerate**
Oversensitive **Jaded** **Destined to be poor**
Self-destructive Devoted to a trivial or futile activity
Hedonistic Leech **Time-waster** Rebellious
Idle
Dangerous—divulger of secrets **Impractical** **Improvident**
Spendthrift/Prodigal **Destructive** Drunkard
Lazy Untalented **Hubristic**

Malign Stereotypes about Writers and Writing

Nice, ain't it? One student, while we were doing the exercise, remarked, "It sounds like Thanksgiving dinner at my family's house." And he is a successful freelance writer with many published books!

Three things to note about this list: it's **harsh, long,** and **salient.**

The harshness is readily apparent; I mean, I can hardly imagine a worse list.

The length indicates the pervasiveness of negative stereotypes of writers in our culture.

Salience means that when I ask students for the negative stereotypes they shout them out so fast I barely have time to write. In contrast, when I do Part II of the exercise (Section 6.4) and ask students to list the positive and truthful attributes of writers and writing, it's often like pulling teeth.

When others maliciously stereotype you we call that bias. When you do it to yourself—when you've absorbed the negative labels into your psyche—we call that internalized oppression. And make no mistake: negative labels undermine our productivity. **No one can move in two directions at once; and if, when you're trying to write, a part of you is thinking that writing is selfish, futile, etc., that part will work in opposition to your productivity (Section 6.5).**

Make a list of the negative ideas you hold about writers and writing, and use journaling and discussions with enlightened friends, colleagues, and others to defuse them. (Just naming some of the canards causes them to lose power, since many are ridiculous on the face of it.) Throughout this process, I would work under the assumption that the labels affect you more strongly than you realize. The tendency is to brush them off, but denial is a strong force, especially when it is aiding and abetting procrastination. Often, the labels are like icebergs: small on the surface, but bigger and more destructive underneath.

At the same time, it's crucial to limit your interactions with people who hold negative ideas about writers, writing, and you personally, because those people can really undermine you. (As always, family members included.)

Section 6.3 How Some Highly Successful Writers See Less-Successful Ones

Many successful writers hold stereotypes about less successful ones. I ask my students to name them, and again get a list that's harsh, lengthy, and salient.

Time-waster   Dilettante   **Foolish**

Wannabe   **Minion/Acolyte**   Inferior

Inconvenient/Distracting   Ignorant   **Unworthy**

Prey, e.g. sexual   **Unimportant—a waste of time**

Naïve   Deficient of talent or drive

Competition   **Inauthentic**

Exploitable

Malign Stereotypes Some Successful Writers
Have about Less Successful Ones

There is probably an element of psychological projection here, with some less-successful writers projecting their own feelings of shame and inadequacy onto more successful ones. At the same time, however, there is no doubt that some successful writers (and editors and agents and academics) treat novices or unpublished writers like crap, and that many literary and academic communities are caste systems. While these behaviors are bad enough on their own, their larger implications are worse, because they're not just offenses against our common humanity but our common mission. Less-successful writers depend on more-successful ones to mentor them—and all successful writers were themselves mentored, so reciprocity, at least, would argue for assuming that role. If a more-successful writer chooses not to embrace the mentor role, that is of course her right, but she at least has the moral obligation to "do no harm." (And, of course, writers who choose to take on teaching gigs have even more of a responsibility to behave professionally. See Sections 2.8 and 3.10 for discussions of the consequences of bad teaching and mentoring.)

Some writers operate under the idea (which they're sometimes clueless enough to state aloud) that an artistic mission somehow justifies bad behavior. This is not just a peculiarly old-school notion—and one ineradicably linked to sexism and exploitation—but a particularly specious and self-serving kind of grandiosity. Writers have as much of an obligation as anyone else, and probably more than most, to treat others well—and that includes their less successful colleagues, no matter how inconvenient or importuning. (Section 4.11 offers kind and respectful ways to avoid getting sucked into unwanted discussions or obligations.)

All that said, many successful writers do treat less-successful ones well, and some are magnificent teachers and mentors. John Gardner was, by most accounts, devoted to his students. And one of my students reported that when she met the poet Seamus Heaney he conversed with her like an equal, confiding his worries about how his next book would be received—and this was *after* winning the Nobel Prize! Years later, when she recounted the conversation, her face glowed, and our entire class felt inspired and encouraged by Heaney's kindness and humility.

The same instructions apply to this section as to the prior one: make a list of those canards you have internalized, and work to eliminate them from your thinking. And always avoid interacting with competitive, mean, or otherwise undermining people, no matter how talented, celebrated, or well connected they happen to be (Section 7.3).

Section 6.4 The Glorious Truth About Writers and Writing

Okay, here's the list of true traits of writers and writing:

Competent   Honest
Imaginative   Intellectual Tenacious   Childlike
Persevering   Necessary   Perceptive   Observant
Builder on tradition   Courageous—self-revealing
Resourceful   Wise   Analytical
Courageous—faces risk and rejection
Generous   Holistic—can see bigger picture
Sensitive   Creative   Rebellious   Fun Inner-driven
Transcendent
Expressive   Reporting/Mirroring   Dedicated
Insightful Empathetic Unconventional   Entrepreneurial
Courageous—willing not to conform
Thoughtful   Noble Individualistic—nonconformist

The Truth about Writers and Writing

It's typically much harder to elicit this list than the prior ones—a sign that students are alienated from their strengths and virtues. This is yet another manifestation of the disempowerment that causes procrastination, especially when the virtues are replaced, in students' minds, with insults and canards.

In fact, I think many people have a love/hate relationship with writers. They admire us for our individualism, creativity, and courage, but resent us for those very same qualities, especially if they themselves have been unable to pursue their dreams, or otherwise regret their life choices.

Also, note how many of the above positive qualities represent freedom and/or a threat to authority. Is it any wonder that authoritarian regimes—or authoritarians on the home front—target writers?

Our lack of "props" is also confounding, and can cause naïve people to think that what we do is easy. As John Gardner put it in his foreword to Dorothea Brande's *Becoming a Writer*:

> Writers, more than other artists, have no visible proof of their specialness once they've achieved it. Visual artists, carrying around their leather-enclosed portfolios, and musicians, bringing complicated and persuasive noise out of tubing or pieces of string and wood, have cumbersome

physical evidence that they are not like other mortals. Writers only use words, as even parrots do.

I like to use the word "shaman" to describe the writer's complex role in society. We are repositories of wisdom, but also danger. We stand apart, but also participate, at least as observers and analysts. We have power and influence, but often of a weird and elusive kind, and we can also be vulnerable. And, like traditional shamans, we have the power to bridge worlds. As John Gardner put it, "When writers are very good at what they do they seem to know more than a decent person ought to know."

Shamanism isn't always the easiest role to live with, but it does have its perks. One night, years ago, I was writing in my peaky attic apartment in a 200-year-old Beacon Hill brownstone. It was a tiny space filled with windows and skylights through which gusty winds poured in; especially at night, I always felt like I was on a ship in the middle of the ocean.

On the night in question, I was sitting and reading, and the dogs were also peaceful. I could hear, along with the wind, the faint music from a party my landlord, Dave, was throwing in his apartment three floors down. Suddenly, I heard the unlikely sound of people climbing the stairs outside my apartment, and after they had stopped, I heard Dave whisper, with a kind of reverence, "A *writer* lives in there."

He had been showing off his building, I guess, and I was one of the things he wanted to show off. I listened while they descended, and even through he was the rich dude who owned the building and I was the broke writer who inhabited the garret, I felt special.

Section 6.5 The Importance of Overcoming Ambivalence

Others may be ambivalent about your writing, but you cannot be. To be fully productive, you need to be clear on what you are doing and why. Writing is hard enough, and procrastination a tenacious enough foe, that even the slightest bit of ambivalence can jeopardize your success. In fact, **the most "stuck" people I meet are those trapped between conflicting values systems or goals.** If a part of you wants to write, but another part thinks writing is trivial, ridiculous, childish, futile, etc., you're unlikely to make much progress.

A major source of ambivalence for many writers is money, because for the overwhelming number of people who choose to write seriously, that choice will make them poorer. Maybe you will work part-time, or maybe at an easy-ish full-time job that leaves you more time and energy for writing than a demanding job would, but that also pays less. Or maybe you will sacrifice salary for a short commute (Section 4.4). Or maybe your household will survive on just your partner's salary. In any case, unless you are very lucky, you are going to be poorer than family members, friends, and others who haven't made similar choices.

In *On Becoming a Novelist*, John Gardner wrote, "If the writer wants everything he sees on TV, he'd better quit writing and get serious about money or else give away his TV to the poor in spirit." (And that was in 1983, when the culture was arguably less materialistic!) See also the quotation from Stephen King in Section 4.4 for other reasons why getting rid of your TV supports your writing.

Along with exploring how many of the canards in Sections 6.2 and 6.2 you've internalized, revisit the other parts of this book and think deeply about how perfectionism, deprivation, and traumatic rejection may be influencing your view of yourself and your work. You've got to get very clear on your mission and the investments and sacrifices that that mission entails (Section 2.2), AND on your willingness and ability to make those investments and sacrifices, because even the tiniest bit of ambivalence can hold you back.

If after doing this work you are still ambivalent (meaning you can't decide whether you want to write, or how much time and energy and money to devote to your writing), then it might make sense to take a sabbatical from writing. Follow your other interests for a while and see where they lead. You may discover another creative outlet, or you may—and this is the likely outcome—wind up back with your writing, only with a fresher outlook and more motivation.

Many writers, when I suggest a taking a sabbatical, freak out, which is a probable sign of over-identification with the work (Section 2.6) and also of "stalling out" (Section 1.10). Writing may enrich our lives, but we shouldn't be afraid to give it up temporarily—and, in fact, many prolific writers plan sabbaticals or hiatuses between books or at other times. A sabbatical is a time to rest and recharge and gain a fresh perspective.

One reason underproductive writers have trouble taking sabbaticals is that, in many cases, they're not giving up actual writing—because they're not actually writing—but only the idea of being a writer, or the illusion of productivity. Painful as that situation is, it's far better to face up to it than deny it, not just because denial is a dead end, but because "facing up" offers a good chance of actually eventually resolving the issues and winding up a prolific writer.

The key to a successful sabbatical is to find something meaningful to replace the writing with. It doesn't have to be something creative: I know one artist who, fed up after decades of struggle and poverty, took an office job in desperation and wound up reveling in the regular salary, medical benefits, regular schedule, decent coworkers, and easy-ish work. And she didn't give up her art, either—just the illusions that (a) she was going to be able to support herself comfortably by it, and (b) she didn't mind the ongoing poverty that resulted from her failure to do so.

In my own case, I took an "enforced sabbatical" in my early forties after a business failure, giving up my dream of being a mogul and instead working as a humble business teacher and coach for a nonprofit organization. At the time, it felt like a huge failure, and I remember pooh-poohing people's congratulations. The job, however, turned out to be one of the best breaks of my whole life. Not only did it turn out that I was an excellent teacher and coach, but I also got to witness at close range the many ways talented and hard-working people fail to attain their goals. It was an incredible lesson, and it led to my most meaningful life's work, including this book.

It helps *a lot,* when trying to find your way as a happy, productive, unambivalent writer, to have role models, and you'll find them at your compassionately objective writers' community or group (Sections 3.9–3.11). True, you'll probably see others who are ambivalent and underproductive, but they are probably beset by perfectionism, internalized oppression, and other problems. Model compassionate objectivity and proper pride, and you'll help not only them but yourself.

Section 6.6 How to Come Out as a Writer

The process of coming out as a writer is similar to that of "coming out" as a queer person—so similar, in fact, that you can read books on coming out sexually and apply most of the principles to your writing. There are lots of books and other resources on this topic, and you may wish to consult some. (I recommend Michelangelo Signorile's classic *Outing Yourself.*)

The cardinal rule is to **stay safe**. Of course, most writers don't have to worry about violence or harsh discrimination the way many queer people still do, but we still have to worry about being labeled, judged, rejected, and ostracized. So come out a little at a time, and at first just to people (e.g., compassionately objective writers, a supportive relative) whom you trust.

The first person you come out to, of course, is yourself—meaning that you embrace your identity and mission as a writer, in full awareness of that mission's complexity, including both its joys and drawbacks. (For most compassionately objective/nonperfectionist writers, of course, the joys far outweigh the drawbacks.)

Out and Proud Writer

Your coming-out process could involve these stages:

1. You come out to the point where you can enjoyably and productively write.
2. You come out to the point where you can actively and joyfully participate in writing communities.
3. You come out to the point where you can be an out and proud writer among friendly and/or sympathetic non-writers. And,
4. You come out to the point where you can be an out and proud writer among clueless or unsympathetic non-writers.

I was once fortunate enough to hear best-selling romance author Jennifer Crusie give a speech to a group of romance writers, editors, and fans, and she showed how it's done. "I'm Jennifer Crusie and I have no shame," she began, speaking in a bold voice, with bold gestures to accompany it. "I tell people I write romance and they just have to deal with it." Later, she said, "I always found those who tried to shame me odd," and exhorted us to not "give away so much of our power just to belong."

You come out via statements (to self and others) and actions. Here are some **Coming-Out Statements**. Speak them in whatever order, and to whichever audiences, feels safe:

- "I am a writer."
- "I write [type of writing or genre]."
- "I love my genre because of these reasons: _____."
- "I have this writing goal: SPECIFY."
- "This is what my process is like: SPECIFY. " (Most empowering to be able to discuss both the strong *and* weak aspects of your process.)
- "Can you help me reach my goal by _____?" (Highly empowering to ask for help!)
- "Even though it's not perfect, I'm so pleased with what I wrote today." (Double points for being compassionately objective!)
- "I love to write because _____."
- "I feel writing is important because _____." (Bonus points for: "I feel MY writing is important because _____.")

Here are some **Coming-Out Actions**. Do them in whatever order, and in whatever context, feels safe:

- Research a class or workshop or group.
- Take a class or workshop, or join a group.
- Procure resources for your writing (Chapter 3).
- Reorganize your schedule around your writing (Chapter 4).
- Change your voicemail message to be more professional.
- Get a business card.
- Start building your professional Web and social-networking presence.
- Research writing careers, markets, etc.
- Write something (even a little bit, and even something informal).
- Submit something.
- Mentor someone.
- Do some research.
- Attend a conference.
- Publish—in any forum (even informal venues count!).

There are two main risks to coming out. One is that you get rejected, which I discuss in Chapter 7. The other is that you get asked difficult questions, which I discuss in Section 6.8. I want you to be cautious about coming out, but not too cautious, because coming out is one of the profoundest acts of self-liberation you can commit—and it doesn't just liberate you, but those around you.

As I discuss in Sections 3.8 and 4.11, many writers get more support and encouragement after coming out than they had anticipated. That's no surprise when you consider that sharing your truth and dreams with someone is a kind of gift that connects them with something beautiful not only in your own psyche, but in theirs.

Section 6.7 Pervasive Deprecations

This chapter lists deprecating ideas about writers and writing that are unfortunately pervasive in our culture. If you're not careful, they can create ambivalence and wear you down. They are also at the root of many of the canards listed in Sections 6.2 and 6.3, and the uncomfortable questions discussed in Section 6.8.

(1) A fundamental hostility to individuality and creativity

John Gardner writes, in *On Becoming a Novelist*, "The first value of a writers' workshop is that it makes the young writer feel not only not abnormal but virtuous"—and it's true that the "real world" is often unsupportive of, or hostile to, creativity. As David Bayles and Ted Orland eloquently put it in *Art & Fear*:

> It may have been easier to paint bison on the cave walls long ago than to write this (or any other) sentence today. Other people, in other times and places, had some robust institutions to shore them up: witness the Church, the clan, ritual, tradition. It's easy to imagine that artists doubted their calling less when working in the service of God than when working in the service of self.

> Not so today. Today almost no one feels shored up. Today artwork does not emerge from a secure common ground ... Making art now means working in the face of uncertainty; it means living with doubt and contradiction, doing something no one much cares whether you do, and for which there may be neither audience nor reward. Making the work you want to make means setting aside these doubts so that you may see clearly what you have done, and thereby see where to go next.

All this takes its toll—and if you add in the fact that our culture actually thinks of itself as supporting and celebrating individualism and creativity, you've got the even worse situation where the artist is both unsupported and blamed for his consequent lack of success.

(2) The decline of writing as a profession

Because so many people equate money with value, and even virtue, the decline of writing markets—and, thus, opportunities for writers to make a living—is a real problem. Just a few decades ago, many writers could support not only themselves, but also a family, by writing nonfiction and even fiction for the "middlebrow" and pulp markets. (The middlebrow magazines were the slick, mass-market ones like *The Saturday Evening Post* and *Collier's Weekly*, while the pulps—who got their name from the cheap, rough paper they were printed on—were mainly science fiction, mystery, "true confession," "men's," and other genre publications.)

More recently, many magazine, newspaper, and other markets have dried up due largely to competition from blogs and other websites. Overall, I think the Internet is a fantastic thing for writers, as I will discuss in Chapter 8, but some of its benefits will take a while to arrive, while its costs, in terms of declining markets, are well under way.

When markets disappear, they take with them not only writers' incomes, but our legitimacy. One of the first questions many people ask upon being introduced is, "What do you do?," meaning really, "How do you earn money?" And there is no doubt that many people think non-money-earning endeavors are a waste of time, and are thus likely to look askance at anyone devoting a lot of her time to such an endeavor.

The decline of paying markets and rise of amateur ones also supports the widespread naïve notion that "anyone can write."

(3) Temporal challenges

In *Outliers*, Malcolm Gladwell discusses how it takes 10,000 hours of intensive practice to achieve world-class mastery of a challenging endeavor. That's roughly equivalent to three hours a day, every day, for ten years—but for someone who can't or won't take that time away from other priorities, mastery will take even longer.

The fact that it takes a long time to get good can put anyone on the defensive. In many fields, however, you at least get paid while you learn. We writers usually have to pay for our own apprenticeship, further reducing our legitimacy in others' eyes.

Another temporal challenge is that books, theses, and other long works take months or years to write. In his *Paris Review* interview, Philip Roth says that whenever he starts a new novel, "I'll go over the first six months of work and underline in red a paragraph, a sentence, sometimes no more than a phrase, that has some life in it, and then I'll type all these out on one page. Usually it doesn't come to more than one page, but if I'm lucky, that's the start of page one."

Roth is successful enough that no one will question his methods—but how would people react if you wrote for six months only to get one usable page? And how would they react if you spend years working on a book with no guarantee of "payoff"? (You probably already know the answers to these questions; see the next section.)

In a perfectionist society that deprecates the true process of creation, the writer will always be on the defensive.

(4) "Fatal Fallacies"

Writers are prone to believe what I call "fatal fallacies," misconceptions about productivity and success that, if not corrected, can create havoc or even doom your career. I list some common ones below; note how many involve dichotomization, trauma, and other perfectionist symptoms (Section 2.7), and also how many support a status quo fundamentally hostile to the creative process.

To not sacrifice yourself 100% to your writing is to sell out. First of all, what does "sacrifice yourself 100%" even mean? Do you give up your entire social life? All material comforts? Bathing?

Second, in the real, nonperfectionist/nongrandiose world, deprivation tends not to catalyze, but degrade, productivity. There's a big difference between working to eliminate lower-priority activities from your schedule and giving up high-priority ones. For more on this fallacy, see Section 1.10.

Relatedly, ***poverty is noble***. In "The Girl Next Door," from his collection *Dress Your Family in Corduroy and Denim*, humorist David Sedaris writes, "Bedroom suites were fine for people like my parents, but as an artist I preferred to rough it. Poverty lent my little dabblings a much needed veneer of authenticity." Many writers (including me!) fall for this fallacy when they're young, but you tend to grow out of it when you realize that not only is poverty not noble, it's a drag and antiproductive. I urge all "starving" writers to read *Money Drunk, Money Sober*, a book about addictive relationships to money that was co-written by Julia Cameron, author of *The Artist's Way*.

Two clarifications:

1) I'm bashing deprivation, not frugality. Frugality is GREAT because it buys you time and freedom—see Section 4.6. But deprivation is taking things too far.

2) I'm not talking about people who are poor because of circumstances beyond their control—for instance, a chronic illness or disability, or trouble finding work in a bad economy.[1] I'm talking about those

---

[1] My free ebook, *It's Not You, It's Your Strategy*, might help. You'll find it at

who make choices that leave them unable to meet their basic material needs, and/or who think that that situation is somehow virtuous.

If your work is coming easily, or you're having fun, then you're doing something wrong. Pure perfectionism—and, moreover, over time your work *should* come more easily, and should be more fun, as you gain mastery (Section 5.8).

In Joyce Carol Oates's 1978 *Paris Review* interview, the very first interviewer comment was, "We may as well get this one over with first: you're frequently charged with producing too much." Charged?!?! Is prolificness a crime? I'll let you speculate on the envy and other emotions and attitudes that could create such a bias. (Oates responded that the issue of productivity is "insignificant.")

And, finally, one of the most damaging of the fatal fallacies, ***publication = legitimacy.*** This one really keeps writers in the hole because (paradoxically) it prevents them from taking the steps they need to take to get published in the first place, including coming out, joining writers groups, and going to conferences.

Jennifer Crusie takes on this one in her essay, "A Writer Without a Publisher Is Like a Fish Without a Bicycle: Writer's Liberation and You,"[2] in which she compares some writers' desperation to be published to some women's desperation, in a prior era, to be married: she notes that, whether you're talking about writing or marriage, "Waiting for somebody else to come along and validate us means giving up all control over our lives."

Marketing guru Seth Godin uses the same analogy in his blog post, *Reject the Tyranny of Being Picked: Pick Yourself,*[3] in which he says:

> It's a cultural instinct to wait to get picked. To seek out the permission and authority that comes from a publisher or talk show host or even a blogger saying, "I pick you." Once

---

hillaryrettig.com.

[2]Jennifer Crusie, "A Writer Without A Publisher Is Like A Fish Without a Bicycle: Writer's Liberation and You," (essay), n.d. (www.jennycrusie.com/for-writers/essays/a-writer-without-a-publisher-is-like-a-fish-without-a-bicycle-writers-liberation-and-you/). Originally appeared in Romance Writer's Report, March 2002.

[3]Seth Godin, "Reject the Tyranny of Being Picked: Pick Yourself," Seth Godin's Blog (blog), March 21, 2011 (sethgodin.typepad.com/seths_blog/2011/03/reject-the-tyranny-of-being-picked-pick-yourself.html).

you reject that impulse and realize that no one is going to select you—that Prince Charming has chosen another house—then you can actually get to work.

Ambitious writers, like ambitious people in any field, must *propel* **themselves into communities they wish to be part of**, and not wait on the sidelines hoping to be invited in. It may initially take some courage to do that, but if you target the right communities you will find them wonderfully welcoming.

Section 6.8 Coping with Difficult Questions

You'd think that having people ask questions about what you do wouldn't be such a big deal. But in a world where most people...

- are suspicious of, and/or outright afraid of, the non-conventional;
- believe in big wins, overnight successes and other perfection-ist tropes;
- have no idea how hard writing is, or how long it takes to complete works, or the time and effort it takes to create and sustain a writing career;
- conflate your value as a human being with how much money you earn;
- believe the canards listed in Section 6.2, and deprecations listed in Section 6.7; and
- are happy to pronounce judgments on people or paths they know little about,

a writer is always going to be on the defensive.

Some of the questions that really irk writers are:

- "What do you do?"
- "What do you write?" (Sometimes followed by: "You write *that*?")
- "Is there any money in that?"
- "Where have you been published?" (Often followed by, "*Where?*")

- "How's the book coming?" (Alt: "When will you be done with that thing?")
- "Why don't you just sit down over a weekend and just finish it?" Or, "Why don't you just go on [popular TV show]?" (Or other "useful" advice.)
- "When are you going to get a real job?" And,
- "Did you hear about XYZ? She just sold her novel for a million dollars!"

In an essay entitled "The Little Author Who Could,"[4] Joanne Levy, who wrote fifteen (!) books before selling her first, eloquently describes the toll these types of questions take:

> Angst, embarrassment, and feelings of failure were pills I swallowed daily along with my multivitamins and orange juice. Family and friends had learned that when they asked how my writing was going, they were going to get a short and crusty answer like, "Shitty" or "it's not," but periodically I would get the question from a well-meaning relative and would have to explain that publishing is a tough business and it was going to take some time (yeah, it felt pretty hollow to me, too, even as I was saying it). Indubitably well-meaning relative would get one of those glazed over looks which I knew meant, "But there are so many books on the shelves at *chain bookstore*, so what's *YOUR* problem?"

I frequently hear writers bemoan the necessity of dealing with difficult, obnoxious, or clueless questions or comments, but don't hear a lot about the specifics of coping. I have a feeling most writers think it's like the weather and you just have to endure. But a little strategy and forethought can help a lot. Below are strategies for (a) increasing your tolerance for difficult questions, (b) maintaining conversational boundaries, and (c) dealing with hostility.

---

[4] Joanne Levy, "The Little Author Who Could," Stet! (blog), February 2, 2011 (backspacewriters.blogspot.com/2011/02/little-author-who-could.html).

Increasing Your Tolerance for Difficult Questions

By far the best thing you can do to increase your tolerance for difficult questions is to work on your own perfectionism and internalized oppression, since they can make you oversensitive, like a burn victim who yelps in pain at the slightest touch. If a part of you actually believes you're "taking too long" to finish your book or thesis, or that writing is a waste of time when it doesn't earn any money, then any hint to that effect from someone else is bound to hurt. In contrast, the more compassionately objective you are regarding your work, the more resilient you will be in the face of challenging questions.

Also, think about your motive when answering questions. If it's to convince the questioner of the validity of your viewpoint—for instance, that money really isn't the most important thing in writing or life—then you're already in trouble. You can't be responsible for what other people think, and certainly won't convince anyone by lecturing. (See my book, *The Lifelong Activist*[5], and Dale Carnegie's classic, *How to Win Friends and Influence People*, for more on this.) The best way to convince people about the value of your path is to live it productively and joyfully.

Your goal for any conversation should simply be to speak your truth, perhaps initially with as little embarrassment or shame as possible, and later on, like Jennifer Crusie, with bold energy and pride.

You might even get to the point where you actually enjoy the questions and value the opportunity for interaction and mutual education. I myself consider questions an homage to my shamanism, and am grateful to be doing something that elicits others' interest.

A special type of difficult question is the nag, which I discussed in Section 3.8. When a friend or loved one repeatedly asks "How's it going?" or "How much did you get done today?" it can stress you out even if they mean well. Use the techniques of collaborative solving (Section 4.11) to help them figure out a better way to support you.

Maintaining Conversational Boundaries

Of course, there could be other reasons you don't like to answer questions. Perhaps you find them invasive, or perhaps you don't like small

---

[5]Hillary Rettig, *The Lifelong Activist: How to Change the World Without Losing Your Way*, Lantern Books, 2006 (www.lifelongactivist.com).

talk. Many writers, I've found, are deep thinkers who aren't comfortable with superficial conversations, especially about their work.

If you're reticent by preference, that's fine; if it's unwillingly (like shyness), consult a therapist. If you simply find the content of the questions challenging, however, then rehearsing a few answers ahead of time should help.

I believe that even the most reticent writer should be able to tell people that she's a writer, since withholding a fundamental truth about yourself creates shame. What you say beyond that, however, is up to you. (I favor a lot of candor, but understand that that approach isn't for everyone.) Delimiting conversations can be tricky, so here are a few tips:

Talk about writing in general. The answer to "Where do you get your ideas?" doesn't have to be some kind of uncomfortable self-exposure, but, "Well, you know, writers get them from all over. Sometimes it's people we know, sometimes it's something we read, and sometimes an idea just pops up in our heads." If your questioner presses for specifics about your work, just say, "I actually don't like to talk about the specifics of my work." Most people will respect that.

Talk about your past works, but not your current work. "I prefer not to talk about the project I'm currently working on" is a great reply that people usually respect. (Or, choose any work that you're comfortable talking about and steer the conversation in that direction.)

Answer without justifying. So you tell someone you've been working on your novel for four years, and they reply, "Isn't that a long time?" Refrain from going into a long, defensive explanation of how complex your novel is, how much research it took, etc., and simply correct the questioner's misinformation: "Actually, it's not. Many novels take years to write."

Avoid the urge to compare your pace with another's—comparisons, as you know, being perfectionist (Section 2.7). If the questioner makes such a comparison, just say that every work, and every writer's situation, is different.

Deflect. E.g., "You know, I really don't like to talk about my projects, but *you* seem very interested in books—what do you like to read?" Deflection usually works because most people like to talk about themselves even more than they like to talk about your writing.

Use humor. If someone asks where you get your ideas, you can hem and haw, or simply say, "Mars." (I guess this wouldn't work so well if you were writing science fiction...)

If they ask how much money you make from your writing, you can embarrassedly mutter, "None." Or you can grin crazily and say, "Oh, millions!"

The great thing about humor is that it often illuminates the naïveté of the original question, both for you and the listener. And if the questioner cluelessly persists, you can keep going:

"No, really, how much money do you make?"

"Enough that right after this party I'm going to stop off and pick up my new Bentley!"

If a listener is simply not getting it, though, I think it's a good idea to switch to one of the other tactics, because while humor is effective, it's also a little hostile, and can be interpreted as condescension.

Keep in mind that ***how* you say something is at least as important as your choice of words: if you yourself are confident and at ease with your choices, all but the most obtuse questioners will get the point.**

Dealing with Hostility

Always assume questioners are innocent until proven guilty. If someone asks me a clueless or even callous question, I try to give them benefit of the doubt, because I've asked my own share of clueless and callous questions over the years. Besides, many of those types of questions are rooted in perfectionism, and given that it's ubiquitous in our society, and that I myself have only lately overcome it, how can I blame my questioners if they themselves are afflicted by it?

If someone is truly insulting or offensive or hostile, however, you shouldn't tolerate that. You have two basic choices: to either not interact with him anymore, or (if you value the relationship) to explain to him why his comment was inappropriate and how you would like to be treated in the future. If you do that and he persists in mistreating you, I would cease interacting with him on any level. This may seem extreme—and it could be difficult, especially in the case of family members—but it's essential. You have to protect yourself.

Not Letting Them Stop You

The most important tip about dealing with challenging questions is to never let them stop you. Here's Joanne Levy again, dealing with her years of fielding questions before she'd been published:

It was really tough; I'm not going to lie. But if I stopped trying, then I would *officially* be a failure and the door would be closed—I would *never* be published. If I kept trying, there was still hope, no matter how slim. It was still something.

I hear the same message from high achievers in every field: "I thought about quitting during a difficult period, but knew that that wouldn't accomplish anything."

So you shouldn't quit either.

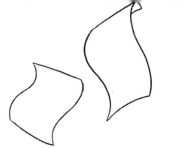

Chapter 7

Coping with Rejection

"Reject your sense of injury and the injury itself
disappears."
　　　　　　　　　—Marcus Aurelius

Section 7.1 **Rejection or Harsh Criticism Can Foment a Block**

An inevitable consequence of coming out as a writer is that you will be rejected. Rejection is never pleasant, but unpleasant-ness is the least of the problems it can cause. Most cases of severe procrastination or writer's block have been fomented by a harsh rejection. The writer may already have been perfectionist, as many of us are until we teach ourselves not to be, but the rejection pushed that perfectionism into overdrive.

I know all this because frequently in classes I will mention a dis-empowering scenario, such as a harsh workshop critique or a nasty comment from a teacher or family member, and someone will say, "You know, that happened to me, and I never finished a piece after that." Or, "I never submitted any work after that." Or, "I stopped writing after that." Often the person wasn't even aware of the link between the trau-matic incident and the block until that very moment.

There's no time limit on how long we're affected by a harsh rejection, either. I routinely talk to people who vividly recall such an episode years or even decades earlier. "Forty years is nothing in the lifespan of toxic feedback," notes Joni B. Cole in her book *Toxic Feedback*. "People forgive, but they don't forget."

I call a rejection that's harsh enough to foment a block a "traumatic rejection."

Rejection takes many forms beyond simple denial (i.e., of publication or admittance to a workshop), including harshness, disparagement, deprecation, dismissal, devaluation, bias, callousness, carelessness, capriciousness, neglect, ridicule, sarcasm, "snark," and ostracism. Also: passive-aggressive withholding of information, time, or other support, and non-accommodation of reasonable requests. (Henceforth, I use the words "rejection" and "criticism" as shorthand for all of these.) Basically, everything that's not an unequivocal acceptance contains elements of rejection.

Rejection also comes from many more sources than we realize, including publishers, editors, agents, teachers, mentors, colleagues (in or out of workshops), readers, reviewers, strangers (especially on the Internet, see Section 7.6), and, of course, your family, friends, neighbors, and day-job coworkers. One writer I know suffered traumatic rejection when she was cruelly cast out of a writer's group she herself had helped found.

Here are some common mistakes writers make in the wake of a rejection:

(1) **We underestimate its impact.** Even a seemingly small rejection in an area you care a lot about can be painful or even crushing—which is why someone who accuses a writer of being "oversensitive" in the face of nasty or callous remark would likely react equally or even more strongly to a similar remark about, say, his parenting skills.

(2) **We fail to recognize it as rejection.** Ignorant or insensitive people sometimes say terrible things under the guise of "constructive criticism," "tough love," or "fun ribbing." Even if you believe someone's motives are basically well meaning—which is not always the case—you shouldn't misidentify the nature of their act, or its effect on you. When, in *If You Want to Write*, Brenda Ueland says, "Families are great murderers of the creative impulse, particularly husbands," she's talking mainly about the kinds of sarcasm and ridicule naïve people think are benign or even helpful.

Joni B. Cole says, "It's wrong to be brutally honest when you give feedback because any kind of brutality is just an excuse to take out your own failures on somebody else."[1]

(3) **We assume that the compliments cancel out the criticisms.** Constructive criticism always begins with something good to say about the writer's work or at least his intentions or efforts, and from there tries to deliver a mix of compliments and criticisms. We often assume the compliments will take the sting out of the criticisms, but that's not always the case, especially if the criticisms are harsh or the writer a perfectionist who mentally filters out compliments.

Because society itself is so perfectionist, you are likely to hear loads of bad advice in the wake of a rejection, such as "Get over it," "Move on, already," or "It goes with the territory." Ignore it all. **It is crucial that you be 100% accepting of your reaction to a rejection, because (a) your feelings are always valid, and (b) judging them will only make you feel worse.** Above all, don't chide yourself for being over-sensitive. Writers feel the sting of rejection not because we're weak, but because what we're doing is difficult and because we have committed to an emotional openness that leaves us vulnerable (Section 6.4).

If you have worked to integrate yourself into compassionately objective communities (Sections 3.8 through 3.12), you should receive much more productive advice of the kinds I'll offer in Sections 7.3 through 7.6.

Section 7.2 Context Counts

The hurtfulness of a particular rejection depends on its context, including these elements:

Who is being rejected. If you are perfectionist, then you will

---

[1]Cole offers loads of great advice to those seeking to give constructive criticism, including: "style matters almost as much as substance." She also suggests creating teachable moments by asking questions such as, "What were you intending to get across with your ending?" "How would you describe your protagonist?" and "Tell me where you're heading with your plot." Teachable moments, she says, "are about reciprocity—the feedback provider and the writer feed off each other in a stimulating way." She also advises those critiquing others' manuscripts to get specific: "Writers ... can handle specifics. It's the generalities that bring them to their knees. 'Your story didn't work for me.' 'I don't get it.' 'This isn't my thing.' These ... only serve to leave writers feeling more at a loss than usual." She also points out that "red-penning every single instance of a recurring weakness in the text is ... wrong."

likely experience rejection much more painfully than if you aren't. The symptoms of perfectionism described in Chapter 2—unrealistic standards of success, over-identification with work, excessive focus on product, excessive focus on external rewards, etc.—make you susceptible. In the worst cases you'll be like a burn victim, reacting strongly to even slight criticism or neutral comments—or even to praise!

Again, this doesn't mean you're weak—only perfectionist. You wouldn't be continuing to write if you were weak. Overcome your perfectionism and you'll automatically become more resilient.

Rejection is also likely to hit hard—and to trigger another unproductive round of "Why am I even doing this?"—if you are ambivalent about your writing (Section 6.5).

Who is doing the rejecting. If, after a mother grounds her teenager, he shouts, "You're stupid—I hate you!" she might be annoyed, but she probably wouldn't be hurt too much. That's because she knows he is acting out of anger and immaturity.

If, on the other hand, her partner or a friend or coworker conveys that same message, she's likely to be really hurt.

Rejection hurts more when we respect the judgment of the person rejecting us, which is a big part of the reason why so many traumatic rejections are perpetrated by teachers or mentors.

Family members and friends are the other big category of traumatic rejecters. We may or may not respect our loved ones, but we trust them—or crave to—and when they violate that trust it hurts.

Respect and trust for certain individuals also often leads us to be blindsided when they harshly reject us—another huge factor in traumatic rejection (see below).

Where it happens. If a rejection happens in public—say, in a classroom or workshop—it is likely to be extra shaming. If it happens via email or text message it's also extra shaming, in part because it implies you weren't important enough to merit a phone call or meeting. (Email, voicemail, and texting shouldn't be used to deliver emotionally difficult messages of any sort—see the section on callousness, below.)

When it happens. Obviously, we're more vulnerable at some times than others. If you're struggling with problems in other areas of your life, you'll likely have less ability to cope with a writing rejection.

Another sensitive time is when you are experiencing situational perfectionism (Section 2.9), a temporary spike in perfectionism that is often the aftermath of a writing success or investment. And, of course, rejection itself can cause such a spike, making you more sensitive to further rejection. **This is probably the mechanism by which many blocks occur: you start with a baseline level of perfectionism and then experience several harsh rejections that are never healed and thus add their own additional layers of perfectionist terror until you are blocked.**

What is being criticized. If someone criticizes a grocery list you wrote, it's probably not going to matter. But if they criticize a book or thesis chapter you've labored over, that's another story. Ditto if you're being criticized over an aspect of your writing you've always prided yourself on, be it analytical rigor, psychological acumen, or the ability to write dialogue.

A common problem is when criticism crosses the line into personal attack: from "there's a problem with this piece" to "there's a problem with your worldview" or even "there's a problem with your character." ("Character" in the sense of your personality and values, not someone you're inventing.) This kind of personal criticism can be highly painful and is inappropriate coming from anyone, but especially a teacher, mentor, or publishing professional.

An even more vicious type of criticism is that which attacks your personal or professional identity, i.e., "You can't be much of a _____ if you do _____." Once, a writer I know who writes on interpersonal dynamics discovered that her agent wasn't returning her publisher's phone calls. When she drew the problem politely to the agent's attention, the agent responded by saying, "Wow, that's not very professional behavior from someone who's supposed to be a relationship expert." Besides its intrinsic meanness and unfairness, the agent's comment is a sterling example of the types of control tactics that publishing professionals (Section 8.1), thesis advisors (Section A.3), and others use to control writers.

Callousness. Callousness represents a negation of our very humanity. Here's Tom Grimes, in *Mentor*, reporting on an incredibly callous rejection from a Master of Fine Arts (MFA) program:

Syracuse turned me down next. But rather than simply sending a letter, the program's staff returned my application manuscript, upon which someone had scrawled and then partially erased the words *B-, boring*. This may have been due to laziness. After all, someone could have used Wite-Out to mask the handwriting, made a copy of the original page, and replaced it with an innocent replica ... Classic rejection letters lie to minimize an author's pain: "We regret." "We wish we could." "We're sorry but due to space limitations." But editors never regret, wish, or feel sorry: they simply avoid being cruel, and the staff at Syracuse hadn't. At best, its response was careless, at worst, mocking and sadistic.

Grimes's anger is justified, and his detailed recollection of a decades-old traumatic rejection is typical: traumatic rejections, as noted in Section 7.1, do tend to imprint themselves with great clarity.

While anyone, including a teacher, can be callous by mistake, **consistently callous rejections are a hallmark of disempowering systems** (Section 8.5). Callous rejections also tend to be blindsiding (see below) because they violate the norms of civil discourse.

One of my students recalled getting a paper back from a teacher that didn't have a single comment on it until the very end, where the teacher had written, "This is where you should have started." (Everyone in class groaned when she told this story.) The teacher might have been rushed or stressed, or he might have felt lazy or uncommitted (which, as you now know, would have been symptomatic of his own disempowerment), but none of those conditions excuses his callousness.

Rejection via voicemail or text message is callous because it sends a message that the rejected person is unimportant enough to merit a conversation. Ditto for form letters, especially if, as is common in publishing, they come unexpectedly in the wake of more personal communications. Emails can be better, but are still inadequate for emotional conversations or those requiring nuance. While we writers may naturally pride ourselves on our wordsmithing, psychologists say it's often the nonverbal elements of a communication that have the most impact.[2]

---

[2] The Wikipedia entry on "nonverbal communication" has a good overview. The phrase "verbal communication," by the way, is often used by specialists to include both spoken and written communication.

Compassionate people strive never to reject anyone, in any situation, callously.

Capriciousness also negates our humanity—we become a mere canvas for the perpetrator's mood swings—but with an extra fillip: we're always in a state of nervous anxiety, never knowing when the axe will fall. Interact long enough with a capricious person, and the entire experience can be traumatizing.

Unfairness is akin to capriciousness. Exploiters often deride fairness as an immature preoccupation in a hard-knocks world, but ethical people do care about fairness, and the opposite of fairness is irrational bias, which most thinking people reject as an intellectual and moral flaw. In any case, if you believe a rejection was unfair, that could well add to your hurt.

Unfairness is common in MFA programs and other educational settings, where a small number of students are often anointed "stars" and showered with attention and support while everyone else is left to languish. (Note the dichotomizing.)

Blindsiding. Blindsiding happens all the time and is a huge cause of traumatic rejection and writer's block. If I tell you I'm going to submit your work to the meanest editor in the world, you have a chance to prepare yourself emotionally for the inevitable harsh critique or rejection. (And you shouldn't let me do that, anyway.) If, however, you get a harsh rejection from someone you don't expect it from—i.e., are blindsided—then you'll probably be unprepared and undefended, and the rejection will hit very hard.

Here are factors that lead to blindsiding:

(1) *Pervasive societal perfectionism.* Many people don't know how to give constructive criticism, or even that they should. They will blithely mouth the most hurtful criticisms, and then, after you protest, blame *you* for being wounded.

(2) *Malpractice.* If a doctor, through ineptness, negligence, or some other gross violation of professional standards, leaves the patient worse off, we call that malpractice. I believe we should use the same term for teachers, mentors, and publishing professionals who, through their own ineptness, negligence, or lack of professionalism, leave writers worse off. When S.J. Culver received a rejection letter *838 days* after

submitting a story, that was malpractice and she was blindsided:

> I was outraged, really *outraged*, when it popped up in my inbox—not because I really thought my story had stood much of a chance at the magazine in question, but because it was the first rejection in some time to catch me off guard. Usually I expect the rejection slips; they turn up like clockwork four months, six months, eight months after I mail off a submission ... My mind is steeled against their inevitable arrival, knowing the odds, knowing I'm no genius. This one was a nasty surprise, though, and for a day or two I was just disgusted.[3]

(More on S.J. Culver's rejection in Section 8.2.)

(3) *Unreasonable expectations.* If you are sure your work will be published by the next editor you send it to, or praised to the heavens at your next workshop, then you are setting yourself up for blindsiding. Often our expectations are grandiose, but sometimes we are disarmed by even reasonable hopes and optimism. Here's Tom Grimes, again:

> Three days later the Houghton Mifflin editor who had recommended my first novel for publication wrote to say I'd "gone off track." Nothing he liked about my first novel existed in my new novel, the rest of which he didn't ask to see. Instead, he advised me to "follow the often-lonely road to literary achievement." Earlier that day, I'd stopped work on page two hundred and seven, mid-sentence ... I opened the blue box, placed the new novel inside it, and didn't touch it again for a decade.

Although it would seem reasonable for Grimes to assume that the editor who liked his first book would like his second, it's never a good idea, when dealing with traditional publishers, to get your hopes up. "Hope for the best, prepare for the worst," is a useful strategy, if you don't let it shade into negativity. (And, as discussed in the next chapter,

---

[3]S.J. Culver, "On Expectations (And A Writer's Lack Of Same)," The Awl (blog), March 17, 2011 (www.theawl.com/2011/03/on-expectations-and-a-writers-lack-of-same).

successful people always try to have a "Plan B.")

The editor rejected Grimes callously, though. He should have called, and he should have also resisted the impulse to offer such silly and patronizing advice.

Section 7.3 Minimizing the Odds of Traumatic Rejection

You won't be able to avoid rejection entirely, but you should do everything you can to minimize the chance of traumatic rejection. There are three main techniques for doing so:

(1) ***Work to minimize your perfectionism and internalized oppression.*** This is key to resiliency, and if you keep at it you'll eventually not care about, or even notice, many rejections. Also, work on setting nonperfectionistic, reasonable goals and having nonperfectionistic, reasonable expectations so you won't be blindsided.

Always remember that there are many reasons your work can be rejected that have nothing to do with its quality, including that the editor was busy, distracted, or biased, or that the market you submitted it to was in financial trouble. (Or the editor might have just purchased something similar to your work.) Of course, a lot of work gets rejected because it is unprofessional—badly crafted, or submitted to the wrong market, or submitted at the wrong time—but there's a lot of randomness in publishing that even the most professional writers are subject to, which is a key reason I advocate self-publishing (Section 8.5).

(2) ***Always strive to deal with ethical, compassionate, and competent people.*** I can't stress this enough, nor can I stress enough the importance of walking away from oppressors and exploiters regardless of the short-term benefit you think you might derive from the association. Not only are ethical relationships far more likely to achieve the desired outcomes, they are also far more likely to evolve into long-term productive partnerships. But the most important reason to avoid oppressors is because relationships with them tend to be disempowering and often culminate in traumatic rejection.

Always **trust your gut**, and quickly exit situations where you don't feel comfortable or safe, where you feel you're being manipulated, or where your investment seems much larger than the other person's. (As a friend of mine says in a different context, "Don't make someone a priority when they've only made you an option.") It's important to leave worrisome relationships even if doing so is difficult, inconvenient, or costly—and to do it fast, before too much damage is done.

It's also important to work with competent people who are capable of seeing a project through. As you now know, there are many reasons why an intelligent and well-intentioned person would be unable to follow through on her plans, including perfectionism, an inability or unwillingness to prioritize, and internalized oppression. To base your success around working with such a person is taking on a huge burden, and a huge risk.

All this raises yet another key difference between underproductive people and the prolific: **underproductive people tend to remain way too long in unproductive situations or relationships, while the prolific, in contrast, are quick to exit them**. The prolific also understand that once in a while they'll leave a situation they should have stayed in; they're okay with that because they know no one makes perfect decisions. They also know that opportunities are abundant, and so another one will eventually come along—in contrast to perfectionists, who tend to think opportunities are scarce and therefore cling to even unproductive situations.

(3) *Be proactive and plan*. Proactiveness means doing the work in this book in an ambitious way, so that when you do get rejected you've got the emotional, community, and other resources to cope.

It also means having a Plan B and maybe even a Plan C—so that, for instance, if you don't get into the workshop of your choice, you've got other options.

Proactiveness also means considering in advance how your published work will affect others. If your writing is likely to annoy or upset or inconvenience someone you care about, it's best to give him notice—after all, he doesn't deserve to be blindsided either. (Often, however, when my students finally "have the discussion" they find that the person they were concerned about not only doesn't mind what they're writing, but actively supports it. So, it's best not to start out with strong assumptions.)

Do you show someone the actual writing that might upset them? I think so—it's the specifics that determine how the piece will affect them. In some cases, I do believe others have a legitimate say over when and how you publish a work—although *never* over what you actually write. These are tricky situations to navigate, though, so consult your mentors, maintain a clear sense of your boundaries, and use cooperative problem-solving (Section 4.12) to let the other person know you care and are willing to work to arrive at the most mutually satisfactory outcome possible.

Don't delay this conversation till the last minute, by the way. For one thing, I've found that the fear that your family (or others) will object to your writing can be a huge barrier to productivity. Also, people's feelings and concerns are legitimate, even if they conflict with your need to publish. If you're afraid you won't stand fast under pressure, I would work on that problem instead of cheating the other person of a cooperative process.

Finally, proactiveness also means you are selective in the information—and, especially, judgments—you take in. Many prolific writers, for instance, only read a few critics whose judgment they trust. Others have trusted family members, agents, or others filter their reviews so that they only see the worthwhile ones.

There is no point in exposing yourself to ignorant or vicious criticism.

Section 7.4 Coping With Routine Rejection: Taking Your Power Back

Rejection hurts most when it is shaming and causes us to feel diminished as a person. Diminishment is a close cousin to disempowerment, which you now know lies at the heart of underproductivity (Section 1.1). Here are two terrific examples of writers taking back their power after rejections.

Carolyn See's boomerang strategy from her book, *Making a Literary Life*:

> In that first hour of rejection, when your liver is exploding and your spleen is on fire, you grope your way through the house to where you keep your "charming note" stationery. You look up the name of that periodical's editor's on the masthead and you write him or her a charming note.
>
> You don't, under any circumstances, write: "Dear Sir or

Madam, Eat shit and die." ...

Try writing something like "Thanks for the bracing experience of your rejection slip! It made me rethink my story once again. I'll be sending you another one in three weeks or so. Because my greatest dream is to see my work in your pages. Maybe next time I'll get a genuine signature on that slip! Or maybe you'll say yes. Wouldn't that be cool? Yours sincerely."

Write it, fold it, address it, stamp it, send it right back *on the same day you get the rejection.*

She continues:

I can't tell you how important this is, how utterly unfrivolous in intent. This simple *thank you* for the rejection is one of the highest forms of spiritual aikido I can think of. ... Maybe [the editors will] read the note and drop it instantly into the wastebasket. Maybe they'll shove it to the back of their desks. It doesn't matter too much what *they* do.

The main thing is that *your* ions will fall back into place, your internal organs will stop exploding, and you might find yourself absently smiling.

See's boomerang works both for alleviating the hurt of the rejection and also for building the kind of author-editor relationship that can lead to publication. (She reports that this process eventually got her published in *The Atlantic Monthly.*)

Chris Offutt's reframing strategy. In his essay "The Eleventh Draft," from the book *The Eleventh Draft:* (Frank Conroy, ed.), Chris Offutt offers one of the most brilliant and delightful re-empowerment strategies I've seen:

The notion of submitting anything to a magazine filled me with terror. A stranger would read my precious words, judge them deficient, and reject them, which meant I was worthless[4]... My goal, however, was not publication, which was still too scary a thought. My goal was a hundred rejections in a year.

I mailed my stories in multiple submissions and waited eagerly for their return, which they promptly did. Each rejection brought me that much closer to my goal—a cause for celebration, rather than depression. Eventually disaster struck. The *Coe Review* published my first story in spring 1990.

As discussed in Section 2.12, rejection (a.k.a. "failure") is not only inevitable but a sign you're operating at an ambitious level. Writers do have to endure levels of rejection that most people can't tolerate— which is a big part of the reason so many people give up on their writing dream—so why not spend some time seeing if you can come up with a clever See-like or Offutt-like way of coping?

Or, even better, craft an empowered career for yourself that puts your acceptances and failures much more directly under your control (Chapter 8).

Section 7.5 Coping With Traumatic Rejection

The strategies in the prior chapter are useful for dealing with the kinds of routine rejections that typically accompany a writing career—or life in general. These rejections sting, and they can wear you down, but they are mostly non-traumatic.

What about the traumatic ones that can foment a block? Here's a process for coping:

(1) ***Overcome your perfectionism and internalized oppression.*** You're probably sick of hearing me say that, but it's fundamental. Don't buy into the oppressor's viewpoint or give away your power. Also, people with strong supportive communities and abundant resources tend to cope much better than those who are isolated and deprived.

(2) ***Prioritize coping.*** Don't try to work through the pain, or

---

[4]Note the harsh punishment, dichotomization, overidentification with the work, and other perfectionist symptoms.

minimize it, or pretend it's "no big deal." Stop your work and focus on healing. This will ensure that you'll be able to resume your work as quickly as possible.

(3) *Cope lavishly.* We're often in shock after a traumatic rejection, and so may not be conscious of the full extent of the hurt. And the tendency toward denial is strong. I find, in fact, that many rejections are like icebergs: small on the surface, but much larger underneath. I would therefore err on the side of caution and assume I'm hurting worse—and need more healing—than I may realize.

If you need a crying jag or a sulk, take it—you're not hurting anyone. (If you need a bunch, take them.) When you're done, move on to journaling, discussions, therapy, and other analytical/healing tools. Explore the situation as fully as possible, and with as much compassionate objectivity as possible. Yes, you want to take responsibility for whatever mistakes you made, but you also need to recognize the actions others took and the role of bad luck in the rejection—and to be sure not to blame yourself for those.

(4) *Avoid the temptation to isolate.* As you know from Chapter 6, that only compounds the shame and deprives you of resources. You need your community now more than ever.

(5) *Take back your power.* You take your power back, mainly, by speaking your truth. If the person who rejected you is compassionate and ethical, call or visit and tell her how her action made you feel; if you've correctly assessed her character, she will probably take responsibility and apologize. Or she could bring up other aspects of the situation that fully or partly exonerate her. That's fine, too. The main point is that she will seriously listen to and think about your statements.

If the person is not, to your knowledge, compassionately objective or ethical in their dealings, or if they are more powerful than you, or if you feel that there might be adverse consequences to speaking out, then you've got a tougher problem. Definitely consult with your mentors, and you may have to limit your re-empowerment to speaking your truth to yourself and your community, coping lavishly, and limiting your future interactions with the person. (Far better, I hope you see, to work with compassionately objective, ethical, and competent people in the first place.)

Section 7.6 **Writing on the Internet**

I can't emphasize enough how difficult writing on the Internet is—or at least how difficult *I* find it. I see bloggers and emailers who write piles each day without apparent hesitation or conflict, but that's not me. I see the Internet as a place of almost constant rejection and perfectionism, and beyond that, numerous conflicts including:

Blurring between personal and public personae. The Internet is a highly intimate medium that's also highly public. How much should you divulge, and when, and to whom? These are bedeviling questions, particularly since once you do divulge the information can go anywhere.

Personae collision. We all reveal different aspects of ourselves to different people and in different settings. I show one side of my character to my friends, another to my siblings, another to my mom, another to my young niece and nephew, and still another to my adult nephew.

These boundaries are much harder to maintain on the Web than in real life, and because the consequences of blurring can be severe, this adds to the difficulties of deciding what and when and where (and whether) to publish.

Collision between personal and professional personae. Even harder to sort out than the conflicts among your personal personae.

Conflicts about fees, licenses, etc. I struggle not just with the immediate practical questions of payments (or lack thereof) and contracts on the Internet, but the ethical implications of my choices.

My own newsletters and blog I of course write for free. But what about contributing articles to someone else's site in exchange for publicity? I am less certain of the benefit of doing that than I once was, not just because some sites have profited spectacularly off the unpaid labor of writers—*The Huffington Post*, which its owner sold to AOL for $315 million, being the best known example—but also because the publicity value of some of the barters I've done was negligible. Should I spend a day or two writing an article for someone else's site when doing so only yields a few hits on my own? (The smart thing, by the way, is not to write an article from scratch, but to quickly repurpose one that you've already written.)

Even more worrisome is that many sites have gotten rapacious in claiming the rights to contributed works. I'm not talking about the major social networking sites, most of which have terms of service explicitly claiming ownership of anything you post on them. (So don't do it! Just link to the post on your site, and make sure your copyright or Creative Commons statement is prominent.) I'm talking about smaller venues. It used to be that when I donated an article to someone, it was taken for granted that they would use it just once. Now, many sites claim unlimited rights to reproduce contributed works in any format or venue—even commercially. They are even worse than the corporate publishers I worked with as a freelancer who were also rapacious, but who at least paid.

Unfortunately, all this is true of even organizations that should know better. Recently, I contributed an article to an animal rights blog (get that? *Rights*) and received a long email back claiming unlimited rights except for the right to be sued for the material, which they considerately left exclusive to me. When I pointed out that the terms were unfair, the editor threw a tantrum (a control tactic, by the way), saying she was "horrifically offended."

This is a complex and constantly changing topic, so I don't have definitive advice except (a) read the fine print, (b) stay informed, and (c) trust your gut.

Writing on the Web often utilizes a different process than writing offline. After a gig filling in for blogger Ta-Nehisi Coates, novelist Michael Chabon had this interesting observation:[5]

> Novelist time is reptile time; novelists tend to be ruminant and brooding, nursers of ancient grievances, second-guessers, Tuesday afternoon quarterbacks, retrospectors, endlessly, like slumping hitters, studying the film of their old whiffs. ... Getting a novel written, or a bunch of novels, means that you are going to miss a lot of opportunities, and so missing them is something you have to be not only willing but also equipped by genes and temperament to do. Blogging, I think, is largely about *seizing* opportunities, about pouncing, about grabbing hold of hours, events, days and nights as they are happening, sizing them up and putting them into play with language, like a juggler catching and

[5]Michael Chabon, "Tai Nasha No Karosha: Reflections on a Week of Blogging," The Atlantic (website), January 14 2011 (www.theatlantic.com/culture/archive/2011/01/tai-nasha-no-karosha-reflections-on-a-week-of-blogging/69573/).

working into his flow whatever the audience has in its pockets.

There's often not just a difference in pacing but in how you perceive the finished product. As a self-identified "writer," I place a high value on the polish of my finished works—an attitude that's somewhat antithetical to blogging and other quick-deadline Web publishing.

The Web lacks editorial safeguards. Serious writers rely on editors and others to review work prior to publication. This gets tricky when you're publishing independently, and especially when you're publishing quickly. It's tempting to skip the editorial review, which means that errors are pretty much inevitable—and that, in turn, brings us to...

The culture of the Internet is deeply perfectionist. You'll find all the major perfectionist symptoms on abundant display throughout the Web, including grandiosity, machismo, dichotomized thinking, labeling, hyperbole, comparisons, and dramatic but unrealistic success stories. You'll also find plenty of nit-picking, harshness, ridicule, sarcasm, and shaming.

Actually, the Web often moves well beyond perfectionism and into outright attack, and often those attacks are nasty and personal. There's also a lot of sexism and other bias, with many women, queers, people of color, or members of other disenfranchised groups getting insulted or harassed when they speak up—and sometimes the harassment carries over into the "real world."

To make matters even worse, all this can happen even in Web communities you would assume to be safe, such as progressive blogs.

The bottom line is that *the Internet can easily seem like one ongoing parade of traumatic rejection.* Chabon again:

> Then there's that whole business of the Comments. Hell, it's bad enough when a book's coming out, and you open wide, and dig your nails into the arms of the chair, and wait for the stink of charred enamel to rise from the reviewers' whirring drills. The pleasure of a favorable notice lasts about three hours and twenty-four minutes; the sting of a bad one settles down to a dull ache that can endure for decades ... Bad enough, like I say, but man, that daily assessment down there in Disqusland—even when it was

mostly, even entirely, sweet and thoughtful and respectful, it was weirdly tough. Tough to withstand, tough to resist. And sometimes, today, tough to read. Maybe after a while a blogger hardens to it, I don't know.

On the Internet, rejection is constant and often vicious. And it takes its toll, having, among other consequences, a silencing effect. Popular food blogger Shauna James Ahern has written an eloquent *cri de coeur* about the ongoing, horrible abuse she endures, and notes that at one point, in the wake of nasty comments about her three-year-old daughter, she almost gave up: "We didn't want our lives public anymore. I thought about taking down this blog."[6]

Recently, I posted a political comment on a blog where I knew many people would be hostile to it. I wasn't trolling[7]: It was a site where I had participated for years, and where many of my views were in line with community norms. This particular view wasn't, however—although there were others who shared it. In fact, the blog owner had published a deliberately provocative post earlier that day, which other commenters had challenged, and I mainly wanted to post to support them.

For about an hour, I fretted over not just the wording of my twenty-line comment, but whether it was even appropriate to post, and whether I was going to be attacked, and, if so, how badly. Part of me wanted to forget the whole thing—I had work to do, after all, and who needs the stress? But I recalled abolitionist Abigail Kelley Foster's famous quote, "Go where you are least wanted, for there you are most needed." So I posted—and I'm happy to report that the blowback wasn't all that bad: a few people called me ignorant and naïve, but no one got really vicious. Afterwards, I was careful to give myself Rewards (Section 2.11), despite my inner perfectionist's disdainful deprecations that "it was only a blog post." The truth was, it *was* a big deal in my morning, and I took a real risk; moreover, I could take pride in standing up for a viewpoint I truly believe in.

---

[6] Shauna James Ahern, "Warm brown rice and grilled vegetable salad," Gluten Free Girl and the Chef (blog), August 30, 2011 (glutenfreegirl.com/warm-brown-rice-and-grilled-vegetable-salad/).

[7] Trolling is when you deliberately post something in opposition to the prevailing culture or norms of a blog, often with the deliberate intention of annoying people or provoking a fight.

Maybe Web participation is easier for most people than it is for me—although I doubt it, given how many people (including nearly all vicious attackers) publish anonymously or pseudonymously. I always publish under my real name, however: partly to show pride in my ideas and values, partly to combat any tendency toward internalized oppression, and partly because anonymity seems such a pain to maintain, and also so easily lost. And so, I continue to wrestle with the above problems, and totally sympathize if you do, too.

I can understand why anyone, and particularly women and others extra-likely to be attacked, would be reluctant to publish on the Web. But don't give up! We need your viewpoint and your voice, to whatever degree you feel comfortable sharing them. Figure out what you hope to accomplish from Web publishing, and devise a strategy for accomplishing it as safely as possible. One thing I always try to keep in mind is that, even if a few people are reacting obnoxiously to one of my posts, there are probably many more people who are quietly reading and thinking (and who see the bullies for who they are). Once in a while, one of those people kindly takes the time to write me and tell me that I've influenced their thinking.

The good news is, on the Web or off, the less perfectionist and more compassionately objective you get, the less rejection will matter. Yeah, it will still be "kinda bad" when someone criticizes your work, and "kinda good" when they praise it, but neither will actually matter much because you will be focused on the work itself, your internal rewards from the creative process, and the appreciation and respect of a few cherished readers whom you know "get it."

Chapter 8

Liberating Yourself from Exploitative Career Paths

For the first time in the history of publishing, writers have the upper hand. Don't piss that advantage away by thinking that this is still 1995.
　　　　　—J.A. Konrath, *The Newbie's Guide to Publishing*

Note: In this section, I focus mainly on book publishing because that's a key aim for many writers, and also because new technologies and business models make it the most exciting and empowered arena for writers today. Also, for all intents and purposes, freelancing for magazines and newspapers no longer exists as a career, due to the Internet and other factors.

Section 8.1 One Writer's Career

*I*f you want to see how the disempowering forces discussed in this book can converge on a writer's career and life, you need look no further than Tom Grimes's memoir *Mentor.* You'll find perfectionism aplenty in it (Sections 2.5 and 2.7), as well as a mentor relationship gone awry (Section 3.10) and traumatic rejection (Section 7.2).

Grimes's real disempowerment begins, however, when he starts selling his novel *Season's End*. From the moment he starts dealing with agents, editors, and publishers, he is manipulated and treated like a hanger-on to his own project. At one point, he spends an agonizing month awaiting feedback from his agent Eric on manuscript changes he had made—and that Eric himself had requested—but won't call him because "Protocol demanded authorial patience. The agent made contact, not the writer."

Later in the sales process, Eric obnoxiously says to him, "Several editors this week want to talk to you to see if you'll be difficult to work with ... No one likes a prima donna." (See the similarly manipulative and condescending "I won't be your mother hen" comment from the thesis advisor in Section A.3.)

But the worst instance of manipulation and control comes when Eric calls Grimes at 3:45 p.m. on the day of his book auction and tells him that it has come down to competing bids between Farrar, Straus & Giroux and Little, Brown and Co.:

> "Okay, let me think about it," I said, "And call you in the morning."
>
> As if he had to tell a child that his dog has died, Eric's voice took on a plaintive quality. "Tom, I can't ask these people to wait until tomorrow. They're sitting by their phones. They've been at this all day."
>
> "I have to decide now?" I said.
>
> "I can't put them off. They want to know, and it's five o'clock."
>
> I said, "I'll have to call you back."

Grimes calls his wife, who has no idea what to do, and then his mentor, Frank Conroy, who recommends that Grimes go with Little, Brown based solely on the larger advance. The decision turns out to be a disaster as *Season's End* is first "orphaned" (the editor who bought it left, and no one else stepped up to champion it to the marketing and sales teams), and then ineptly marketed as a "baseball book" instead of a literary novel. It sold few copies and got disappointing reviews from *The New York Times* and other important venues (although good ones elsewhere). Grimes, who had been pumped up by Conroy and others to expect stratospheric success, was devastated, and later suffered severe mental illness in part due to the experience.

Bad vs. Good Mentors

One of the most heartbreaking aspects of *Mentor* is how Grimes repeatedly blames himself unfairly for setbacks caused by others. "The paramount reason [for the book's failure] was my stupidity. First, I sold my book after considering my options for less than fifteen fraught minutes." But he asked for the time and wasn't given it—and nor did his mentor tell him to insist.

Also: "It's clear to me now: I'm a failure as a writer because I've overreached; my ambition was larger than my talent." But it was Conroy who irresponsibly inflated Grimes's ambitions and hopes from the beginning, and who never took responsibility for doing so. Moreover—and this is not unusual in tales of disempowerment—in instance after instance, Grimes appears to have made reasonable decisions in the absence of information and support, and to have advocated for himself. Within moments of meeting Grimes at Iowa, for instance, and based solely on the fragment of the novel Grimes had submitted with his application, Conroy offers him "the best agent in America" (his own agent, Candida Donadio). I admire Grimes for maintaining his cool *and* focus at that moment, as he responds: "Thanks. Is it okay if I don't commit right now ... I'd rather write the book without that pressure." (At that moment, he's actually doing both his job and Conroy's, who, as the mentor, should have been the voice of pragmatic caution.)

Conroy also offers Grimes a prestigious scholarship, which Grimes shrewdly turns down in favor of teaching assistantships he thinks will aid his future job prospects.

Of course, Grimes was aided in his self-blame by others who either didn't take responsibility for their actions, or blamed him for problems he didn't cause—primarily Conroy, but also Eric:

> Little, Brown mailed Eric twenty-four review clippings: each positive, each approximately twenty-four words long, and each from a newspaper's sports section. With a trace of exasperation and complaint in his voice Eric said, "Tom, I can't do anything with these," meaning, the reviews were worthless. He couldn't use them to promote the book ... I don't believe Eric intended to make me feel responsible for the length and nature of the reviews ... nevertheless, he did.

Some of Grimes's decisions did turn out to be wrong, but of course you can't predict or control outcomes, so there's no point feeling bad if you've honestly done your best (Section 2.10). Grimes's most serious mistake, it would appear, was his continued reliance on Conroy, Eric, and other inept mentors; and one of the most excruciating aspects of *Mentor* is the occasional appearance of competent mentors who stand in stark contrast. These include a woman at a party who tells him, "The next time you get an offer from Farrar, Straus, take it," and Sam Lawrence, a renowned publisher who looked kindly on Grimes and his work and advised him, "The next time someone tells you that you have fifteen minutes to decide what to do with a book you spent two years writing, you tell him to go fuck himself."

Early in *Mentor*, Grimes notes in passing that while working to support himself as a writer he had managed two successful businesses in Manhattan. He's clearly a competent person who had also managed to rise from a difficult background. Only in a fundamentally disempowering system would such an achiever fail so short of his goals and blame himself so unfairly.

Section 8.2 More Disempowerment

Grimes is not the only writer to have gotten treated like crap by publishing professionals, only to subsequently blame himself for his own disempowerment. S.J. Culver is another. I mentioned her article on the effects of having gotten a rejection slip *838 days* after sending out the manuscript in Section 7.2. Elsewhere in the same article she writes:

> On my computer's hard drive languish five partial drafts of the novel I began writing in 2008. All of the drafts are between 100-200 pages in length. I don't think any of the abandoned drafts are terrible, which, in a way, is worse than thinking they're just unworkable. Those drafts make me think the problem is simply that I cannot finish a book-length work. I don't have the stamina, the attention span. I have game, but I can't close. Some of this paralysis is surely caused by ineptitude—if I knew how to write a novel, I would have written the damn

thing by now—but I'm suspicious of the effects of the writer's gospel of resignation.

That Culver is *not* lazy, unfocused, inept, etc., is abundantly illustrated by "the short list of things I did with my life" during those 838 days, which includes:

> I completed an MFA in creative writing, taught five semesters' worth of college freshmen how to write, and, after 149 job applications, landed a full-time position with health insurance and a 401(k). I wrote a dozen more stories and the beginning of a novel. I sold reviews and articles to various markets. I actually *published the story in question in another magazine.*

The main lesson Culver appears to derive from her traumatic rejection is that she should learn acceptance. "This mantra of acceptance is everywhere. Acceptance of the difficulty of the writing task. Acceptance of the waiting. Acceptance of the greatly flawed and hugely problematic enterprise of mainstream publishing. Acceptance—grimly—of rejection itself." But I don't think she really believes that. For one thing, she lacks the subversive glee of Chris Offutt when he describes reframing his goal from acceptance to "a hundred rejections in a year" (Section 7.4). And she writes:

> Low expectations are not a recipe for good self-care. You get sour; you drink too much wine; you stop reading because everything you read makes you even more sour; you go on diatribes against successful young writers in the kitchens at parties. You definitely are not working out. Eventually you wear a hole in one of the elbows of your bathrobe and instead of taking it off, you think, "That makes sense. It's nice to have a little air circulating around. They should make all the bathrobes this way."

What she's describing actually sounds less like acceptance and more like learned helplessness, an almost inevitable result of systematic disempowerment. On some level, however, she seems to understand the unfairness of it all, since her anger peeps out at times. She notes at the start of her article that "I have too much personal integrity" to name the magazine that rejected her, only to add, "That was a joke; I don't; I'm just scared of editorial blacklists."

Section 8.3 The Bad Deal for Writers That Is Traditional Publishing

This entire book is about the costs, to writers, of disempowerment, and so I cannot in good conscience recommend that any writer get involved in a disempowering system—and that means I can't recommend you go the traditional book publishing route, which typically consists of:

- Sending query letters to dozens of agents or editors; then spending months or years waiting and hoping you've engaged someone's interest.

- If you do engage someone's interest, submitting a book proposal and/or partial manuscript (first three chapters); and then waiting more weeks or months. (I suppose we should be grateful that the publishers finally relaxed their long-held iron-clad rule against "simultaneous submissions," which meant that writers could only submit to one editor at a time and had to wait for months or even more than a year before they could even submit to another.)

- If the editor is interested, being asked to submit a full manuscript—and waiting yet more weeks or months.

- Having little or no say in important marketing and sales decisions. We saw how Tom Grimes's book got miscategorized as a baseball book; another (pretty egregious) example are the many books by non-white authors, and with non-white protagonists, that somehow wind up with white people on the covers.[1]

- Having to shoulder nearly the entire burden of marketing and sales yourself. Most publishers will list your book in a catalog; send out review copies (but not strongly advocate for reviews); create a Web page on their site for you

---

[1] See, for instance, Kate Harding, "Publisher whitens another heroine of color," Salon (website), January 19, 2010 (www.salon.com/life/broadsheet/feature/2010/01/19/cover_whitewashing/index.html).

(perhaps with a "video trailer"); print up advertising post-cards; and brief their sales teams, if they have one. They *might* even help organize—but often not pay for—a book tour, and they might pay for some ads, or give you or some bookstores "co-op" marketing dollars to promote your readings. Generally speaking, the better known you are, or the more salable your book is considered, the more support you'll get—but even many successful writers get little support.

While publishers may say (and even believe) that the above represents an extraordinary commitment, it really isn't—especially since they don't hold themselves accountable for the result (see the Diamant story in Section 8.8). And it doesn't even begin to match the effort you will be expected to make marketing and selling your book, which usually consists of spending hundreds of hours and thousands of dollars each year on a website and other online promotion, and still more time and money traveling to give readings or appear at conferences

- All of the above, usually for a minimal advance and a royalty payment of around $.50–$2 per book.

Oh, and:

- No loyalty. A couple of generations ago, some publishers prided themselves on not just finding and nurturing talent, but sticking with a productive writer through the (reasonable) highs and lows of her career. These days, however, conglomerate-owned publishers dump even reliably selling authors to make room in their catalogs for the latest celebrity tell-all or faddish bestseller.

Mind you, all of the above is when the publishing process goes *as planned*. Like everything else, however, it can go awry. Stories of agents and editors who are incompetent, uninvolved, overworked, or simply go AWOL are legion. I know one writer who politely inquired why her agent had missed an important meeting, only to be told, in essence, "I have thirty writers like you, so if you're not happy with my work we don't have to do business."

I also know writers who have been stuck in "revision hell": being asked by an agent or editor to revise their submission, then waiting months to hear back, and then being asked to revise and wait again. That's months or years of excruciating extra work and suspense, with no guarantee of publication.

In *Be the Monkey*, an ebook on self-publishing co-written by Barry Eisler and J.A. Konrath, Konrath notes:

> My publishers have made a lot of mistakes. Some of them big. Some of them which cost me, are costing me, money. Talking to other writers, I know I'm not alone. Almost every writer I know has gotten screwed by their publisher, in one way or another. I know hundreds of writers, and I can count on one hand the number of my peers who have no publisher complaints. Bad covers, title changes, editing conflicts, slow payments, unclear royalty statements, orphaned books, bad launches. The list is so long that I have to wonder if we're not being intentionally screwed.

The situation is better, in some ways, with the small presses, but still far from ideal. Small presses often care more about your work, and so they often do a better job at editing and production. They may even give you more say in the marketing and sales process. But most won't give you an advance, and they'll still expect a major investment from you in terms of marketing and sales while offering little support or recompense in exchange.

Of course, there are many good people in publishing—people who care deeply about books. However, there's only so much that even they can do in the throes of a fundamentally disempowering system.

It doesn't have to be that way, as we'll see in the next chapter.

Section 8.4 Self-Publishing: The Only Way to Go

Contrast our examples of disempowered writers with these:

> Brunonia Barry self-published 2,500 copies of her novel *The Lace Reader*, sold them via an aggressive marketing campaign, and then signed a $2 million deal with William Morrow/HarperCollins.

Neuroscientist Lisa Genova self-published *Still Alice*, her novel about a woman afflicted with early-onset Alzheimer's Disease, after spending nearly a year unsuccessfully trying to interest agents and editors in it. She promoted it aggressively via a website that became an online hub for information about Alzheimer's, and also via a blog on the Alzheimer's Association website. She eventually sold it to Simon & Schuster for more than $500,000.

Julia Fox Garrison never considered approaching agents or publishers with her memoir *P.S. Julia*. "Instead of wasting my energies trying to appeal to agents and publishers, I was able to put all my time into my vision of how I wanted my story presented. It was like giving birth, and I was very protective of my baby."[2] Instead, she self-published it and marketed it aggressively; it was eventually purchased by HarperCollins, which released it under the title *Don't Leave Me This Way*.

Christopher Paolini wrote his first novel, *Eragon*, when he was fifteen. His family's company published it, and Paolini promoted it by giving readings at more than a hundred libraries, bookstores, and schools across the United States. Eventually writer Carl Hiaasen saw the book and introduced Paolini to his editor at Alfred A. Knopf, under whose imprint it later became a bestseller.

My friend Ann Herendeen spent six months seeking an agent or publisher for her genre-busting first novel, *Phyllida and the Brotherhood of Philander*, a bisexual Regency romance, then decided to self-publish. It attracted a devoted cult following and was eventually bought by an editor at HarperCollins, which has also published her second book *Pride/Prejudice*, a bisexual version of you-know-what.

---

[2]Piper, "She's Looked at Life From Both Sides Now," Smith (blog), August 4, 2006 (www.smithmag.net/memoirville/2006/08/04/shes-looked-at-life-from-both-sides-now/).

By self-publishing, these authors opted out of the disempower-ing system I've been describing, at least until they were able to enter it more on more equal terms. It's not incidental that at least two of them had business experience (Paolini and also Barry, who co-owned a games development company with her husband): this accounts not just for their marketing prowess, but, I'm guessing, their unwilling-ness to submit to a disempowering system. Businesspeople learn early on that unequal, disempowering relationships are a dead end (see next section).

The rationale for self-publishing only intensifies with ebooks, where "publishing" amounts to creating a digital file, and "distribution" to sending that file over the Internet. The current ebook self-publish-ing star is young-adult fiction author Amanda Hocking, who, after enduring "countless rejections from book agents,"[3] sold hundreds of thousands of her ebooks on Amazon, and then landed a $2 million contract with St. Martin's Press.

Hocking is a spectacular example, but hardly unique:

> Writer Karen McQuestion spent nearly a decade trying without success to persuade a New York publisher to print one of her books. In July, the 49-year-old mother of three decided to publish it herself, online. Eleven months later, Ms. McQuestion has sold 36,000 e-books through Amazon. com Inc.'s Kindle e-bookstore and has a film option with a Hollywood producer. In August, Amazon will publish a paperback version of her first novel, "A Scattered Life," about a friendship triangle among three women in small-town Wisconsin."... "All of this time I have been trying to get traditionally published, I was sending my manuscript to the wrong coast," says Ms. McQuestion.[4]

It's perhaps not surprising that savvy novices are turning to self-publishing and e-publishing. What is more surprising—and even

[3]Tara Bannow, "Amanda Hocking Signs Four-Book Deal With St. Martin's Press," March 24, 2011 (www.huffingtonpost.com/2011/03/24/amanda-hocking_n_840169.html), originally published by the Associated Press.

[4]Geoffrey Fowler and Jeffrey Trachtenberg, "'Vanity' Press Goes Digital," *Wall Street Journal*, June 3, 2010 (online.wsj.com/article/SB100014240527487049120045752 53132121412028.html).

more damning of traditional publishing—is that successful writers are also embracing it, an example being *Be the Monkey* co-author Barry Eisler, who opted out of a $500,000 deal with St. Martin's Press:

> I'm confident I can do better financially over the long term on my own ... But it's not just the destination that matters to me; it's also important that I enjoy the trip. And ceding creative control over packaging, not to mention control over key decisions like pricing and timing, has never been comfortable for me. It might be okay if I thought my publishers were making all the right decisions, but when your publisher is doing something you think is stupid and that's costing you money—something like, say, saddling your book with a closeup of an olive green garage door, or writing a bio that treats your date and place of birth as a key selling point ... or otherwise blowing the book's packaging—it can be pretty maddening.[5]

Other successful writers who are also turning to self-publishing include science fiction writer F. Paul Wilson, who anticipates making "as much as $5,000 to $10,000" a month e-publishing his out-of-print books, and *Be the Monkey*'s Konrath, who "says he's already earning more from self-published Kindle books that New York publishers rejected than from his print books."[6] And literally the day I was writing this (June 23, 2011), J.K. Rowling announced that she would be self-publishing ebooks of the entire *Harry Potter* series. Lest there be any doubt about my viewpoint, I'll state it plainly: **self-publishing is the only way to go.** Maybe you'll do it as your primary career strategy, or maybe you'll do it to build your audience so you can win a more equitable deal with a traditional publisher. Or maybe you'll combine self-publishing and traditional publishing throughout

---

[5]Barry Eisler, "Why I'm Self-Publishing," The Daily Beast (blog), March 24, 2011 (www.thedailybeast.com/articles/2011/03/24/barry-eisler-explains-self-publishing-decision.html).

[6]Both the Wilson and Konrath stories are from the *Wall Street Journal* article cited in footnote 4. Regarding Wilson's story, note that when traditionally published books go out of print, the rights to them typically revert to the author. This story also illustrates how traditional publishers often give up on books that still have a lot of life—and sales—left in them.

your career. But it's hard to envision an empowered writing career that doesn't involve at least some strong element of self-publishing.

All this is definitely true for fiction writers, and it will also be true for many nonfiction writers, except, perhaps, for celebrated entrepreneurs, popular experts, trendy memoirists, and others who can command a big advance from a traditional publisher.

Is self-publishing easy? No and yes. "No" in the sense that no ambitious venture is truly easy. "Yes" in that it's a rational enterprise in which your result depends largely on the quality of your effort and investment, especially in the areas of marketing and sales. That alone is a big improvement over traditional publishing, which for many writers has basically been a misery-generating crapshoot. But don't take my word for it—here's best-selling author and Internet marketing guru Seth Godin (who has also given up traditional publishing in favor of self-publishing) on why even obscure authors should self-publish:

No Knight, No Shining Armor.

"Sure, Seth can do that, because he has a popular blog."

Some people responded to my decision to forgo traditional publishers (not traditional books, btw) by pointing out that I can do that because I have a way of reaching readers electronically.

What they missed is that this asset is a choice, not an accident.

Does your project depend on a miracle, a bolt of lightning, on being chosen by some arbiter of who will succeed? I think your work is too important for you to depend on a lottery ticket. In some ways, this is the work of the Resistance, an insurance policy that gives you deniability if the project doesn't succeed. "Oh, it didn't work because we didn't get featured on that blog, didn't get distribution in the right store, didn't get the right endorsement..."

There's nothing wrong with leverage, no problem at all with an unexpected lift that changes everything. But why would you build that as the foundation of your plan?

The magic of the tribe is that you can build it incrementally, that day by day you can earn the asset that will allow you to bring your work to people who want it. Or you can skip that and wait to get picked. Picked to be on Oprah or American Idol or at the cash register at Borders.

Getting picked is great. Building a tribe is reliable, it's hard work and it's worth doing.[7]

The fact that you're reading this book shows that self-publishing can work even for someone much more obscure than Godin. I'll tell you the steps I took to get here in Section 8.9. First, however, let's examine the essential differences between empowered and disempowered careers—one of the most important topics in this entire book. And then we'll explore the details of strategy and marketing for empowered self-publishing writers.

Section 8.5 Disempowered vs. Empowered Careers

It is very important to your writing, and your life in general, that you understand the difference between disempowered and empowered careers.

Disempowered careers:

- *Are vague and irrational.* The goal ("to have a best seller") is often ill-defined, and so is the path for getting there. Luck plays way too large a role, so it's hard to make wise choices and you can't predict the outcomes of your efforts. (Note how closely this irrational, luck-dependent scenario gibes with, and supports, perfectionist grandiosity; Section 2.2). Two related problems are:

  Faddishness. Publishers are notorious for jumping on

---

[7]Seth Godin, "No Knight, No Shining Armor," Seth Godin's Blog (blog), November 11, 2010 (sethgodin.typepad.com/seths_blog/2010/11/no-knight-no-shining-armor.html). © 2010 Seth Godin. Used with permission. (By "Resistance," by the way, he's referring to Steven Pressfield's conception of procrastination, from The War of Art.)

the latest fad—be it drug memoir, chick lit, or something else—and then just as abruptly jumping off. If your book happens to even vaguely fit that fad, lucky you—although you might regret it later if your book gets hideously mis-marketed. But if your book doesn't fit the current fad, you're going to have a tough time getting noticed.

As alluded to by Godin above, **overinfluential and often arbitrary gatekeepers** with disproportionate power over your fate. In publishing, these aren't just editors or agents, but teachers in MFA programs who connect favored students with agents and publishers (Section A.8), and the legions of overworked, underpaid, underqualified, low-level staffers who are often the first-line reader at many agencies and publishers.

- *Are unstrategic/unplanned.* Of course, you can't plan within an irrational system.
- *Don't leverage your strengths.* (Or others'.) As Grimes's story illustrates, it's hard to act effectively within a disempowering system. Your strategic, creative, business, and other talents will all largely go to waste.
- *Force you to spend time on low-value activities.* For instance, mailing out dozens of query letters, or spending hours trying to convince your publisher to make sane marketing decisions.
- *Mire you in overgiving and codependency* (Sections 4.8 and 4.9). For instance, jumping through hoops to get an agent or editor, and then doing most of the work to maintain that relationship. Also, lots of boundary violations—e.g., relationships that merge the professional and personal—and lots of unspoken needs and motives.
- *Reject or underutilize 21st-century technologies and business models.* Even into the 1990s, many agents and editors were not accepting queries via email. More recently, many publishers remain behind the curve on ebooks and social media.
- *Tend to isolate you or embed you in unhealthy communities.* Such as bitchy, competitive workshops or cult-like

coteries of acolytes of famous writers or editors.

- ***Unsustainable, financially, emotionally, and otherwise. Also, negatively impact the rest of your life.*** How much inequality, rejection, poverty, and stress can you take?

Disempowered careers are also characterized by:

- ***Unequal access.*** See, for instance, Tom Grimes's interactions with his agent (Section 8.1).
- ***Automatic bias/disrespect.*** Consider the term "slush pile," which agents and editors use to refer to their stack of unsolicited queries or manuscripts, each representing some writer's cherished dream.
- ***Disparity in investment, and return-on-investment (ROI).*** You spend years writing a book and someone spends minutes evaluating it. Or you spend years writing it, and considerable time and money promoting it, but get only a minute fraction of each sale.
- ***Devaluation of your needs.*** For example, for a prompt reply to a submission, or prompt payment, or a clear royalty statement, or a cover that reflects the book's intent.
- ***Harsh or callous rejections.*** See, for instance, the Grimes and Culver examples in Sections 8.1 and 8.2.
- ***Misaligned incentives and objectives.*** Meaning, people get rewarded for the wrong activities—or no activity. For instance, booksellers who get full refunds from publishers when they fail to sell your book, and therefore have no incentive to actually sell it— especially when the latest celebrity tell-all just flies off the shelves. Or, the amount of effort you want your publisher to put into marketing and selling your book versus the amount they're actually prepared to put into it, given that they've got dozens of books— including that tell-all!—to promote this season.
- ***Rigidity.*** It's the publisher's (or editor's) way or the highway. (Another perfectionist symptom, by the way; see Section 2.7.)
- ***Short-term thinking.*** Publishers often abandon books if they don't sell strongly within the first 90 days. (And yet another perfectionist symptom.)
- ***Victim-blaming.*** Despite all of the widely recognized

shortcomings of traditional publishing, if a book doesn't sell, the publisher is likely to blame the book or writer.

Empowered careers, in contrast:

- *Have precisely defined goals, and are rational.* The goal is clearly defined, and so is the path for getting there. The role of luck is minimized, and there are no overly influential gatekeepers.
- *Are planned and strategic.* Strategic means the plan is crafted by working backwards from goals. (See next section.)
- *Leverage, and build on, your strengths,* and those of others. Also, *let you invest most of your time in high-value activities* (Section 4.8), such as writing, building your audience, and supervising the Web developers, marketers, and bookkeepers whom you can, in an empowered career, afford to hire.
- *Support clear and healthy boundaries.* Responsibilities are transparent and rational, and everyone's responsible for meeting their own needs but also motivated to support everyone else in meeting theirs.
- *Leverage 21st-century technologies and business models.* The bulk of these are hugely empowering of writers—which may, in fact, be why publishers have been so slow to embrace them.
- *Engage you in healthy, egalitarian communities.* For instance, the professional writers' associations (romance, science fiction, mystery) mentioned in Section 3.9.
- *Are financially, emotionally, and otherwise sustainable.* In fact, they add joy, meaning, and sustainability to the rest of your life.

Empowered careers are also characterized by:

- *Equality of power and access.*
- *Respect.*
- *Reasonable returns-on-investment (ROI).* In most cases, a writer who self-publishes a salable book can expect to make much more money per book than one who goes with a traditional publisher. How much? For a paperback book, you should aim for *at least* a 50% profit over your production and marketing costs (Section 8.9). For

an ebook, you should expect to retain anywhere from 60% to 100% of the sale, depending on whether you sell the book off your own site or off another site that takes a commission. You'll have to subtract credit card fees (usually 2% to 3%), and perhaps the cost of an inexpensive shopping cart service, from the above profits. But even after you do, your profit will far outstrip the measly 5–10% royalty payment you could expect to earn from a traditional publisher.

- **Compassionate rejections.** Because (1) you're dealing with equals, (2) codependency is minimized, and (3) everyone is operating in a climate of empowerment and abundance, instead of disempowerment and scarcity. Also **consideration of your needs**, for the same reasons.

- **Aligned incentives and objectives.** The freelance artist, editor, and marketer/Web developer whom you hire to assist you—and who probably want you to hire them again for your next book—are far more likely to care about doing a fantastic job than your publisher's overworked and underbudgeted marketing team.

- **Flexibility.** You can try different publishing or marketing tactics and see what works. Flexibility is a hallmark of empowerment, and one of the really fun aspects of self-publishing.

- **Long-term thinking.** I.e., in terms of what's best for your career and life, instead of having to reactively chase the latest fad.

- **Problem-solving, rather than blaming, orientation.** And when conflicts arise, they are resolved cooperatively (Section 4.11)

Can you be empowered in a disempowering system? There are two answers to this:

(1) Perhaps, but why bother? There's plenty of empowerment in the world.

(2) To do it, you need to know exactly what the rules are AND you have to be at the top of your game. In fact, that's precisely how successful authors have always succeeded—by treating publishing like the business it is, and ignoring grandiose misconceptions (Section 2.2), pervasive deprecations (Section 6.7), and especially disempowering strictures concerning how writers are "supposed to" behave—e.g., that they're supposed to be grateful for the opportunity to be published, and satisfied with the crumbs from the publisher's table.

In the absence of today's fabulous print-on-demand and Web technologies, those authors didn't really have a choice but to work within the system. We do. So, I repeat: Why bother? The fantastic Konrath quote that I began this chapter of *The Seven Secrets of the Prolific* with bears repeating:

> For the first time in the history of publishing, writers have the upper hand. Don't piss that advantage away by thinking that this is still 1995.

Section 8.6 Empowered Careers Begin with a Clear Vision and a Plan

What is your goal for your writing?

It is very important that you answer this simple seeming, but perhaps not so simple, question.

Do you want fame? Fortune? The admiration of a select few?

To achieve certain aesthetic or creative goals?

Or simply to enjoy yourself and revel in self-expression?

Or some combination of all of the above?

Further, what does each of your goals mean to you? By "fame," do you mean you want to get on a prestigious bestseller list? Or do you mean you want to be a recognizable name in your niche or genre—so that, although you're not one of the superstars, you still have those gratifying experiences where strangers email you and tell you how much your work means to them? (Hint, hint...)

And what is a "fortune?" Would you be content with half an income a year? (Perhaps because someone else in the household is providing the other half.) Or a full income? And what constitutes a "full income"? $50,000? $100,000? $250,000? More?

And how soon do you want it?

Are you prepared to write a book every year or two, in a profitable genre, and market the heck out of all of them—investing a lot of time and money in the process—so that maybe in ten years you're supporting yourself entirely through your writing? Do you have the time, energy, and focus to do that?

Or do you want or need to take things slower?

Remember that it's fine to have ambitious goals: what makes a goal grandiose is not simply its scope but whether you are prepared to make the necessary investments and sacrifices to achieve it (Section 2.2).

After you're done clarifying your goals, quantify them and give them deadlines. Then, create a plan for achieving them. Here are some tips for planning:

- ***Work from models.*** Find writers whose success you wish to emulate and study how they got to where they are. Also, join a writer's community and interact with local successful writers (Sections 3.9 and 3.10), even if their successes aren't exactly of the type you're after. You'll still learn a lot.

- ***Plan backwards from your goals.*** Write down your goals for the next couple of years, and also five and ten years from now. Then write down the series of steps that will get you there, and what you want the result of each step to be. (Example: "Step 3. Attend XYZ Writer's Conference. Desired Result: Meet Writers A and B; learn tricks for marketing historical novels.")

- The steps in your plan should be ***baby steps***—easily attainable—and your estimate of the yield from each step should be conservative. E.g., "My aim in meeting Writer A is not to get him to agree to include me in his anthology, but to get his permission to follow up after the meeting on that topic."

- You should also write down the ***resources*** (e.g., money, time, assistance, mentorship) you'll require to accomplish each step. Remember: The prolific resource themselves abundantly (Section 3.4).

- ***Don't overplan.*** A two- or three-page document that you consult and update regularly will help enormously in keeping you on track.

- Important! ***Show your plan to your mentors*** and ask the important questions, "Will this plan get me to where I want to go?" "Did I leave anything out?" "How can I strengthen it?" And, "Are there any people you know whom I should talk to, or resources you know of that could be useful to me?"

Section 8.7 Two Key Questions

There are two key questions you're going to need to answer:
    (1) Do I want a publisher or an audience? And,
    (2) Do I want to be in business?
Let's take them one at a time.

    Publisher vs. audience? I hope that by now you've learned to separate your desire for a publisher from your desire for an audience. In the past, you often needed the former to get the latter—although not always, as there were self-publishing triumphs even in the bad, old pre-Internet days, including the Boston Women's Health Book Collective's *Our Bodies, Ourselves* and Julia Cameron's *The Artist's Way*. (Both dealing with empowerment, by the way.) These days, however, writers are fully empowered to build their own audiences via the Internet and allied technologies, independent of the help of a publisher.

    If you're one of those writers who feels you must "be published" to be legitimate, please revisit the section on that fatal fallacy in Section 6.7 and do your best to overcome it. It's so much more productive, not to mention fun, to focus on your craft and audience-building than it is to knuckle under to a disempowering system.

    Am I in business? Most writers follow one of the three career paths summarized in the table below:

    (I omit from this analysis the wonderful emotional and community benefits of a creativity-centered lifestyle, including joy, fulfillment, and the camaraderie of wonderful people, all of which can be derived from any of the paths.)

    To be clear, *any* of the paths is a good choice if it syncs with your values and needs. The "Business/Hobby" path is a bit risky in that it can easily devolve into a "worst of both worlds" scenario where you wind up doing all the work of a business without getting the payoff. That and the "Hobby" path are fine, however, *unless* you're choosing them because you're afraid to try the "Business" path. (In that case, take a business class at a local community college or microenterprise organization, and also hang out with professional writers with a business orientation—business ain't so bad.)

    I'm partial to the Business and Business/Hobby paths not just because it's good to get paid for our efforts, but because getting paid helps us "rationalize" (in the sense of making rational) our interactions. It also helps put the brakes on overgiving—and when you and those around you are all focused on exchanging fair value, the result can be a

	Business Path	Business/Hobby Path	Hobby Path
Income Goal	All or most income from writing and writing-related activities (e.g., teaching, lecturing).	Some income from writing and writing related activities.	No income from writing and writing related activities.
Supporting Goals	1) Yearly robust profit that, over time, yields income growth and wealth accumulation.	1) Small or intermittent profit, which yields income supplement but probably no wealth accumulation.	1) No income or wealth impact. (In fact, you're probably putting money into your writing for a Website, memberships, workshops, etc.)
	2) The largest possible audience for your work.	2) A somewhat larger audience than your immediate circle.	2) Audience is typically limited to your immediate circle or a little beyond.
	3) Tax deductions and other financial benefits.	3) Tax deductions and other financial benefits.	3) No tax deductions or other financial benefits.
Time Investment	Full time, with approximately 50% of work time devoted to marketing, sales and management.	Less time overall, and a lesser percentage devoted to marketing, sales and management.	Overall time need variable, and no need to market, sell, manage.
Compromises	1) You'll probably need to compromise the type and style of your writing at least somewhat to maximize salability and income.	Less income than a serious business, but more business "chores" than a hobby.	No income from writing, but also no "chores."
	2) A lot of your income goes back into marketing and sales.		
Lifestyle Impact	Possibility of leaving day job (big time and happiness win!). Also, a full-time writing career can be incredibly fulfilling.	No possibility of leaving day job. Risk of regret from wondering what you could have achieved had you gone all out?	No possibility of leaving day job. Risk of regret from wondering what you could have achieved had you gone all out?

kind of miracle. "After all these years, everything is finally working like it should!" a musician friend of mine said, after she had left the chaotic and underpaid world of performing and become a well-paid voiceover artist. "I market, I use my referrals, I sell, and voila! I get work!"

The primary goal in business, after ethics, is **profit**, or a net gain of income over expenses. Profit is the hallmark of a healthy business, and it creates not just business sustainability, but health, wealth, and happiness in the entrepreneur. More on profit in Section 8.9.

Because of the financial implications of the choices, you should consult your accountant before deciding.

Section 8.8 Marketing (and Sales)

First, three success stories:

When her publisher did little to market her first novel, *Mama,* Terry McMillan (later famous for *Waiting to Exhale*) sent, at her own expense, thousands of letters to bookstores, libraries, colleges, and other organizations in African-American communities asking them to buy and support it. Thanks to her efforts, it sold out its first edition and went through two more reprintings in just six weeks.

When Anita Diamant's publisher was ready to pulp[8] unsold copies of her first novel, *The Red Tent*, which told the story of Dinah, the sister of Joseph (of "coat of many colors" fame), she convinced them instead to send free copies to rabbis. The rabbis promoted it within their congregations and communities, and it eventually became a bestseller.

Spencer Johnson spent years sending copies of his business-advice book *Who Moved My Cheese?* to CEOs of major corporations, some of whom bought thousands of copies for their staffs. It, too, became a bestseller.

The first two lessons you should draw from these stories are that **marketing is powerful**—which makes sense; corporations wouldn't spend billions on it each year if weren't—and that **writers can be great marketers**. The latter should come as no surprise, given that marketing is all about communication, observation, and analysis, three skills

---

[8]Yes, traditional publishing is so dysfunctional that it will even destroy a perfectly good product rather than take a little trouble to come up with new ways to sell it. (The Diamant and Johnson stories are from Al Ries and Laura Ries, *The Fall of Advertising and the Rise of PR*. New York: Harper Paperbacks, 2004.)

many writers have in abundance.

The implied third lesson is that **you should market**. Marketing is your vehicle to whatever success you are after, whether it's fame, fortune, or the respect of your peers (and the job opportunities that flow therefrom). Besides, marketing goes with writing like PB goes with J: once you've written something you're proud of, don't you want as many people as possible to see it? Marketing is just the thing for that.

People make a big fuss about sales—no one's written a play called *Death of a Marketer*, after all—but it's marketing that creates the customers. If you market effectively, customers will visit your website, come to your reading, or stop by your conference table primed to buy. Then, all you have to do is finalize the transaction (more on this, below).

The goal of marketing is to create a clear image in the *right* customer's mind of who you are and what you are selling. Marketing is what impels the reader with a yen for an action-packed romance novel with a fun, quirky heroine to Jennifer Crusie, or the one who wants a suspenseful thriller served up with a goofy side of humor to J.A. Konrath, or the one who craves acutely observed comic essays about life and love to David Sedaris.

Marketing is therefore about creating a perception—but the first person you have to do that for is yourself. If you're on a Business path (see last section), you've committed to doing a lot of marketing, and so you need to see yourself as a marketer as well as a writer. (Ditto for Business/Hobby, albeit to a lesser extent.) If a part of you is thinking marketing is weird, pushy, or a distraction from your "real" work, please do some journaling around those ambivalences, because they will hold you back.

Twentieth-century marketing was all about broadcasting—meaning, I send out my message to many passive recipients, who are not empowered to respond. Twenty-first-century marketing, however, is all about interactivity, reciprocity, and community-building. It's about asking for people's opinions—even about things like what your heroine's name should be, and whether her dog should be a basset or a corgi. (Or—heaven forfend!—a cat.) It's also about telling them the story behind the story; letting them enter your world and life and work process to whatever extent you're comfortable.

And it's about showing up—because although the Web is a great billboard, it's still weak for sales. Many people want to see your face and hear your voice before they'll buy (see below).

If all this sounds like a lot of work, you're right: it is. Marketing does take time, so be a good writer and do your time management as discussed in Chapter 4. If you've got twenty hours a week to "write," it may be that you apportion eight or ten of those to your marketing, sales, and management. Maybe you'd rather not do that—and, if so, I sympathize. But that's the path you signed up for. If you really object to time spent marketing, then settle on your writing as a Hobby and be done with it.

Be aware that the minute you start marketing, you basically become a public figure. In fact, that's the point! And if that squicks you out, I wouldn't blame you one bit, because once you become a public figure, you are not only psychologically exposed but vulnerable to others' misbehavior. People can—and will—say mean things about you or your writing. They'll visit your website and start trolling around or otherwise behaving badly (Section 7.6). They'll mock you for your mistakes, and also for your accomplishments and virtues.

In person, you'll meet some tedious people, obnoxious people, importuning people—maybe, if you're unlucky, a harassing person or two. (The techniques in Section 4.9 will help with the first three types, at least.)

I won't deny it—that's all a drag. And I'm guessing that some successful writers would gladly give up the "public figure" part of the job description if they could. But they can't, and so eventually they learn to cope with it the way one copes with bad weather or dental work or the bad part of any job—meaning, they mostly ignore it. It also goes without saying that, along with the bad'uns, you'll meet many, many terrific and supportive people, and that the life of a successful writer is, generally speaking, fantastic.

There are lots of different ways to market, so you can play to your strengths. If you like to give readings or workshops, you can do that. If you like to write blog posts and articles, you can do that. If you like schmoozing at professional meetings or other venues, you can do *that*. (The best approach is a combination of all three, but you can emphasize the one(s) you're most comfortable with.) But all these tactics involve public exposure, and so you'll have to come to terms with that. I suggest getting out there a little at a time, and taking the time to adjust between steps; gradually, you'll get more used to it. (This all also amounts to a coming-out process, so also refer to Section 6.6.)

You can try a pseudonym, but that's a dicey strategy in the Internet age. Eventually you'll be found out, and in the meantime your ability to market will be impaired. Some writers use pseudonyms to enhance the salability of their books—for instance, some writers of historical romance use old-fashioned-sounding names, and writers who write in multiple genres often use a different name for each—but that's different because they're not doing it to hide, and don't care much if they're found out.

Marketing is a huge topic, one that people have written entire books, and libraries, on. Below are some general tips, followed by a strategy for getting started. I highly recommend J.A. Konrath's *The Newbie's Guide to Publishing* not just for the "how to" details, but insight into the mind and methods of a writer who is also a relentless marketer. Also, read fun marketing classics by authors like Harry Beckwith (*Selling the Invisible*) and Al Ries and Jack Trout (*The 22 Immutable Laws of Marketing*); and you should also be sure to read the works of new media marketing gurus like Seth Godin (*Permission Marketing* and his newsletter) and Adam Singer (his "The Future Buzz" newsletter).

Here are some more tips:

- **Work from models.** Don't reinvent the wheel: find writers whose success you wish to emulate and see how they market themselves. Study their websites, subscribe to their newsletters, read their press releases, and see what conferences they show up at—and how they behave when they do.
- **Think in terms of segments.** Novice marketers want to market to everyone, but pros know that that's both impossible (you don't have enough time or money) and ineffective. Instead, they market to those segments of the population most likely to buy their product. The three success stories mentioned at the beginning of this chapter show how spectacularly well this works, the segments in question being African-American cultural gatekeepers, rabbis, and CEOs.
- **Know your reader.** After figuring out your segments, write "customer profiles" of a typical reader in each segment. These can include age, sex, location, job, education, wardrobe, family structure, upbringing, religion, and whatever else interests you. (Character building: a classic writer's exercise—see, I *told* you writers could market!)
- Next, **adapt your writing, website, and promotional**

materials as completely as possible to your target segment's expectations and needs, so that when members of that segment encounter you they immediately think, "Yes, I want that." Specifically, market to your customer's *needs*, be they for entertainment, intellectual gratification, or life-changing spiritual insights—as well as, on a more prosaic level, content delivered via his favorite mobile platform, or using large fonts so he doesn't have to hunt for his reading glasses.

Every aspect of your work, marketing, and public persona should delight and powerfully attract your customer, including not just the book content, title, and cover but your website and newsletter (see below). *Marketing lives or dies on the details.* If you use a wrong word, wrong color, or wrong font—or if your messaging is just muddled—you've lost impact. If the customer has to fight his way past an ugly cover, confusing book summary, or hard-to-navigate website … well, he won't. (Most customers spend at most a few seconds contemplating whether to buy a book, especially from an unknown author.)

It also helps if you show up for readings and other events looking somewhat the part. You don't have to take it as far as Christopher Paolini, who dressed in "a medieval costume of red shirt, billowy black pants, lace-up boots, and a jaunty black cap"[9] for *Eragon* readings—although he wound up with a bestseller for his efforts!—but an evocative hat or tie or shirt can go a long way.

The advice to adapt your writing to the needs of the market may raise the hackles of writers who feel I'm suggesting a corruption of the creative process. My advice is to focus on the market as much or little as you want to, keeping in mind that sometimes even just a pinch of marketing can greatly increase a book's salability.

If your goal is wealth and fame, however, you'll almost certainly have to have a strong market focus.

Obviously, all this puts some pressure on you to get the marketing exactly right, but don't get all perfectionist about it. Many writers (and other businesspeople) evolve and refine their marketing message over time. Actually, you never stop doing it: I've been working on my current one for ten years and continue to improve it. Which brings us to...

---

[9]From Chrisopher Paolini's website (www.alagaesia.com/christopherpaolini.htm).

- ***Persevere.*** Marketing builds over time. You often won't see an immediate result from a specific marketing endeavor, and yet the cumulative impact of all your marketing should be to steadily increase the size of your mailing list (see below), your Web traffic, and of course your sales. This long-term effect can make it hard to tell which marketing tactics are really working; a good guide is when a particular effort actually results in a meaningful online or offline contact with another human being. And, finally:

- ***Start marketing before you finish the book.*** In fact, before you begin it. Start now!

Here's a simple plan for getting started, and building your audience:

First, start building your email mailing list. This is your most crucial marketing asset because, quite simply, the more people you communicate with, the more you can sell to. So put everyone you know on the list and keep relentlessly adding to it. There's no upper limit to how many you want —hundreds is better than tens, thousands better than hundreds, etc.

What will you do with the names? Glad you asked. Communicate with them, is what: meaning, send newsletters (see below) and other promotional mailings. For that reason, it's best to store them in a combined mailing list manager/newsletter program or service. MailChimp and Constant Contact are well-known services that can produce gorgeous emails with fancy fonts, art, etc., but for many writers they're too complex and expensive. Good content is really what your customers want, and so many writers do well, at least initially, with a program like PHPList that creates simpler emails but that is also cheaper and easier to use.

While you're building your list, have someone create the first version of your website. Make sure she's a pro who understands not just HTML and Java but how to use search engine optimization, social media, multimedia, etc., to build traffic and sales.

Remember, you don't want a boring informational site: you want a hub, a community, a hive of activity. (Recall how Lisa Genova built her site into a hub for Alzheimer's disease information and support.) You'll probably want a blog where you can post articles about your work in progress (or the work you hope to be writing), as well as relevant current events and extras that bring the whole experience to life. (Recipes are always a big hit, but make sure you test them or you'll get hate mail.) Encourage comments and conversations. Ask questions. Pose challenges. Survey. Hold contests. Do giveaways. Do a charity event. And, of course, ask people to sign up for your mailing list.

Now you've got the basics. From this point forward, every one to three weeks, repeat this marketing cycle:[10]

- ***Post a short article on your blog.*** It should be useful and/or entertaining and/or timely. A current events "hook" is great—the article of mine that resulted in the most hits was one that discussed perfectionism in the hit movie *The King's Speech.*[11]
- ***Send it out in newsletter format to your mailing list.*** (If you've done what I've suggested above and subscribed to other writers' newsletters, you should know how the newsletter should look and be organized.) After the article you can do a *mild* sales pitch if you've got something to sell. Remember that "newsletters" that do nothing but sell get trashed, while those that offer valuable and/or fun information are read and retained.
- Then, ***link to your post on Facebook, Google+, Twitter, LinkedIn, etc.*** Don't post your article on any site where you don't retain full ownership. Besides, you don't want to build the traffic on Facebook, etc., but on your own site.
- Next, ***"syndicate" the article by getting it reprinted on other websites***—always after confirming that you retain ownership, and always with a link back to your own site. Establish cross-promotions with other authors. Konrath is big on the need for writers to promote and otherwise help each other, and he's absolutely right. Let's all work together to help all writers succeed!

Reach out to relevant sites and communities. If you're writing a history of Norway during World War II, for instance, reach out to

---

[10]Adam Singer discusses the importance of a regular posting cadence, and offers other good tips, here: Adam Singer, "Still Making These 4 Mistakes? You're Not A Media Company Yet," The Future Buzz (blog), June 14, 2011 (thefuturebuzz.com/2011/06/14/media-company-mistakes/).

[11]Hillary Rettig, "Perfectionism in the 'Tiger Mom' and 'The King's Speech,'" February 26, 2011 (hillaryrettig.com/2011/02/26/perfectionism-in-the-tiger-mom-and-the-kings-speech/).

websites about Norway and WWII.

Then repeat it all again in one to three weeks.

That's it: A basic, yet effective, marketing engine, designed to help you build your mailing list and website traffic—and sales. Over time, and by studying your mentors, you'll refine your process so that it works as well as possible.

Beyond all this, you can (and should):

- *Do podcasts and multimedia.* Right now you can register your own "channel" on YouTube for free, and then start filling it with movies. But post these on your own site as well.

- *Publish articles and short stories in magazines,* even if they don't pay well—or at all. Konrath recommends doing this because many magazines have large circulations, and so it's essentially free, or even paid, publicity. Also, *publish diverse stuff,* so that diverse audiences will get to know you. Varying your genre, length, settings, types of characters, themes, etc., is a sure way to attract people who wouldn't otherwise encounter you and your work.

- *Get testimonials from influential people and reviews from influential venues.* See next chapter.

- *Sell ebooks cheap.* Cheap yields lots of sales and promotion. See next section.

- *Give your writing away for free,* including articles, chapters, Podcasts, etc. If you're lucky, your free stuff will go viral, but even if it doesn't, it should help build your name recognition and increase website traffic and sales.

  Some writers are afraid that giving stuff away will cannibalize their sales, but so far the evidence strongly suggests otherwise.[12] As tech publisher Tim O'Reilly famously said, "Obscurity is a far greater threat to authors and creative artists than piracy."[13]

- *Sell services and products other than books.* Teach. Coach.

---

[12]Cory Doctorow, "Free Ebooks Correlated with Increased Print-Book Sales," BoingBoing, March 4, 2010 (boingboing.net/2010/03/04/free-ebooks-correlat.html).

[13]Tim O'Reilly, "Piracy is Progressive Taxation, and Other Thoughts on the Evolution of Online Distribution," Openp2p, December 11, 2002 (openp2p.com/lpt/a/3015).

Edit. Also, if you can figure out how to sell non-book products based on your writing, like t-shirts,[14] that's even better.

- **Give public readings/visit bookstores.** I'm conflicted about these, since they are important to building an audience and making sales, and yet expensive in terms of both time and money. (And the time expense isn't just the time you spend traveling but the time you spend handling the logistics.) Also, they work better for some books than others, and you'll probably encounter some kneejerk anti-self-publisher bias when you approach venues.

  But it's probably still worth doing, if you do it right. Konrath's done a lot of these, and in *The Newbie's Guide to Publishing* describes how you can do them on the cheap (stay at fans' houses, etc.). He also does a lot of quickie bookstore visits while en route to other destinations, and that's a great, low-cost tactic, too.

  If you can get a paid speaking gig from a library, university, school, business, or community organization, that obviously changes everything. (You can also read in people's houses and they'll pass the hat around for you, in which case you could get anything from very little to a good chunk of change to show for the night, in addition to book sales and free food.) My approach is to try to get at least one paid gig (or expenses-paid, at least) per trip, and then schedule some free or discounted events around it.

  Some writers are also using videoconferencing technology to do low-cost remote book tours, which is just one more example of how modern technology is hugely liberating for writers and readers alike.

As mentioned at the start of this chapter, the purpose of marketing is to bring potential readers to you. Then when they show up, you need to "close the sale," as the salespeople say. It's not hard! Greet them: Don't just sit at your table like a lump or wait for them to make the first move. Hand them a copy of your book and invite them to take a look. Have a fun conversation, ask questions, and LISTEN to their

---

[14]Margaret Atwood (!) at www.cafepress.com/DeadAuthorTshirtsandOtherStuff. More authors should do stuff like this.

replies carefully (listening provides not just great market research, but a compelling sales tactic; read Dale Carnegie's *How to Win Friends and Influence People*). Then ask them to buy it, e.g., "Sounds like we've got a good fit, here—how about you buy one and I'll sign it!"

This may be challenging at first, but eventually it gets routine. Watch how other writers handle themselves and you'll figure out how to do it.

Section 8.9 Another Writer's Story

Well, we're almost at the end of the book! When I do workshops, I typically say goodbye to everyone during the last break, since once the workshop ends people tend to fly out the door. So I will say goodbye and thank you now, and then again a bit later, in the epilogue.

I thought a good way for me to wind down would be for me to share with you the process and major decisions by which I self-published *The Seven Secrets of the Prolific*—not necessarily because I think my process was exemplary, but because I think it will be helpful for you to see how one writer (me!) made the transition from "being published" to "publisher." So here it is. (Of course, many of the technologies and business models I discuss will be obsolete practically the day I write about them, so do your own research.)

Building a Team. The best decision I made was the very first: to not go it alone. I had done some research on self-publishing and was pretty sure I could handle the details if I had to—plenty of writers do—but why would I want to? Recalling Time-Management Principles #2 and #4 (Sections 4.4 and 4.5), I wanted to stick as much as possible to my high-value activities, and bring others on who could contribute their high-value expertise, contacts, and other resources to the project.

So about six months ahead of my intended publication date, I asked my friend Chris Sturr of LeftUp Publishing (www.leftup.org) to help me manage the overall project and produce the paperback book. Chris knew *exactly* what to do, including details like getting the copyright and ISBN, and he also did editing and layout. He also had an existing relationship with premier print-on-demand (POD) service Lightning Source, Inc., so the printing logistics were quite easy.

I also signed on Lee Busch (www.lbdesign.com), a friend who not only does brilliant Web and print design work, but is a brilliant marketing strategist who knows vast amounts about search engine optimization, social media, multimedia, and e-commerce.

In Section 4.8, I discussed the wonderful benefits of working within an empowered community—benefits you sacrifice when you go it alone or overgive. By working with Chris and Lee I got a much better result than I could have achieved alone, and with hugely lowered stress. Both were great at what they did, incredibly easy to work with, and cared a lot about me and my project.

It's worth mentioning that I didn't just hire Chris and Lee, I *listened* to them. From my own coaching of others I know that an inability or unwillingness to listen to advice hampers many people's success. In all areas of my life, I always seek out the best possible advice and then do my best to follow it.

An alternative to hiring Chris and Lee would have been to go with one of the full-service POD companies that offer editing, design, marketing, fulfillment (customers can order right from their websites) and other services. (Lightning Source offers none of these, but provides great printing at a rock-bottom cost.) Many writers use these companies and are happy, but I honestly doubt that I would have gotten as good a result as I did with my dynamic duo of caring experts—and I was happy to keep my money "in the family."

A final "team member" worth mentioning is Smashwords.com, which Chris and I chose to create the ebooks. Feed Smashwords a text file, and its software will automatically format it for the most popular e-readers, mobile phones, and other platforms. Smashwords also acts as a retailer/distributor, selling the work (for a 15% commission) from its site, and through affiliates like the Apple store (for up to a 40% commission.)

Planning, Profitability, and Pricing. I knew from the beginning that I wanted this book to be a profitable venture, earning more money being a huge motive to self-publish in the first place. So I did what responsible business people do and created a **profit-and-loss statement** (P&L, also called an income statement) that projected my income and expenses month by month over the first couple of years of the project. The hard part of a P&L isn't the math, by the way—that's simple addition, subtraction, and percentages—but anticipating expenses, justifying your sales figures (if you say you're going to sell thirty books a month, you have say where and how you will do it), and then having the stomach to cut costs and raise prices, probably more than you want to, to ensure profitability.

I calculated my upfront capital needs to be $12,892.82 (P&L precision!), with about $3,600 of that going to printing 1,500 paperback copies (1,300 for me to sell, and 200 to give away to bloggers and others for promotion). The rest would pay for ebook production (some additional formatting and other work required), art, improvements to my website, and other online and offline promotion (see "Marketing" section, below.)

Obviously, I could have started with a smaller print run (although the per-book printing price would have been higher) or invested less in marketing—and if my "crowdfunding" (see below) turns out to be weak, I may have to do just that. But 1,500 seemed like a reasonable number for me to sell within a couple of years, and I also have enough faith in the book that I really wanted to print a lot of copies to use for marketing.

Pricing is a very important consideration, since it has a strong influence on sales. I initially thought a $19.95 price (plus shipping, handling, and applicable taxes) for the paperback would be reasonable, but couldn't make the numbers work. So I wanted to price it at $24.95. However, a bookseller persuaded me to price it at $29.95 so that he and other retailers (including me, at my readings and speeches) could offer discounts. (Customers *love* discounts.) A price of $29.95 also ensures that I get a healthy profit even after discounts and even after PayPal takes its 2.9% cut from sales made via www.hillaryrettig.com.

At $29.95, I will have to sell 431 books just to cover my startup costs. With discounts, of course, the number will be much higher.

The ebooks were a simpler calculation, since (a) they cost almost nothing to produce and are therefore profitable at any price, and (b) savvy authors treat them not as profit centers but loss leaders—meaning, something they sell cheap to catalyze other business. So my plan is to follow the examples of Amanda Hocking, J.A. Konrath, and other self-publishing heroes and price low: the full ebook at $3.95 and each chapter at $.99.

Capitalization/Crowdfunding. I could have scraped together the $12,892.82 startup costs myself, but that's not just bad business—businesspeople like to hold on to their cash—but outmoded and unhealthily isolationist 20th-century thinking. Twenty-first-century thinking, in contrast, is to "crowdfund" via an online appeal that not only engages your audience and gets them to invest, but attracts new audience members and gets them to invest as well.

So I put up a pitch up on the crowdfunding site IndieGoGo.

com asking people to prepay for their books and offering a big discount if they did. My target was $7,500: lower than what I needed, but I knew that it would be far better to succeed publicly at reaching a low target than to fail publicly at reaching a high one. Honestly, I wasn't at all sure I could even reach that number—$7,500 is a lot of money to ask for, especially if you're asking for it mainly in $25 increments—and I only had around 1,600 people on my mailing list. Part of me was terrified I'd only raise a thousand or two, which would be a mortifying public failure.

The fundraising turned out to be a lot more work and stress than I had anticipated. A good crowdfunding pitch turns out to have a lot of components, and some require a lot of thought. For instance, you have to decide on which levels of "contributions" you'll accept, and which perks you'll give for each level.

You also need to post book excerpts, testimonials, and updates.

And you also need to stay in touch with your community more or less constantly throughout the fundraising process, giving progress reports, answering questions, and exhorting people to pay.

AND it all has to be done very professionally, or not only will people not pay, but you'll damage your reputation.

A lot of the fundraising examples I studied were either extremely witty, *très* artsy, or both, and many included professional-looking videos. After studying these for a while, I started to feel totally inadequate. But I soldiered on, doing my best to come up with what I thought was compelling fundraising text.

Lee read my first attempt and wasn't impressed. "You need some *drama*, honey. Pathos. A mission," he wrote after reviewing it. And then he helped me revise. Honestly, I don't think I could have written it without him.

The two main crowdfunding sites, by the way, are Kickstarter and IndieGoGo. Kickstarter wasn't an option for me because they don't accept self-help projects. IndieGoGo did, and seemed business-friendlier in general. IndieGoGo also pays out the funds as you collect them, as opposed to Kickstarter, where you only get paid if and when you meet your fundraising target. So IndieGoGo was a great choice from the standpoint of cash flow.

As I write this, my IndieGoGo site has been live for about four days and I've raised just under $2,500, or one-third of my goal. So I am saved from the "mortifying public failure" of only raising "a thousand or two," but still have a ways to go. I've been hustling like mad—sending out announcements and personal emails to dozens of people, including some I haven't communicated with in a while. I'm sure I will have sent out hundreds of emails before this is all over. I am determined to meet my target.

You'll have to check the blog at www.hillaryrettig.com to see how I did. But even now I can tell you that crowdfunding was a very worthwhile project because it got me to think about my project in a very customer-focused way. And getting back in touch with some people I hadn't communicated with in a while was also a nice plus—and many of them did buy the book.

Art. Being a "word" person, I tend to devalue art and design. But experts agree that a good cover is crucial to book sales, so I knew I'd have to have some good art.

I also knew I wanted the cover and other illustrations to be fun cartoons that would defuse the seriousness (and, for some people, scariness) of the topics I cover, and so I was thrilled when Chris introduced me to the wonderful cartoonist Barry Deutsch (www.amptoons.com). I paid him around $1,300 for the cover plus interior illustrations.

When I got the first draft of Barry's cover cartoon, it was a thrilling moment! And then when Lee embedded it into a full-fledged cover design, I was thrilled all over again! Seeing that cover was hugely motivating, so in the future I'll do my covers earlier in the process. I can't convey how absolutely proud I am of the cover of this book, and how happy it makes me feel every time I look at it.

By the way, Barry's got his own passionate fan base, so I'm hoping that some of his fans will buy this book. For every one who does who wouldn't have otherwise heard about me, it's the equivalent of lowering his fee.

Marketing and Sales. I described the basic marketing strategy I use in the last section. Here are some other things I'll be trying for this book:

Testimonials (a.k.a. "blurbs"). These are hugely important to sales, but most of the writers and other luminaries I solicited for my first book, *The Lifelong Activist,* either didn't respond or turned me down. So I am a bit discouraged about this tactic. However, I'll be setting aside two hundred copies of *The Seven Secrets of the Prolific* to mail to influential bloggers and others in hopes that they blurb me and/or review or recommend the book. (Total cost of copies and mailing will be around $1,600.) And I'll do my best to reciprocate for those who support me.

I probably won't be sending review copies out to book reviewers at newspapers and magazines because many are biased against self-help and self-published books.

Workshops and speeches. I'm putting a calendar and budget together in which I aim to visit a different state each month and a different part of the country each quarter. This doesn't sound like much of a commitment—and the truth is, I'd like to do much more—but, as mentioned in the last chapter, travel costs money, and trip logistics take up a huge amount of time. Hopefully one day I'll be famous enough that people will seek me out and beg me to do workshops—speaking of which, if you'd like me to give a workshop at your organization, please email me at hillaryrettig@yahoo.com!

Public Relations. My topic—overcoming procrastination and writer's block—is a perennial, so this might work for me. Hiring a PR agency would be expensive—a good one costs thousands each month—and also a bit of a crapshoot. But I've worked in journalism and know how PR works, so I'm going to try to cultivate a few good journalist connections myself and see if I can get them to write me up.

I'll also try Konrath's technique of publishing articles in magazines.

Fulfillment. Lightning Source, as mentioned earlier, does not do fulfillment. That means that shortly after Chris submits the final galleys I will be receiving several boxes of books at my home. As orders for the paperback come in, I'll pay a neighbor to stick each book in an envelope and mail or UPS it. (Keep the money in the family...)

The ebook orders will be fulfilled automatically via Smashwords.

Time will tell how my strategy will play out. Hopefully this book will sell well enough to merit future editions in which I can discuss the results I obtained.

Regardless of sales, though, I can tell you that the effort of self-publishing was totally worth it. It was an intellectually and emotionally rewarding experience that allowed me to work with, and learn from, amazing people.

One thing is also for sure: that evolving digital technologies, and the resultant new business models, are firmly on the side of the self-publisher. I'm particularly looking forward to ubiquitous "tip jars," which will allow someone to read one of my blog posts anywhere on the Web and, if they like it, to easily (with a single click) send me a buck or two. And I'm sure there will be other technologies that will be even more profitable, exciting, and empowering to writers and readers alike.

To be continued...

Arrows All the Time

The Greek writer Longinus said that the creator must be ready when the "arrow of inspiration" strikes. What the prolific know is that there aren't just a few arrows out there: it's arrows all the time. You just have to eliminate the barriers to your receiving and working with them.

If you've started the work in this book, you are well on your way. Keep going, and always strive to remain within the light and warmth of compassionate objectivity. Also, resource yourself abundantly, manage your time, optimize your writing process, eliminate ambivalence and internalized oppression, avoid (and heal from) traumatic rejections, and create an empowered career. The results, for both your work and your life, should be amazing.

Appendix

Publishing without Perishing

Advice for Graduate Students, MFA Students, and Other Academic Writers

Section A.1 Why, Why, Why?

Why an appendix on academic writers?

And why should non-academics read it?

One answer to the first question is that grad students and non-tenured faculty are among the most oppressed and exploited writers out there—which is really saying something. Another is that academia has elevated perfectionism to an art form: it's academia, after all, that insists that its denizens either "publish or perish."

The answer to the second question is that the plight of academics can illuminate that of other writers.

In my discussion, I focus mainly on graduate students in the liberal arts; however, much of what I say also pertains to postdoctoral fellows, untenured faculty, and even undergraduates in the liberal arts and beyond. In Sections A.8, A.9, and A.10 I deal with problems specific to MFA (Master of Fine Arts) and other graduate writing programs.

I expect this section to be controversial, and even to offend some people, but I didn't set out to offend: in fact, I tried hard to be fair. Many thesis advisors (and other committee members, of course) have good hearts and motives, but are undermined by the system they work in; as for the rest—the uncommitted or incompetent ones—well, at least they're not out there building bombs or growing tobacco. I'm also aware that by the nature of my work I'm going to disproportionately see the stuck and unhappy grad students, and so my sample is skewed.

But I can't ignore what I constantly see in my workshops, coaching, and elsewhere: that many academics are very poorly treated, with consequences detrimental to them *and* society. Scholarship is precious, after all, and the more we undermine our scholars, the more wisdom and perspective we lose.

Section A.2 The Rules of the Game

Graduate school presents itself as a classic apprenticeship opportunity in which you work long hours over many years for a poverty salary, receiving in exchange instruction, mentorship, and an entree to the field. I believe that that contract, as played out in academia, is fundamentally unfair, because a graduate student's teaching and research often yield his university tens or even hundreds of thousands of dollars in tuition and research funding, while he only receives a small fraction of that in compensation. Still, students willingly enter into these contracts, so the situation might not be so bad if the universities actually lived up to their half of the bargain. The trouble is they often don't. Many graduate students are given minimal mentorship, and many are "mentored" destructively—with the student himself being blamed, of course, if he underperforms as a result.

Moreover, the career payoff is, in many cases, illusory. In her April 2010 *New York Times* article, "The Long-Haul Degree,"[1] Patricia Cohen cites a study that found that more than a third of 2008 humanities Ph.D. students remained unemployed a full year after getting their degree. Of course, academia is happy to continue exploiting those unemployed Ph.D.s with poorly paid, part-time, no-benefit, no-advancement "adjunct" and "instructor" gigs.

Obviously, not all grad experiences are awful or exploitative, and some are wonderful. But the bad stories I hear are truly awful...

---

[1] Patricia Cohen, "The Long-Haul Degree," *The New York Times*, April 16, 2010 (www.nytimes.com/2010/04/18/education/edlife/18phd-t.html).

Section A.3 A Symposium on Academic Oppression

Consider the below, said to a graduate student by her thesis advisor:

> "Graduate school is not about babysitting, and I'm not going to be your mother hen. If you want that, go to a community college."

It is:

1. Insulting and demeaning.
2. Snobbish (and ignorant), with the dig at community colleges.
3. Possibly sexist, directed as it was to a female student (by a female advisor, by the way). I doubt the professor would have used the term "mother hen" to a male student, although she might have.

And, above all,

4. Controlling and intimidating. "Don't bother me," is what this advisor is really saying. "Just do great work, get it published, and let me share in the glory and collect the grants. But if you run into any problems, solve them yourself."

Of course, the advisor never bothered to delineate which requests for help she considered reasonable and which she didn't: vagueness is a tool of oppressive systems. If the advisor had really stopped to think it over she would see that (a) the vast majority of her students' needs are reasonable, and (b) it's also her job to cope with those students who are basically competent but require more support than average. She would also see that her strategy of setting up a straw-person in the form of an over-needy student and using that straw-person to control her actual students is not only dishonorable but an abdication of professional responsibility.

I can't entirely blame the professor, however, because her quote reflects the pervasive macho propaganda about how tough graduate school is supposed to be: how it separates the "wheat" from the "chaff," the "serious scholars" from the "dilettantes," etc. Graduate school is "sink or swim," students are told, and anyone asking for more than the bare minimum of help (or any help at all, in some cases) is looking to be "babysat," "handheld," or "coddled." (All of the terms in quotes were actually said to graduate students I know by their advisors—and note the grandiosity, dichotomization, labeling and other perfectionist symptoms.)

Oh, and "let's face it: not everyone can handle intellectual work, and if we open the field up to everyone it will simply devalue it." (The straw person argument again.) Oh—and I almost forgot!—if you've got significant personal responsibilities or problems that you need to balance with your scholastic activities, too bad, and the fact that you're even asking indicates your lack of seriousness.

Of course, it's particularly grating when you hear those kinds of messages from advisors in fields related to social justice.

In *Mentors, Muses & Monsters:* (Elizabeth Benedict, ed.), my Grub Street Writers colleague Christopher Castellani wrote that his MFA program "had a sink-or-swim philosophy. You were a writer with innate talent, or you weren't. The program's goal was to anoint the real writers and spare the 'nonreal' ones from years of heartbreak." (See the section on "unfairness" in Section 7.2.) Fortunately, Castellani subsequently attended the Bread Loaf Writers' Conference, where some of the perfectionist damage was healed:

> By the end of my stint ... I don't feel "real" or "not real," and I begin to understand that such a distinction is meaningless, that the questions should be: Am I working hard? Am I learning? Am I digging deeper, embracing complications? Am I "failing better"?

Do I think the "mother hen" professor is a monster? Of course not: she's probably a decent person who is trying to juggle multiple responsibilities with inadequate support from her own superiors. The "mother hen" comment might have even been an effort to help her student by clarifying the rules for their interaction, which is more than many advisors do. Still, her comment was, at the very least, inept; and whether or not she meant to manipulate her student into not feeling comfortable asking for help, that was the result she got.

And I've heard worse stories, much worse—like the one from the graduate student whose advisor told her, "Graduate school is about wrestling with your demons, and I hope I don't wind up to be one of them, but if I do, so be it." And (surprise, surprise) the advisor did indeed prove himself to be a demon by stealing his student's work and publishing it himself. His justification was that of oppressors everywhere: that the victim drove him to it (in this case, because she was supposedly too slow to publish). And, not surprisingly, he also committed other egregious sins, including neglect, cruelty, and sexism.

This student actually had nightmares in which her advisor raped her. Is it any wonder she had trouble writing?

It's not just advisors who are abusive, by the way. Another awful story I was told was of a graduate student at an Ivy League college (which I'll call College X) who, after learning that her brother was diagnosed with cancer, went to the departmental administrator to do the paperwork for a leave of absence to be with him, and was told, "This is College X, and we don't take leaves."

Section A.4 Advice for Graduate Students I: Managing Your Relationship with Your Advisor

(1) My most important advice for graduate students is to ***never work for anyone who is cruel, exploitative, or negligent***. I don't care how brilliant or charismatic they are—and charisma, by the way, often masks narcissism. I also don't care how amazing their CV is, or how many doors they can open. Also, don't work for someone who is flaky, irresponsible, or a tantrum thrower. Without a foundation of honesty, integrity, compassion, and basic fairness in your relationship with your advisor, you are very vulnerable. (Hopefully you'll get this advice before you've chosen an advisor, but if you've already done so it applies throughout your career, and life.)

(2) ***Delineate boundaries and expectations with your advisor.*** Honestly, it's really her job to do this, but she might not know how, or even that she should. So you should. Ask how she prefers to work and communicate with her students, and accommodate those preferences as much as possible.

Set up a regular weekly or biweekly meeting, and save as many of your questions or concerns for that meeting as possible. (Obviously, in cases where you truly need fast input, you shouldn't wait.) This is true even if you see your advisor all the time casually, since casual conversations are not a substitute for formal meetings.

(3) **Be a good colleague.** Show up for seminars, and participate. If you're shy or otherwise inhibited, seek professional help, since that can hinder your career.

Join a committee. Forge ties with other faculty members, as well as postdocs, other grad students, and administrators. Don't isolate yourself, even if (especially if!) you're behind on deadlines. Building a broad base of support in and beyond your department is not only a good career move but gives you protection in case your advisor becomes problematic. There are few people more professionally vulnerable than a graduate student locked in tight orbit around a dysfunctional thesis advisor.

Of course you will need good time management (Chapter 4) to ensure you're balancing your responsibilities properly.

(4) **Especially in times of crisis, give credence to your own thoughts and feelings.** If you are feeling under-supported, misused, exploited or discriminated against, you probably are. Seek help, starting perhaps with someone outside the organization (e.g., a coach or therapist who works with academics).

And remember: You didn't get this far by being weak or thin-skinned, so don't let anyone tell you you're being weak now. Anyone who says that, or that it's your job to grow a thicker skin (Section 7.1), is ignorant, if not an active oppressor.

(5) **Especially, though not exclusively, for women: watch out for sexism and sexist critiques.** Sexism remains rampant in academia, and I rarely meet an underproductive female academic who hasn't experienced serious—and, in some cases, devastating—sexism, sexual harassment, or sexual exploitation. Again, your priorities should be to (a) give credence to your own perceptions of, and feelings about, the situation, and (b) seek help.

If someone labels your concerns "complaints," "whines," or "nags," be aware that those words have strong sexist connotations, and are often used to deprecate women's valid concerns, and silence their voices.

(6) **Follow the advice in this book.** Make a plan, with deadlines and deliverables, for getting your degree. Do your time management. Work to eliminate perfectionism. Ask for help early and often. Equip yourself with abundant resources. And, most especially, work in

community. Community doesn't just provide support and grounding but tried-and-true solutions to many of the problems you're likely to encounter.

(7) ***Remember that graduate-level writing requires a different process than undergraduate writing.*** Some graduate students I know could write a decent undergraduate paper in a single sitting without breaking a sweat, but when they tried the same trick in graduate school they ran aground (Section 2.5). When starting graduate school, adjust your writing process to handle the longer and more challenging assignments. Don't forget to ask your advisor and others for help!

(8) ***Unionize.*** It's a fundamental tool of empowerment. Check out the website of the Coalition of Graduate Employee Unions (www.cgeu.org) for more information.

Section A.5 Advice for Graduate Students II: When Researching and Writing Your Thesis

9) ***Professionalize***, by which I mean invest time and money in tools and techniques that will boost your effectiveness, including a good computer and backup system and specialized software tools (Section 3.6). Make abundant use of your university's writing center, and if you need counseling or coaching, go right out and get it. Your institution probably offers it for free, but if it doesn't or if it's not working for you, do your best to pay for it elsewhere. Group sessions are cheaper, or you might be able to find a therapist who offers a sliding scale. Your school probably also has some graduate student support groups, or you could organize one using meetup.com—an empowering act that doesn't have to take up too much time.

10) ***Jettison as many other responsibilities as possible.*** Reducing commitments not only frees up time but reduces stress, so get your family and friends to take on as many of your responsibilities and chores as possible, or hire someone. Also, take a leave from as many projects, committees, and campaigns as possible. Be ruthless and "overdo it": even if you think you'll be able to handle a certain commitment while writing, you'll almost certainly be glad later if you give it up now.

If you have a spouse who can support the family while you write, give up the teaching gig. If a family member or someone else offers a gift of money or an easy-term loan, take it if you don't think doing so will lead to uncomfortable family dynamics.

If there are responsibilities you can't delegate, understand that it will take you longer to finish your thesis than someone without those responsibilities. This point would seem obvious, but I constantly talk to grad students who are kicking themselves for not working at the same pace as less-encumbered colleagues.

11) ***Be cognizant of your work's activist and emotionally challenging aspects.*** Many research projects either intentionally or unintentionally challenge the status quo, and therefore can be considered activist as well as academic projects—and, often, graduate students get hung up because they don't realize what that implies.

When you add activism to scholarship, you add layers of intellectual, emotional, and strategic complexity. Intellectually and emotionally, your work could challenge not just you but your committee members or others. Strategically, it could limit your career options.

It's wonderful if you want to combine academics and activism, but do so knowingly and with abundant support from other scholar/activists. In particular, you will have to figure out how to balance your activism with your career goals, especially if you're hoping for a job at a leading institution—which is not necessarily a sell-out, by the way, since we need radical viewpoints inside the system as well as outside it. It's also not a sell-out to (a) incorporate your radical views gradually into your works, so that your thesis might not actually be that radical, (b) collaborate with non-radicals, or (c) present a conventional/non-threatening appearance that makes it easier for others to accept your message.

For more on what an activist mission entails, see my book *The Lifelong Activist* (Lantern Books, 2006) at www.lifelongactivist.com.

Relatedly, many underproductive students I speak with, especially in fields such as anthropology, sociology, psychology, or history, have fears and/or conflicts around their research topic. Sometimes they've got anxiety or even trauma from a stressful or dangerous field research experience. Make sure you're aware of any such fears or conflicts, and seek professional help in coping with them.

And, finally,

12) ***If you think academic writing is somehow special, and so the advice in the rest of this book doesn't apply to you, get over it.*** Academics commingle with other writers in my classes, and the advice

helps them as much or even more than the others. (More, because of the huge amount of perfectionism in academia.) Thinking your work is too complex, intellectual, esoteric, or otherwise special to follow the basic rules of writing productivity is nothing but perfectionist grandiosity.

Section A.6 Regarding Academic Couples

Academics often marry or partner with academics, so perhaps it's not surprising that I work with many underproductive academics who are married to prolific partners. Almost always, the underproductive person in a heterosexual couple is the woman, a fact we can attribute mainly to sexism. (Women still tend to have a lot more household and caretaking responsibilities, and to suffer from more discrimination.)

Having a prolific partner puts enormous pressure on a perfectionist writer, since the partner is a constant reminder of how much the perfectionist is "failing." To make matters worse, prolific partners' attempts at "helping" are often counterproductive. The usual tactic is nagging, but even gentle nagging (e.g., "Did you get any writing done today?") is only likely to create anxiety and feed the underproductive partner's perfectionism.

In some couples, the prolific partner is a harsh critic, not necessarily because he's mean but because he himself is resilient and can't understand why others aren't. But here, as elsewhere, harsh criticism is counterproductive.

If you're the underproductive partner, it's your job to state your needs and maintain your boundaries. If it sets you back to have your partner critique your work, stop asking him to do it. If his reminders are stressing you out, tell him to stop. If you need more time to write, ask him to do more chores, or discuss hiring someone.

If you're the partner of an underproductive writer, the best thing you can do is model compassionate objectivity (Section 2.10). Also, listen to her needs and strive to meet them generously. If she asks you to do the dishes so she has more time to finish her thesis, offer to do the laundry too. (Better yet, pay others to do it.) It's natural to want to ask her how her day's writing went, but if doing so stresses her out, refrain.

If your relationship is already charged because of her procrastination, it's probably best not to offer advice—but if you do, make sure it's not misguided, e.g., "C'mon, honey, you know in this business you need a thick skin."

If she hasn't read this book, suggest it to her.

Section A.7 Advice for Advisors

First of all, thank you.

Thank you for being a caring advisor, and for being willing to improve your skills in this vital area. Proper supervision does take time, but can boost not just your students' productivity but your own. The trick is to devote generous time to students at the beginning of their graduate careers, and also when they need help: this not only helps them to be more self-sufficient but empowers them to take on tasks you might not otherwise be able to delegate, such as helping with grant proposals, organizing meetings, and being a mentor to others. (See below for delegation tips.)

In contrast, if your students feel undertrained or under-supported, or if they feel there's no one they can turn to for help, they are likely to become disempowered and run aground—thereby requiring much more of your time over the long run.

The first thing to do is analyze your own methods for supporting your students and identify any barriers or obstacles (Section 1.1) that could constraint your effectiveness. Supervision is hard, and no one does it perfectly. Beyond that, there are probably elements in your own situation that are disempowering, including time constraints and people ineffectively supervising and supporting you. Acknowledge your deficits and constraints, make a plan for overcoming them where possible, and do the best you can.

When you start working with a student, ask about her experiences, needs, and expectations, and clarify your own. The gap between undergraduate and graduate school responsibilities is often both huge and unacknowledged (perfectionism, again!). Compared with undergraduates, many graduate students have:

- Many more, and much harder, scholastic responsibilities;
- Many more, and much harder, professional responsibilities beyond the scholarship; and
- Many more life responsibilities.

And yet, many advisors expect students to leap this gap with little or no help—and judge them harshly if they can't. If you do acknowledge the existence and breadth of the gap, however, it only makes sense that, even though graduate students are older than undergraduates and have been selected for commitment and competency, they still have a legitimate need for abundant support, particularly at the beginning of their graduate careers.

Also, **be aware that many students have the mistaken idea that the same processes and techniques that allowed them to excel as an undergrad will allow them to excel now.** Helping your student understand exactly what graduate-level research and writing entails, and which techniques have worked for prior students, could make all the difference.

Help your student create a time budget, and when he begins his thesis, a plan for research and writing. Familiarize him with your school's writing center and other resources (maybe provide him with a list, which you can have your students maintain). Think of him as having a team to help him, with you being the team leader. (You can refer him to the writing center for help with composition, for instance, while you focus on his ideas and analysis.) Set up a regular meeting time where you can relaxedly discuss non-urgent matters, while encouraging him come to you promptly with the urgent ones.

The key to helping students be prolific and reasonably independent is to set clear guidelines for them in the areas outlined in this book: compassionate objectivity (antiperfectionism), resourcing, time management, writing habits, internalized oppression, etc. Don't just give them a copy of this book, however: ask *specific* questions to uncover any triggers or obstacles (Section 1.1) that may impede progress. (Recall the Joan Bolker comment I quoted in Section 2.15, in which she invokes a hypothetical diligent advisor asking a student, "Do you really want to take on all of Henry James's novels in your thesis?") Remember that **simply asking a student how her work is going without delving into specifics is nagging, not support.** The student may appreciate that you cared, but you're not providing the context for meaningful problem-solving.

Be aware that some barriers may be linked to your field or your student's thesis topic. Some students researching intense topics like war or oppression wind up being more affected by them than they anticipated, and some working on controversial topics wind up being more fearful of the career or social ramifications of their choice than they anticipated. In both cases, by the way, the student is likely to be either unaware of these fears or in full-on perfectionist "shaming mode" about them.

One of the most damaging aspects of academia is its hypercompetitiveness. **Never compare your students with each other or anyone else**, and also discourage them from making comparisons. Remember that even seemingly "good" comparisons can backfire by causing situational perfectionism (Section 2.9).

Especially discourage irrational perfectionist comparisons (Section 2.7), such as those with scholars who have been in the field longer, or who are researching fundamentally different topics, or who are luckier (say, in their personal circumstances or the timing of their work).

All of this comes down to **explicitly** teaching the student how to be an effective scholar and coworker. To not be explicit is to expect your student to absorb the needed information and strategies automatically, just by being around you and other academics—a risky and fundamentally irresponsible strategy.

It's particularly important that you tell your student you want him to come to you if he's experiencing productivity problems or if he has a personal problem that is interfering with his ability to work. Many students believe it's inappropriate or even ill advised to discuss such problems with their advisor, so they retreat into shame, isolation, and underproductivity that only worsens over time. You don't have to get involved in your student's personal problems, and probably shouldn't, but you can provide understanding and referrals.

If a student who is falling behind doesn't approach you for help, you should intervene promptly.

Finally, delegate responsibly. Delegation shouldn't be about dumping your unwanted tasks onto your students, but about working collaboratively with them on projects that support not just your team and/or department but their own growth as scholars. Delegate only to the extent that it doesn't compromise a student's own work—which means, delegating only very lightly until you and he figure out a good balance.

As any good manager knows, effective delegation itself takes a lot of time. If you give your student a meeting to organize and it takes him ten hours to do it, expect to spend two or three hours supervising. That's still a wonderful net yield of seven hours.

Section A.8 Some Unvarnished Thoughts on MFA Programs and the "Literary-Industrial Complex"

MFA programs promise training and mentoring that will improve your writing, but often don't deliver. Tim Tomlinson, in the introduction to *The Portable MFA in Creative Writing*, writes, "Many people find it hard to believe that I passed through two years of an MFA program, four separate workshops, and received not so much as a comma back on a manuscript. But it's true, and my case was not exceptional."

I can believe it, because I've heard many stories of absent MFA teachers and neglected MFA students. One MFA graduate told me in a typical comment that "Though the faculty were great, most were over-committed writer-teachers and only quasi-present. My peer group did most of the teaching." She attended one of the most highly regarded programs, by the way.

And when teachers aren't absent, they're often inept or negligent. Tomlinson offers ten types of ineptness, including teachers who believe writing can't be taught ("enables lazy teaching"), those with a "Moses Complex" ("Anything that doesn't fit into their narrow definition [of good writing] is treated as an abomination."), and those who fail to "establish any critical vocabulary with which to assess manuscripts" ("... the critiques are almost guaranteed to be either dull or chaotic or both."). Teachers with these failings will inevitably leave a trail of damaged and discouraged—not to mention, financially cheated—students.

Gross negligence and ineptness are far from the worst you hear about MFA programs, however. In my classes and elsewhere, I regularly hear about teachers who were hostile or belittling, who encouraged vicious criticism within groups, who marginalized students because of who they were or what they wanted to write, or who committed sexual discrimination, harassment, or exploitation. (See the section on teacher malpractice in Section 2.8.)

And then there's the hero worship and favoritism, which are present in many educational settings but often taken to an extreme in MFA programs. Favoritism is not just demoralizing (and, sometimes, devastating) for the students who aren't favorites, but often a mixed blessing for those who are. Here's Jane Smiley, from her essay "Iowa City, 1974," in *Mentors, Muses & Monsters* (Elizabeth

Benedict, ed.):

> ... [T]here was a story going around that one of the instruc-
> tors had taken a particular shine to the work of one of our
> fellow students. He expressed his admiration for her poten-
> tial by devoting himself to trashing her work. He would have
> her into his office, and then subject her to brutal line-by-
> line criticism, making her defend every word, every phrase.
> He "held her to a very high standard" and only praised her
> when she met it. ...Thank God, I thought, that I was not
> this teacher's pet.

I've already mentioned the unhealthy mentor-protégé relationship at the center of Tom Grimes' memoir *Mentor* (Section 3.9). Here's
Grimes on what it was like to be the favorite of Frank Conroy, director
of the famed Iowa Writers' Workshop:

> Frank had guided, defended, praised, and, in a way, iso-
> lated me from my classmates. With the exception of
> Charlie, I existed apart from everyone. I had Frank's
> approval, friendship, and affection. When it came to
> most of the other students, he barely knew their names.
> And I imagined my classmates thinking, *Tom Grimes
> was published by Frank Conroy's publisher. He didn't write
> a good book; he received an undeserved gift.*

All this brings us to one of the root problems with graduate writing
programs: that most of the teachers teach primarily to make money—
which means, inevitably, that many will have little or no aptitude for
teaching, or interest in it, or even respect for it. Grimes quotes Conroy
about accepting the Iowa directorship: "Forty, broke, unemployed and
in debt, I accepted an offer to come to Iowa ... more from a sense of
desperation than any deep conviction that I'd know what to do when
faced with a roomful of young writers."

And so these broke and desperate, but not necessarily skilled or
committed, teachers wing it, which means that even when their intentions are good they can leave a trail of woe.

Finally, to top it all off, MFA faculties are also notoriously unhelpful with, and often openly disdainful of, problems with procrastination

and blocks. So good luck handling any disempowerment you may be experiencing—and that the program itself might be causing.

About Those Career Advantages...

What about the supposed career advantages an MFA confers? Mostly illusory. First of all, even if MFAs did confer a huge advantage on graduates, there simply aren't that many opportunities for writers or writing teachers to start with. Here's Jane Smiley, again: "Every so often, a tall, big-shouldered editorial power would swoop into Iowa City and ... court one or two [students], then return to New York." That's one or two students out of dozens. And Tom Grimes, discussing a reunion with three other Iowa graduates, "We represented a typical workshop graduating class: three out of four hadn't survived as writers."

To survive as a writer, you need to make the leap from the literary magazines to writing that pays real money—usually books, screenplays, and feature magazine articles. Unfortunately, that's the point where the value of an MFA shrinks to near zero. Despite pervasive propaganda to the contrary, many agents and editors, when being candid, will admit that an MFA degree confers at best a slight edge.

What about teaching? An article entitled "What Becomes of an MFA?" by Daniel Grant in the February 26, 1999, *Chronicle of Higher Education*[2] cited a University of Florida at Gainesville survey of its MFA graduates that found that:

> Roughly 60 percent were teaching on the college level (although more than half of them were adjunct faculty), 10 percent were working in publishing or actual writing (technical writing, for the most part), another 10 percent were employed in fields unrelated to writing, and the remaining 20 percent were pursuing another degree.

So, fewer than 30% of graduates got a permanent teaching gig—and it's safe to assume that many of those were part-time. It's probably also safe to assume that many of the approximately 5% who wound

---

[2] An admittedly old study, but I haven't found a more recent one: Daniel Grant, "What Becomes of an M.F.A.?," The Chronicle of Higher Education, February 26, 1999 (chronicle.com/article/What-Becomes-of-an-MFA-/45719/).

up doing technical writing initially had another career in mind, since technical writing is not what people enroll in an MFA program to learn.

Finally, it's also safe to assume that the percentage of success-ful careers among the 10% who didn't respond to the survey is even lower than among those who did. (Kudos to the University of Florida at Gainesville for at least surveying its students and publicizing the results—most schools don't.)

Tomlinson, in *The Portable MFA in Creative Writing*, says liter-ary agent Noah Lukeman always answers those who ask him what he thinks of MFA programs thusly:

> Take the $35,000-$50,000 you're going to spend on the degree, buy yourself a good laptop and printer and a bun-dle of paper, and go off to a cabin and write. At the end of two years, the worst that can happen is you have nothing. Less than nothing is what you'll almost certainly have at the end of your MFA program, because, besides nothing, you'll also have a mountain of debt.

Some will probably claim that I—and Tomlinson, Lukeman, and Anis Shivani, author of an essay entitled, "The Creative Writing/MFA System is a Closed, Undemocratic Medieval Guild System That Represses Good Writing"[3]—are biased against MFA programs, writ-ing programs, or even literature in general. What I really have a bias against is obfuscation in the service of exploitation, the kind of thing that confuses smart and dedicated people into thinking that teachers who are only "quasi-present" are "great."

Section A.9 MFA Programs Cost Too Much

The abovementioned career-related concerns wouldn't matter so much were not MFA programs so hellishly expensive. (Although the con-cerns about neglectful, inept, and abusive teaching absolutely still would

---

[3] Anis Shivani, "The Creative Writing/MFA System is a Closed, Undemocratic Me-dieval Guild System That Represses Good Writing," *Boulevard*, Fall 2010, (www.boulevardmagazine.org/shivani2.pdf).

matter.) Most cost $35,000 or more.

I'm not disputing a program's right, or even need, to charge high prices. I'm not even arguing that those prices are high relative to the services provided (assuming they are, in fact, provided). I simply want to call attention to the effect these prices have on students from non-wealthy families. (Their effect on contemporary literature I'll leave to others to discuss.) In her essay "My Misspent Youth,"[4] Meghan Daum describes how she wound up nearly $70,000 in debt largely due to her MFA:

> Even as I stayed at Columbia for three years and borrowed more than $60,000 to get my degree, I was told repeatedly, by fellow students, faculty, administrators, and professional writers whose careers I wished to emulate, not to think about the loans. Student loans, after all, were low interest, long term, and far more benign than credit-card debt. Not thinking about them was a skill I quickly developed.

Telling a young writer not to worry about debt is irresponsible in the extreme, especially given how badly the profession pays. It's particularly galling that many of those advising her not only profited directly from her indebtedness via tuition payments but had what most MFA students are destined never to achieve: a full-time, writing-related job with a decent salary.

Daum's essay is part of a growing genre I call "debt lit," in which highly educated people tell how they got into huge debt, often via student loans, and often for postgraduate creative or liberal arts degrees. Another example is Beth Boyle Machlan's essay "How Scratch-Off Lottery Tickets Have (Not Yet) Changed My Life".[5]

> All I know is that in spite of her upscale upbringing and four degrees from name-brand schools, the Irish girl is back in a Brooklyn basement, overeducated and utterly screwed. It's

---

[4] Meghan Daum, "My Misspent Youth," October 18, 1999 (www.meghandaum.com/by-meghan-daum/22-my-misspent-youth).

[5] Beth Boyle Machlan, "How Scratch-Off Lottery Tickets Have (Not Yet) Changed My Life," The Awl (blog), September 7, 2010 (www.theawl.com/2010/09/how-scratch-off-lottery-tickets-have-not-yet-changed-my-life).

possible to romanticize poverty. It is not possible to romanticize debt. If they could foreclose on my education like a house or a car, I'd happily pack it up, pull out my memories of each and every course—"Tudor and Stuart England," "East Asian Art"—and leave them stacked neatly at the curb. ("Take my Ph.D.—please! ") Hell, I'd even downgrade, trade in my ivy and the New England Liberal Arts degree for any of your better state schools. But I can't, and so I'm fucked.

In partial defense of the MFA and graduate programs, their conveniently irresponsible attitude toward their students' indebtedness merely mirrors that of higher education as a whole. Thankfully, that attitude is finally being questioned. In a watershed article in the May 28, 2010, *New York Times*, "Placing the Blame when a Student Lands in Debt,"[6] financial columnist Ron Lieber wrote about Cortney Munna, a 26-year-old woman from a middle-class family who graduated from New York University with a liberal arts degree and more than $100,000 in student loan debt. "So why didn't N.Y.U. tell Ms. Munna that she simply did not belong there once she'd passed, say, $60,000 in total debt?" Lieber asks. The N.Y.U. spokesperson's answer—that it should be the family's decision whether to get into debt—is disingenuous, since no one's asking N.Y.U. to make the decision but simply to advise.

In the original article Munna states, "I don't want to spend the rest of my life slaving away to pay for an education I got for four years and would happily give back." In a follow-up piece she repudiated that statement, but said, "In retrospect, it's absolutely clear to me that I should have thought more about the cost of the education versus career prospects."

The bottom line is that you can get most or all of the important things an MFA program provides outside an MFA program, and far more cheaply *and* reliably. You can take high quality classes at a community writing program. You can pay a teacher or editor (who might actually *teach* at an MFA program) for individual help. You can immerse yourself full-time in a creative community via conferences and retreats. You can even get quality time with celebrity writers, editors, and agents via contests, conferences, and auctions, or plain old

---

[6] Ron Lieber, "Placing the Blame as Students Are Buried in Debt," *The New York Times*, May 29, 2010 (www.nytimes.com/2010/05/29/your-money/student-loans/29money.html).

networking (Section 3.9).

If an MFA program is not financially onerous for you, and you can enroll in a great program with teachers who really care, then that could be an amazing experience. But proceed carefully, especially if you expect the degree to yield a career benefit.

Section A.10 Don't Procrastinate by Going to School, or Staying in School

One final piece of advice is not to procrastinate by going to school, or staying in school. I see people who do this all the time, and some of them wind up with multiple degrees and a boatload of debt, but no solid career prospects.

This falls squarely under the category of procrastination mimicking productive work (Section 1.8). The "educational procrastinator" always seems to believe that it's the *next* degree or certificate that will greatly improve his odds of employment, so getting that degree always seems like the right idea. Only he's not really motivated by the need for the degree so much as a fear that he won't be able to find work, or otherwise succeed in the work world.

I fully understand the desires both to stay permanently in school and to avoid the work world; still, for someone who needs to earn a living these are not options. Also, staying in school out of fear is not the same as staying because you love learning: it is a fear-based strategy likely to yield a life of bitter disappointment.

If you believe you are unemployable, or don't know how to do an effective job search, download my free ebook, *It's Not You, It's Your Strategy* from www.hillaryrettig.com. Also, get a good career coach.

For those terrified of a drone-like life doing meaningless work in cubicles, educate yourself on the many interesting and meaningful types of organizations out there, including nonprofit and community organizations, health organizations, and start-up businesses. Many would welcome a creative and ambitious candidate from a nontraditional background, particularly if you've got a relevant volunteer gig or two under your belt.

Index

CPSIA information can be obtained at www.ICGtesting.com
Printed in the USA
BVOW04s0847110414

350365BV00004B/4/P